THE INTERNATIONAL
RELATIONS OF THE
PALESTINE
LIBERATION
ORGANIZATION

THE INTERNATIONAL RELATIONS OF THE PALESTINE LIBERATION ORGANIZATION

Edited by
AUGUSTUS RICHARD NORTON
and
MARTIN H. GREENBERG

With a Foreword by
JERROLD D. GREEN

Southern Illinois University Press
Carbondale and Edwardsville

Library of Congress Cataloging-in-Publication Data

The International Relations of the Palestine Liberation Organization /
  edited by Augustus Richard Norton and Martin H. Greenberg.
      p. cm.
    Bibliography: p.
    Includes index.
    1. Munaẓẓamat al-Taḥrīr al-Filasṭīnīyah. 2. International
relations. I. Norton, Augustus R. II. Greenberg, Martin Harry.
DS119.7.I497 1989
322.4'2—dc19   88-29338
ISBN 0-8093-1533-5   CIP

to
MARION E. NORTON
and
AUGUSTUS NORTON

CONTENTS

FOREWORD
JERROLD D. GREEN

No modern national liberation movement has been as badly misunderstood, both purposely and unintentionally, as the Palestine Liberation Organization (PLO). Those sympathetic to its aims as well as those violently opposed to it have failed to come to grips with the true character of the organization. More specifically, it seems, frequently, to have been easier or politically more expedient to distort the character of the PLO than to understand it as it is. Among those who have adopted this pose are the obvious—Israel and the United States—and the much less obvious—the Arab states, the Soviet Union, and Iran.

Only the ideologically most rigid still cling to the notion that the PLO does not really represent the Palestinians. Yet recognizing Palestinian reliance upon if not great affection for the PLO accomplishes very little. Furthermore, the organization's failures at least equal its successes and its weaknesses its strengths. But it is sheer folly for the organization's friends, foes, and competitors to remain so ill-informed about it. One does not have to love the PLO to recognize that it is an important organization. It is a significant force in Middle East politics and is, for many, synonymous with Palestinian nationalism and self-determination. Why is this the case? What are the strengths and weaknesses of the PLO? How does it work? Where does it get its funding? What is its precise role in Middle East politics, in Great Power rivalry in the region?

For some, these are questions of greater importance than for others. This is a consequence of the PLO's major weakness: its uncertain status. Although the organization has many of the obligations of a sovereign state, it has few of the rights, allowing those with whom it interacts to dismiss it with great ease and, at other times, to elevate it out of all proportion. States have territory, they have capital cities, they have populations living collectively within a single border, and they have permanent neighbors. For the most part, this is not the case for the Palestinian people or for the Palestine Liberation

Organization. Those who disagree with the PLO or envy its position can simply dismiss it, unlike "normal" governments which cannot be shunted. And just as quickly Arafat can be transformed into a quasi head of state.

Views of the PLO often tell us far more about the viewer than they do about the Palestinians. There are those who believe that to study the PLO objectively is somehow tantamount to endorsing its agenda or its methods. However, to evaluate the true role and significance of the PLO we should stop trying to determine how we feel about it and begin to study it using the same concepts that we bring to the study of other complex organizations. Those who deal with the PLO try to have it both ways: they magnify or minimize its legitimacy, constituency, and significance as a means to enhance their own political fortunes rather than promote understanding of the PLO itself. The readers of this volume however, are not dealing with the PLO; they are trying to comprehend it. And our understanding of the organization has—for too long—been colored by the actions of political actors rather than by what can be found in field research, libraries, and disinterested analysis. Position papers substitute for systematic investigation. Given the rapid and at times contradictory permutations that characterize international politics, opinions about the PLO have come to replace facts. And the attitudes of the relevant actors—both in the Middle East and those dealing with it from afar—are so contradictory and self-serving that their utility for understanding the PLO is nil.

An obvious example was the abortive attempt initiated by the United States Congress to force the closure of PLO information offices in the United States since they are considered to represent a terrorist organization. At the same time, Secretary of State George Schultz met with two leading PLO supporters, Professors Edward Said and Ibrahim Abu Lughod. Although the Department of State attempted to legitimize the meeting by trying to obscure the professors' political views and portraying them as just "two American citizens," the two made no secret of their ties to the PLO and their membership in the Palestinian National Council. Thus, one branch of the United States government met with the PLO while another was trying to close down its operations in the US.

This indecision is not unrelated to Israeli perceptions of the PLO. Clearly Israel knows as much about the PLO as anyone. Certainly the efficiency with which the Israeli Mossad assassinated Abu Jihad (Khalil al-Wazir) showed a tactical understanding of the PLO that is probably without peer. Yet Israel's problem is ideological/political not military or analytical. As long as Israel can persuade the world that the PLO is a terrorist group rather than a national liberation organization, then Israel can continue to treat its conflict with the Palestinians as a military rather than political one. Put somewhat differently, it is easier for Israel to turn all Palestinians into "terrorists" than to accord them a measure of political recognition as a group with any legitimate political agenda or aspirations. At this point, given the paralysis that afflicts the Israeli government, it is simpler to fight with Arafat than to negotiate with him. Yet even this convenient arrangement has caused Israel a measure of discomfort and uncertainty.

In the early days of the political insurrection which has engulfed the West Bank and Gaza, official Israeli pronouncements alternated between accusations that the PLO was "behind everything" to sober statements that the PLO had no responsibility at all for the uprising. Blaming the PLO contributed to the denigration of Palestinian nationalism. This was belied however, by the Israeli tendency to argue, on alternate days, that the PLO does not represent the Palestinians and thus could not possibly be behind the insurrection. Israeli analysts, as opposed to political spokesmen, undoubtedly knew the true story. But there was something almost comical about the manner in which the government tried to inflate and deflate the organization simultaneously.

Arabs have also politicized the PLO in a fashion that has distorted general understanding of it. For example, this was the case at the Amman summit conference of 1987 where the primary agenda item was Iran and the expansionist policies of Ayatollah Khomeini. King Hussein, who hosted the conference, used the gathering as a vehicle to shift the focus of Arab politics away from the Arab-Israel conflict, where little progress was being made, and toward the Iran-Iraq War which provided a genuine and sorely needed means to call for Arab unity. In addition, the king was motivated by resentment toward Yasser Arafat who had not, in Hussein's opinion, supported their 1985 agreement. The 1985 Hussein-Arafat Agreement was meant to promote an international peace conference which would embed Palestinian representation within a broader Jordanian delegation. Although Arafat originally agreed to this arrangement, vociferous opposition to it in the higher echelons of the PLO forced him to reconsider. Ultimately the agreement disintegrated and Hussein felt bitterly betrayed by Arafat. He no doubt took some pleasure in relegating the Palestine issue, the PLO, and Arafat himself to a back-seat position in the Amman proceedings. Indeed, in the English language version of the meeting's resolutions, the PLO was not even mentioned as it was in the Arabic. This diminution in the status of the PLO as well as the attendant humiliation of Arafat illustrate the manner in which the PLO can rise and fall in importance with far greater ease and speed than can a sovereign state. For Jordan, as it is for the United States and Israel, the PLO is a political organization more easily manipulated than dealt with consistently.

Among others who have a long but inconsistent record of dealing with the PLO is the Soviet Union. Breaking ties with Israel in 1967, the Soviets have historically attempted to portray themselves as friends of the "Arab cause" with a special commitment to the Palestine issue. In recent years however, the Soviets have recognized that by siding with the Arabs and breaking ties with Israel they had opted out of a more influential and meaningful role in Middle East politics. The US, despite its pro-Israel bias, has still been able to maintain good relations with a number of Arab states in the region. Thus, while Washington had influence on both sides, Moscow had influence on only one. In an attempt to assume a position of greater regional influence, the Soviets have been compelled to temper their support for the PLO somewhat. This explains the recent meeting in Moscow between Gorbachev and Arafat in which the Soviet leader indicated that the PLO "was going to have to learn to live with Israel." In light of Moscow's desire to placate the moderate Arab states and to establish ties with Israel, support for the PLO was downgraded and the organization demoted, perhaps temporarily.

Iran is another country whose ties with the PLO appear to have changed. From the euphoria that characterized the first Arafat-Khomeini meeting in Tehran immediately after the Iranian Revolution, we can trace a definite cooling between the two. For the early enthusiasm which brought them together has given way to the fact that the differences that divide them are more powerful than the factors that could unite them. The PLO is Pan-Arab in orientation; Iran is Pan-Islamic. The PLO needs broad Arab support by the very countries that are supporting Iraq against the Islamic Republic. Iran's opposition to Israel is abstract; the PLO's is not. The point is that the realities of political life have forced the Iranians to turn their attentions elsewhere and a once close PLO-Iranian tie has fallen victim to the political realities of a region where pragmatism—not ideology—reigns supreme.

What distinguishes the PLO from virtually every other national liberation organization is the fact that it has more than twenty-two ethnically, religiously, and linguistically similar states in support of its basic goals. This strength is also its weakness. Many of these states, in exchange for their support, make significant demands upon the PLO. This support tempered by competing demands explains how Yasser Arafat maintains his position and yet why, at the same time, he appears so indecisive. For a hallmark of Arafat's leadership has been his attempt to maintain good relations with all states in the Arab world. The challenge of satisfying Libya/Egypt or Syria/Iraq simultaneously, for example, is daunting if not impossible. His efforts have diluted his credibility while making him difficult to totally dismiss since at any given moment some state in the region supports him. It has also prevented any Arab state from relying on or politically supporting him too consistently for none trust him completely.

For every friend Arafat has in the Arab world he automatically has an opponent (the opponent of the state that may currently be supporting him). These factors, when combined with the geographic dispersal of the Palestinian people, the inability of a large proportion of them to organize politically due to Israeli and Jordanian occupation, and the ambivalence with which their cause is viewed by the Arab world promotes a situation of great uncertainty while permitting radical swings of political support and opposition. The PLO cannot live without Arab support. On the other hand, recent history has demonstrated time and again that every Arab state is willing to fight Israel to the last drop of Egyptian blood. Put somewhat less crudely, it is appropriate to ask what Arab support has really meant over time to the Palestinians? What is it worth today? The uprising on the West Bank and Gaza has once again shown that only the Palestinians will struggle without reservation for their cause. Arab support since 1948 has been of minimal practical value as empathy with the plight of the Palestinians in and of itself has accomplished little. Recent events on the West Bank and Gaza clearly indicate that the Palestinian people and the PLO have moved into a new era replete with both new challenges *and* opportunities.

The International Relations of the PLO goes a long way to clarify and expand upon many of the issues briefly raised above. One of the volume's strengths is its decidedly objective, systematic, and nonpartisan approach. Furthermore, few existing scholarly analyses of the PLO examine it as an international actor, preferring instead to focus on the constant, debilitating competition for power within the organization. Every chapter in this volume is concerned with the organization's foreign relations, and each contributes to an understanding of how the PLO continues to exist while lacking a genuine home base and trying to mobilize a widely dispersed and often inaccessible constituency. The PLO is a major factor within Arab and Middle East politics, and it has often been the casualty of Great Power rivalry in the region. And what virtually every contributor to the volume concludes is that all parties with whom the PLO has dealings are likely to confront a daunting array of challenges which will continue to make the Middle East the world's most volatile political setting. One can only hope that these challenges can be met in a fashion that will permit all parties in the region to maintain their dignity and humanity.

THE INTERNATIONAL
RELATIONS OF THE
PALESTINE
LIBERATION
ORGANIZATION

1 INTRODUCTION
AUGUSTUS RICHARD NORTON

B orn of cynicism and the desire of the Arab governments to oversee and constrain the passions sired by the most emotive issue in Arab political culture—the plight of the Palestinian people—the PLO has attained its extraordinary prominence in a political life that spans only twenty-five years. However, if the popular personification of the PLO is the gun-toting and keffiya-wearing guerrilla, a more accurate image would place a pin-striped suit in the guerrilla's wardrobe. The PLO extols military struggle in its political program and in its pronouncements, and most of its component resistance organizations have gained notoriety through the use of political violence, but it is diplomacy that has eked out a prominent place for the PLO in world politics. Judging from its energetic campaign to build and sustain international support, the Palestine Liberation Organization (PLO) has shrewdly determined that the road to Palestine may run through Paris, Dakar, Moscow, Vienna, and more than a hundred other cities where the PLO maintains diplomatic or quasi-diplomatic posts or information offices. Today, the PLO is deeply embedded in the international political system, thanks largely to its remarkable success in establishing and sustaining a wide range of ties with states.

A cursory review of the world's major newspapers reveals that the PLO earns more news coverage than most Middle Eastern states and often more by far than major states like West Germany, Mexico, and France. Yet it has also accumulated an impressive array of foes and detractors, notably including Israel and, at one time or another, all of the major Arab states, with the notable exception of its most stalwart supporter, Algeria. Whatever sentiments the observer might harbor toward the PLO, its visibility and high diplomatic profile emphasize that while the PLO may still be a long way from attaining its central goal of establishing an independent state in Palestine, it is hardly an ephemeral political actor.

In leading international relations texts, the PLO is often offered as the quintessential example of a nonstate or transnational actor. The author of one of America's most popular international relations textbooks observes: "The PLO exerts considerable leverage in international politics—more than many states—in its efforts to found a state of its own. Until these efforts definitely fail or succeed, such a 'state in waiting' remains classified as a transnational actor."[1] Scholars allude to the autonomy—unusual for all but states—enjoyed by the PLO. "The role of [subnational groups] in foreign-policy formulation hardly needs emphasis, but only in rare instances (the Palestine Liberation Organization is one such) do they act importantly without the intermediary instrument of a national government."[2]

Although scholars of international relations have recognized the PLO's unusual salience in the international system, academics focusing on the Middle East have all too often allowed prejudices and biases to color their analyses of the PLO. For the most part, the authors writing in this volume have striven to avoid this pitfall and, instead, have examined the PLO as a statelike actor on the international stage.

THE PLO AND THE PALESTINIANS

The Palestinian tragedy would neither be as widely known, nor arouse as much grass roots support outside of the Arab world were it not for the activism of the PLO. Of course, activism is too bland a word for many of the outrages, the hijackings, the murders and the gruesome slaughters that focused the world's attention on the question of Palestine. In fact, critics and opponents of the PLO argue that it has gained notoriety through the use of physical and political intimidation, terrorism, and miscellaneous chicaneries. Civility and revolution are hardly synonymous, and the PLO has committed its share of despicable acts, but the PLO's central role in regional and international politics can hardly be explained as the product of thuggery.

Despite its defects, the PLO is seen by the vast majority of the Palestinians as the indisputable and indispensable embodiment of their nationalist aspirations. This trend in support began with the stunning Arab defeat of 1967, which served to demonstrate that if Palestine, or a portion of Palestine, was to be restored to the Palestinians, it would be the work of the Palestinians, not the Arab states.

In all there are 4.5 million Palestinians, the majority of whom are dispersed throughout the Arab world. Only two million live in historic Palestine; 700,000 are citizens of Israel and live within the pre-1967 boundaries of the state, 800,000 reside on the West Bank and 500,000 live in the Gaza Strip. One million Palestinians live in Jordan, many as citizens of the kingdom; 400,000 struggle for survival in Lebanon, where only a few have been granted citizenship; 300,000 are in Syria; 250,000 reside in Kuwait, where many Palestinians have prospered; and 200,000 are scattered through the other Gulf states or live in Iraq and Egypt. The remainder have found homes in Europe, Latin America, and North America.

Wherever they are found, there is little question that the PLO has gained the allegiance of the vast majority of the people it claims to represent. No one who has traveled among the Palestinians in the West Bank or Gaza, in the refugee camps of Lebanon, Syria, or Jordan, or throughout the rest of the diaspora could honestly observe otherwise. There is simply no viable alternative. As one of the US government's leading experts on the PLO has noted, "the PLO has come to represent a kind of surrogate state and identity for an alienated and landless Palestinian constituency."[3]

The PLO is a complex organization, and while it is usually treated here as a unitary actor, this should not be taken to mean that the authors do not appreciate its abundant diversity. Although eight resistance organizations comprise the PLO, Fatah (founded in the 1950s) has become the dominant component of the organization. (It is instructive to remember that Fatah was hardly welcomed onto the Arab political stage; Jordan and Egypt tried to stamp it out even before it got started.)[4] The leader of Fatah, Yasser Arafat, doubles as the chairman of the Executive Committee of the PLO (on which Fatah holds three of the fifteen seats). To speak of the PLO is often—but not always—to speak of Fatah.

The PLO has suffered deeply divisive struggle and competition, and it is far from a finely tuned, internally cohesive body. Yet, the organization is more united today than it has been for years. Fractiousness remains a defining characteristic, but it is important not to underestimate the extent to which Fatah defines the thrust and content of the PLO's policy. For instance, the Popular Front for the Liberation of Palestine (PFLP), whose rejectionist stance has frequently constrained Arafat's freedom of action in the past, has moved closer to Fatah recently. In fact, after two absences in thirteen years, provoked by the PLO's willingness to accept a state on the West Bank and Gaza, the PFLP rejoined the Executive Committee in 1987. As one scholar has noted, "contrary to claims constantly made in the West, most PLO organizations are willing to confine their national aspirations to any part (within limits, of course) of historic Palestine presented to them."[5]

Although it lacks the prime attribute of a state—namely land over which it

exercises sovereign authority—the PLO does perform many functions normally associated with a state, particularly within the Arab world where it
frequently enjoys the right to extradite, tax, and represent the Palestinian
Arabs. [6] The PLO has resisted numerous calls to declare itself a government-
in-exile, yet it encompasses a wide range of "state-like" departments,
centers, agencies, and welfare institutions, in addition to the resistance
organizations that are normally associated with it. [7] The Palestine National
Council (PNC) is the supreme lawmaking body of the PLO, and even though
membership is by nomination rather than by free elections—which would be
impossible considering the political conditions and the dispersion of the
Palestinians—it is viewed by most Palestinians as their legislature. In
practice, the PNC acts as a policy-sanctioning, if not a policymaking body. It
is noteworthy that less than a third of the PNC's 315 members are drawn from
the guerrilla groups. [8] As one Palestinian scholar observes in a capable and
well-argued study, in the diaspora it is the web of cultural, economic,
educational, and political units subsumed by the PLO that have been the
bridge between the solidarity of the resilient Palestinian family and broader
membership in the Palestinian nation. These institutions have insured "that
the Palestinians have not become prisoners of their microbonds of solidarity." [9]

THE PLO AND PEACE

The task that has consumed much of the energies of US Middle East
diplomacy in recent years is the search for a formula that would provide for
Palestinian participation in a negotiated solution that would quiet Israeli
fears and satisfy Palestinian aspirations. This difficult and, thus far, fruitless
search has foundered repeatedly on the issue of the PLO's role in any
settlement process. Simultaneously, Israel has faced significant frustration in
its attempts to cultivate alternative Palestinian representation, most dramatically in October 1976 when relatively free elections on the West Bank led to
the electoral victories of a slate of pro-PLO mayors.

Even some Israeli scholars who emphasize their commitment to Zionism
and the survival of the Jewish state, and admit their preference for interlocu-
tors other than the PLO (usually Jordan), have come to the realistic conclusion that Israel's best option for peace is an Israeli-Palestinian settlement
negotiated with the PLO. [10] As Mark Heller observed in a widely read and
carefully reasoned book, "a settlement on this basis would probably leave

Israel in a better overall position than would a continuing political stalemate or any of the other potential outcomes."[11]

In real life there is usually a difference between the preferable and the possible, and few experienced Middle East hands—whether in government or academe—believe that peaceful resolution of the Palestine question is possible without the participation of the PLO. From the standpoint of some US and probably most Israeli officials, the PLO is hardly a preferred interlocutor, but it is indubitably a novel approach in the first place that presumes one adversary should choose the representative of the other. The unanswered question, in the view of many observers, is whether peace is possible *with* the participation of the PLO.

THE PLO'S QUEST FOR FRIENDS, SUPPORT, AND LEGITIMACY

Politics are usually motivated by interests, not altruism, and quite understandably the PLO is engaged in a number of relationships that are grounded in reciprocal exploitation and shared or parallel political interests. The body of scholarly and popular writing on the PLO is large, as indicated by the selective bibliography in this volume; nonetheless there have been relatively few efforts to explore and analyze the diplomatic dyads in which the PLO is a participant. Many of the bilateral relationships involving the PLO are couched in the polite language of diplomacy and justified in terms of principled commitment, yet the case studies presented in this volume suggest a more mundane calculus. Simply put, the PLO's relations with states have often been informed by a "What's in it for me?" mentality. Thus, pragmatism and opportunism often seem the guiding constants, and if the PLO has at times been the exploiter of a relationship, it has also found itself in the role of the exploited as well.

Some of the PLO partners in diplomacy have sought to use relations with the PLO as a lever with which to gain entry into lucrative Middle East markets. The most obvious such example has been Greece. Five days after Prime Minister Andreas Papandreou came to power in 1981, Greece became the first Western European country to grant diplomatic recognition to the PLO. Papandreou's left-wing politics partially help to explain the move, but another decisive factor seems to have been the desire to gain export opportunities in the Middle East.[12] Thus, the PLO has been no more immune to manipulation or empty gestures of support at the hands of the powerful than any other player on the global scene. In the rough-and-tumble of international relations, the experience of the PLO has been rather prosaic, even if the fact that a nonstate actor like the PLO should have such relations in the first place is clearly exceptional.

The stature enjoyed by the PLO in the eyes of its followers is in large measure a result of the active role it plays in regional and international politics. This role has grown, especially since 1974, when the Arab summit in Rabat recognized the PLO as the "sole legitimate representative of the Palestinian people." Over the ensuing period the PLO has cultivated an impressive number of international ties, extending from the Middle East, to Europe, Asia, and even Latin America. Some of the most interesting of these relationships are treated in the chapters which follow. It does bear emphasizing that several of the PLO's relationships have been jeopardized by its support for violence prone irredentist groups. For instance, although Turkey has long maintained a position supportive of the PLO (while also maintaining diplomatic ties with Israel), PLO support for Armenian and Kurdish groups has diluted Turkish support. [13]

This is not, however, a book about the misdeeds of the PLO, or about the reprehensible tactics it has sometimes used and supported; there is already a large and not altogether commendable literature of that genre. Instead, the authors will leave this aspect of PLO activity to the terrorism mavins who have taught us all that myopia, tautology, and vacuousness are no bars to success, so long as the "right" villain is selected. After all, it is never one's friends who are terrorists, only one's enemies. [14]

It should be emphasized that the contributors bring to this book a variety of perspectives on the Middle East, and they hardly share a consensus on an appropriate answer to the question of Palestine or on the significance of the question in the first place. Nor do the contributors or the editors necessarily agree on the merits or demerits of the PLO or the validity or invalidity of its claims. Some of the contributors are well known for their work on the politics of the Middle East, while others have brought their expertise on other regions of the world to bear on this subject. All of the contributors are expressing their personal views and arguments, and their writings should not be construed to necessarily represent the positions of other persons, institutions, or organizations.

All of the chapters are published here for the first time. Each selection was commissioned in order to provide a rich assessment of one or more facets of the many relationships in which the PLO is involved. Some selections focus on specific state-PLO dyads, while others survey relations in a regional context. The revealing composite that emerges from this volume is that of an organization whose struggle for recognition and legitimacy has been conducted with a heavy dose of pragmatism and has met only uneven success.

Ronald D. McLaurin's chapter, "The PLO and the Arab Fertile Crescent," focuses on the geographic and political epicenter of the Palestine question. He provides a rich, if deeply critical, analysis of the PLO's nearly constant struggle to maintain its autonomy and its freedom of action among states jealous of the PLO independence and not hesitant to co-opt and control the PLO in whole or in part. Its flawed strategy of survival has mixed rhetorical victories with real defeats, hardly a formula for success. In McLaurin's view, extremism has had a seductive appeal for the PLO, for all too often it has succumbed to the logic of military struggle, which served only to illustrate its weakness and dissipate its modest power. Ever susceptible to external manipulation, the PLO has often been preoccupied with fending off the encroachments of its Arab brethren. McLaurin is sharply skeptical that the organization has the capacity to escape seduction by the tempest of extremism, but he does note a decade-long evolution toward peaceful settlement. Notwithstanding this evolution, the picture that emerges from this chapter is of an organization that will continue to be hampered and diverted by the interplay of politics in the Arab world.

On the heels of McLaurin's pessimism, it is important to emphasize that despite its faults the PLO has sustained its following among the Palestinian people. In this regard, Rashid Khalidi's chapter, "The PLO as Representative of the Palestinian People," is especially pertinent. The watershed popular uprising which began in 1987 has shown that the PLO continues to be seen as the only credible representative of the Palestinians. This is not to say that there is no criticism. There is plenty. In fact, while popular support for the PLO is a fact, so is widespread criticism of the organization for its ineffectiveness, its poor leadership and its corruption. Yet, the PLO is the only feasible representative in the view of most Palestinians.

The dependence of the PLO on the Arab regimes has been a constant problem for the PLO, and as Chris P. Ioannides illustrates in his chapter, "The PLO and the Islamic Revolution in Iran," it was with a view to breaking this dependence that Arafat strove to establish relations with the new Islamic Republic of Iran. Iran offered the possibility of a new coalition and a new military balance in the region. Arafat's dilemma was that he strove to maintain ties with Baghdad while establishing ties with the new regime in Tehran. As the author notes, in the aftermath of Camp David it was hoped that an alliance with the new regime in Iran would compensate for the loss of Egypt's considerable weight in the Arab-Israeli conflict. In short, through an alliance with Iran, the military option of the rejection front would be kept open.

Arafat and Khomeini differed over fundamental goals. For the PLO the aim is to create a state to take its place among the states of the Middle East, whereas for Khomeini it is to secure Palestine for the *umma* (the Islamic community). Islam plays a considerable role in shaping the political culture in which the PLO must function, but the PLO is not an Islamic movement, nor is Fatah despite the fact that most of its members are Muslims. In contrast, Khomeini's fixation with Palestine does not stem from nationalism, but from Palestine's role in Islam. Indeed, for Khomeini and his followers, the state is an instrument for the fragmentation of the region.

The PLO's difficulties with Iran were compounded by its support for the Mujahedin-i Khalq, who violently opposed the Shah but came to be adversaries of Khomeini's Islamic Republic, and by its uneasy and subsequently hostile relationship with Shi'i Muslims in Lebanon, who resented the state-within-a-state that the PLO erected in their country. Ioannides capably explains this complex web of animosity and disaffection, and he demonstrates that the decisive blow to the relationship was the Gulf war, which prompted the PLO to try to walk a fine line between Iran and Iraq and thereby earned the scorn of Iran. From the halcyon days of 1979 when Arafat was received like ahead of state in Tehran and handed the keys to the former embassy of Israel, the PLO came to be derided by the Iranians for its ineffectiveness against Israel, especially in comparison to the Lebanese Shi'i militants who played such a key role in forcing Israel to withdraw from all but a fraction of Lebanese soil.

John Reppert is a careful student of Soviet politics, who combines the skill of the scholar with the talents of a soldier-diplomat. In his chapter, "The Soviets and the PLO: The Convenience of Politics," he shows that the Soviets have pursued a cautious policy in the Middle East, and nowhere more so than in the context of the Arab-Israeli conflict. The USSR was slow to embrace the PLO, and it did so only after the Arabs had clearly consecrated the organization.

As Reppert argues, the Soviets were stung by the loss of Egypt and were anxious to counterbalance the loss. If Soviet frustration with Egypt helped to make the PLO an attractive partner, the episode also illustrated that Moscow's calculation was based on opportunism. If a weakening of ties with Egypt could facilitate relations with the PLO, then a strengthening of those same ties could make the PLO dispensable. This is precisely the dynamic that defines Soviet-Syrian relations, often to the considerable disadvantage of the PLO.

Yet the PLO and the Soviet Union have found complementary roles for one another. The Soviets want to be recognized as a principal player in the region and the PLO has reciprocated this desire by calling for a negotiating formula that would facilitate a Soviet role. The PLO is also a surrogate in those Arab states where the USSR has weak or nonexistent diplomatic ties, most importantly Saudi Arabia.

Given the choice though, the Soviets consistently favor the predictable behavior of the state over that of a revolutionary movement, and they have never been comfortable with the fractiousness and the counterproductive use of violence that has often described the PLO. Thus, forced to choose between movement and state, they consistently choose the state. This is not to say that they have not tried to resist or avoid the choice, as when Syrian forces intervened against the PLO and its allies in Lebanon in June 1976. Yet Syria is the main Soviet ally in the region, and the balance of Soviet policy has always taken this into account.

If they did not already have serious cause to doubt the value of their relations with the USSR, the events of 1982 gave the PLO plenty of cause to do so. The USSR, like most of the Arab states for that matter, stood by quietly as the Israeli army plowed through Lebanon. As if by way of a delayed response, the PLO tried to play by the rules laid out in the Reagan plan of 1 September 1982. The US plan called for negotiations between Jordan and Israel, toward the goal of establishing an autonomous Palestinian region under Jordanian control. Throughout 1985 Yasser Arafat and King Hussein attempted to construct a mechanism whereby Jordan would take the diplomatic lead in negotiations with Israel. Though eventually futile, Arafat's efforts were not simply a tactical flirtation between old enemies, but a serious attempt to parley weakness into negotiations. The pointed Soviet rejoinder was a stunning aloofness when, in 1985, the PLO camps in Lebanon came under fierce attack from Lebanese Shi'i militia intent on preventing the PLO from reestablishing the armed presence that the Israeli invasion of 1982 had expunged. By 1987, when it was already clear that the Arafat-Hussein initiative had reached a dead end (largely due to Arafat's inability to overcome recalcitrants in the Fatah leadership—a perennial problem), the Soviets got back in the act, notably in April 1987 when Moscow pressured Syria to stop the camp fighting. Simultaneously, the USSR played an important role in repairing some of the most serious tears in the rent fabric of PLO unity.

In his chapter "The People's Republic of China and the PLO," Raphael Israeli has done an effective job chronicling a less well known, but still important relationship. More than any other relationship, this one was born of the isolation of both parties. For the PLO, China was a port in the storm, and for Beijing the PLO was an antiwestern revolutionary force at a time when it was isolated diplomatically. Even before the Arab states had officially designated the PLO the legitimate representative in 1974, the PRC was according the PLO this mantle.

Support for the PLO was not just anti-US, but a way of diluting the relationship with the USSR. Despite it quest for legitimacy, the PRC refrained from endorsing hijacking and terrorism. After the PRC had broken out of its long period of diplomatic isolation, it seemed to lose its enthusiasm for the PLO. In August 1975 it supported Henry Kissinger's diplomatic efforts, which served to undermine Soviet influence. In the next few years the PLO lost further esteem, in the eyes of the Chinese, by supporting Vietnam in 1979.

The warm relations fell victim to improving US-PRC ties. True to form, as the PLO was being pummeled by Syria, a USSR ally, the PRC reinvigorated its support. But, in general, with growing respectability the PRC has mellowed her position. The author ends with the tantalizing thought that PRC relations with Israel are possible and not foreclosed by Beijing's relationship with the PLO, a possibility bolstered by Israeli arms sales to China.

Robert Thomas Barrata, a specialist on Latin America with research experience throughout the region, reviews PLO ties in Latin America in terms of cultural affinity, mutual interests, and material gain (oil) and in light of the presence in selected Latin American countries of influential citizens of Palestinian origin. Not surprisingly, considering the immense diversity of Latin America and its politics, Barrata's chapter provides a rich picture that serves to emphasize the extent to which the PLO benefits tactically from the immense emotive appeal of the Palestine issue in Arab politics yet suffers strategically as a result of its problematic alliances with nonstate actors that challenge existing Latin American governments.

The volume ends with a preliminary, but carefully wrought chapter by Adam Zagorin, who combines solid credentials as a student of the Middle East with the skills of a professional journalist. Zagorin has done an admirable job pulling together some difficult and inaccessible information on the finances of the PLO and of Fatah in "Auditing the PLO." The substantial ties the PLO has established in the financial world illustrate, perhaps as no other factor does, the mundane permanence of the organization, as well as its substantial stake in the international system. Zagorin concludes with some hints as to how the PLO's assets might be used to reshape the PLO's actions and policies, yet he sagely observes that the PLO's complex infrastructure enhances its ability to endure pressure, whether diplomatic or military. Thus, the irony is that the very factors that have undergirded the PLO's international role may serve to forestall innovation and diplomatic risk-taking.

That the PLO plays an active role in the international system is amply corroborated by the contributions in this volume. But the organization remains a statelike actor, and its activism on the international stage has not empowered it to transcend its station as a political simile. Notwithstanding its significant accomplishments, the PLO remains only an organization in quest of statehood. The challenge facing its leadership is to convert its unusual prominence into sovereignty, and, if the chapters that follow are any guide, that challenge remains a profound one.[15]

NOTES

1. John Spanier, *Games Nations Play: Analyzing International Politcs* 4th ed. (New York: Holt, Rinehart, and Winston, 1981), 57. See also Charles W. Kegley, Jr. and Eugene R. Wittkopf, *World Politics: Trend and Transformation* (New York: St. Martin'sPress, 1981), 103.

2. Bruce Russett and Harvey Starr, *World Politics: The Menu for Choice* (San Francisco: W. H. Freeman and Co., 1981), 56.

3. Aaron David Miller, "The PLO and the Peace Process: The Organizational Imperative," *SAIS Review* 7 (Winter-Spring 1987): 95–109. Quote on p. 96.

4. Helga Baumgarten, "The PLO, Its Struggle for Legitimacy, and the Question of a Palestine State," *Jerusalem Journal of International Relations* 9 (September 1987): 99–114. Quote on p. 106.

5. As'ad AbuKhalil, "Internal Contradictions in the PFLP: Decision Making and Policy Orientation," *Middle East Journal* 41 (Summer 1987): 361–78. Quote on p. 375.

6. Mohamed E. Selim, "The Survival of a Nonstate Actor: The Foreign Policy of the Palestine Liberation Organization," in *The Foreign Policies of Arab States*, Bahgat Korany and Ali E. Hillal Dessouki, eds. (Cairo: American Univ. in Cairo Press, 1984; and Boulder: Westview, 1984), 197, 240; see esp. 209–10.

7. See Cheryl Rubenberg, *The Palestine Liberation Organization: Its Institutional Infrastructure* (Belmont, MA: Inst. of Arab Studies mono. series, no. 1, 1983). In a 1987 interview, Yasser Arafat, chairman of the Executive Committee, the PLO's ruling body, did refer to the PLO as a "state in exile." For the text of the interview see *American-Arab Affairs*, no. 23 (Winter 1987–88): 1–8.

8. Rubenberg, 7–10.

9. Shafeequ N. Ghabra, *Palestinians in Kuwait: The Family and the Politics of Survival* (Boulder, CO: Westview, 1987), see 164–67; quote taken from p. 165.

10. See Mark Heller, *A Palestinian State: The Implications for Israel* (Cambridge: Harvard Univ. Press, 1983).

11. Heller, 147.

12. Greek-PLO relations have been examined in an unpublished 1986 paper by Michael Asimos.

13. See George E. Gruen, "Turkey's Relations with Israel and Its Arab Neighbors: The Impact of Basic Interests and Changing Circumstances," *Middle East Review* 17 (Spring 1985): 33–43.

14. For a critical perspective on the phenomenon of terrorism in the Middle East see Augustus R. Norton, "Opprobrious Violence: A Commentary on Terrorism in the Middle East," forthcoming in an edited volume commissioned by the International Ass'n. of Chiefs of Police.

15. The editors would like to thank Ms. Elizabeth Wilson for her assistance in checking and rechecking many of the bibliographic entries throughout this volume.

2 THE PLO AND THE ARAB FERTILE CRESCENT

R. D. MCLAURIN

PLO interactions with the Arab countries of the Fertile Crescent have been the organizations most intensive and extensive. This is true for several reasons. First, and most importantly, Palestine is itself part of the Fertile Crescent. Fertile Crescent relations are, therefore, the relations of neighbors. By no means can this be taken as an indication that they are uniformly or even predominantly friendly; relations with neighbors are often highly contentious, and it is not a misreading to place PLO relations with the Fertile Crescent states in that category. A second — or perhaps an adjunct to the first — important reason for the salience of these relations is that Israel, the PLO's nemesis (in fact, its sometimes nemesis), lies in the Fertile Crescent. While we are not addressing PLO-Israeli relations here, Israel's presence in the Fertile Crescent directly affects and has affected PLO relations with Jordan, Lebanon, and Syria. That is, the Palestine/Israel geographic and political entity in the Fertile Crescent focuses the primary conflict upon Israel and its neighbors, neighbors who have been unable to escape this confrontation. Moreover, the fact that the Palestinian leadership has had as a principal goal to maintain the participation of the Fertile Crescent Arab states in the confrontation has been another dominant theme of the relations and one with the most far-reaching implications. The other side of the coin is also germane — because of their proximity to Israel, the salience of the conflict and of the PLO to these states is also very high.

There is another and very central reason for the importance of the Fertile Crescent in the international relations of the PLO, a reason that again affects in the most far-reaching ways the nature of the Fertile Crescent states and their interrelations, and therefore the interaction of the PLO with those states. The absence of a clear focal point for loyalty or nationalism in this area is an underlying theme. Throughout the Arab world the ambivalence between Arab nationalism and state nationalisms remains an acute problem. In the

Fertile Crescent this problem is compounded by the attraction of local or regional nationalism as well as loyalties that are not national in nature at all.

HISTORICAL BACKGROUND

The modern states of this area have no real history as political entities. They date from the end of the First World War at the earliest. Palestine, Lebanon, and Syria are geographical names stretching back into antiquity, but among them only Palestine had any political (which is to say administrative) significance until about five hundred years ago when Mt. Lebanon became an autonomous region. Apart from the boundary separating what became Transjordan (and later Jordan) from Palestine,[1] borders were arbitrary and fluctuating. Little wonder, then, that the growth of nationalism in the states of the Fertile Crescent is even now very tentative.

This is not to say that the area had no history or identity prior to World War I. Syria and Palestine were geographical concepts that took on political meaning. Leaving aside the issue of Palestine for the moment, the confusion of the geographical and political meanings of "Syria" has had an especially important consequence. Even today, Syrians—which is to say nationals of the *political* entity of Syria—frequently apply the *geographical* concept to politics. Thus, many Syrians believe that Palestine is rightfully part of Syria,[2] just as many see Lebanon as part of Syria.[3] There are also Palestinians and Lebanese who subscribe to these views. We shall point out that this ambivalence is at least in part responsible for the very aggressive and at times imperialistic Syrian role on Palestinian issues.

Similarly, the absence of a sovereign Palestinian entity facilitated the emergence of a multitude of claims concerning rightful sovereignty over Palestine. The Israeli case is merely one, and the most successful. However, the Egyptian and Jordanian reactions to the 1948 crisis were no less moves to assert their own interests in Palestine. PLO obsession with its role as the "sole legitimate representative" of the Palestinian people reflects something of this history.

But the problems of Fertile Crescent nationalism do not stop there. In the period since 1975 it hardly seems necessary, against the backdrop of events in Lebanon, to point out the salience of religion in the Middle East. Yet, the issue is quite important with respect to Palestinian issues, too. Palestinian leadership and political relations and organizational and behavioral cohesion have involved sectarian loyalties much more than many would care to admit.

In its creation, the PLO was a product of inter-Arab relations more than it was of the conflict with Israel. To such a degree was this true that the PLO must be viewed as having two origins.

The official birth of the PLO was its creation by the Arab League. It was recognized as a creature of the Egyptian government. Following the Suez War (1956), some Arab leaders raised the possibility of constituting a Palestinian entity or government in exile. The various forms of this suggestion demonstrate clearly that it was much more a reflection of inter-Arab rivalry than of concern for the Palestinians or the Palestinian cause.[4] The debate over the form this Palestinian entity should take continued for four years, but these were years in which Gamal Abdel Nasser was a dominant force in the Arab world, and eventually it was his own position that prevailed. An Arab summit conference, convened in Cairo at the end of 1963, agreed to create a Palestinian entity and to name Ahmad al-Shuqairy as its head.[5] This "entity" became the PLO. Most Arab states seem to have perceived the PLO as an Egyptian tool. Interestingly, at least some Palestinians and others saw it from a different perspective: "the PLO was widely regarded . . . as a device to enable the Arab governments to pass the responsibility of confronting Israel to the Palestinians and thereby avoid shouldering it themselves."[6]

The second set of roots leading to the modern PLO is much more important in understanding the nature of its development and interaction with the Fertile Crescent countries. This historical beginning is the story of Fatah, which has been treated in its overall outline quite adequately elsewhere.[7] Fatah, which was organized and retained a strong base of support in the Gulf, received operational support—without which it would surely have disappeared—from Syria as a means to combat Egyptian influence among the Palestinians and in the Arab world. In the period before the 1967 war, it is not inaccurate to see Fatah as a Syrian-dominated organization, even though its leadership was not distinctly different from what it has been in the years since.

The PLO was not merely a creature of Egyptian policy; it was a reflection of Egyptian and other Arab governments in its reluctance to challenge the existing political order. Fatah and the other guerrilla organizations, by contrast, challenged the status quo in their use of cross-border raids which incited Israeli reprisals.

It is certain that in respect of the Palestinians, as in so many other ways, the 1967 war brought fundamental change. After the 1967 war—in which the PLO was humiliated—al-Shuqairy was discredited and a new leadership installed. Meanwhile, the *fida'iyin*, who had captured the imagination of the

Arab world (and to a great extent the rest of the world) with their daring raids—so much in contrast to the abysmal performance of the Arab armies in 1967—appeared the wave of the future, the only hope. Having established better relations with Egypt, an Egypt that in any case was less dominant in 1968 than prior to the June War, the guerrilla organizations were essentially given the control of the PLO.

When half the seats in the PNC were given to the commando organizations, a precedent was established that continues to the present day, a precedent of maintaining a broad base of leadership that is not limited to one group or philosophy. In practice, the key Fatah group around Arafat has played the dominant role in the PLO but from the outset determined it would not force its views down the collective throats of the Palestinians and would practice a form of leadership by consensus.

The history of the PLO, then, is closely related to the history of Fatah. It should not be inferred, however, that Fatah has been the principal factor in the turning points of the PLO's international relations or that Fatah itself is a monolithic organization. Indeed, to some extent the dissension within the PLO reflects the disunity of its primary component. Notwithstanding its anti-establishment and somewhat revolutionary beginnings and the shop-worn revolutionary rhetoric, the group around Arafat has shown itself to be dominated by political conservatism. From the outset, and particularly from the time this conservative mentality came to establish its clear-cut leadership over the Palestinian movement, the first priority among the extremists within the movement has been to preclude the leadership from taking initiatives in accordance with its natural inclinations.

The preferred method for preventing the triumph of pragmatism—which is popularly referred to as "defeatism" or, more recently, "liquidationism"—was to follow a double-safety process of proliferating extremist organizations at the same time ensuring that the extremist elements within the pluralist Fatah leadership were not diluted. This approach has dramatically affected the Palestinians' prospects of any resolution to the Palestinian problem and their relationships with Jordan, Lebanon, Syria, and Iraq.

From the time Fatah began carrying out operations, the PLO's relationship with Syria has been especially important. However, the Syrian government was one of the first to close its border with Israel to PLO operations. Therefore, Jordan became very important both as home to large numbers of Palestinians and as a front. When the Jordanian army expelled the PLO from Jordan in 1970 and 1971, the remaining front, that of Lebanon, took on added importance. Yet, the crucial question was always how best to resolve the

Palestinian problem The Fatah/PLO shibboleth of "armed struggle" never made military, political, or any other sense. The fact that it was a shibboleth, rather than a tactic, condemned the PLO pragmatists to a career of frustration in their goals and conflict in their international relations.

PLO leadership is divided on means; it is divided on ends; and it is divided in both national and local loyalties, for it is in many respects a microcosm of the Palestinian people in exile. What PLO leadership is *not* is equally important: it is not representative of the West Bankers. This is not to deny their support for the PLO. The Palestinians who remained behind—both in the first war and in 1967—have never been allowed to develop their own leaders. Israel evicted some; others were killed. The result is that the PLO is an external leadership, external to the only Palestinian land with any chance of ever becoming part of a Palestinian polity—the West Bank and Gaza.

It suffices to note that the interests of the West Bankers and those of the PLO leadership often differ. The West Bankers' first concern at present is to salvage what they can of the West Bank for Arab control, to preserve what they can of their lands, rights, and identity. While it is true that a portion of the PLO leadership recognizes and supports this as a principal goal, a very large portion does not. Many do not come from the West Bank, but from pre-1967 Israel. There is a much greater nihilism and drive for vengeance from among this group, a group that will never recover its own land in Palestine.

Over the past decade the PLO can be said to have evolved toward acceptance of a peaceful (i.e., negotiated) solution to the Palestinian problem. Clearly, the PLO posture toward negotiations is to welcome them. We have not discussed this element of PLO international relations for several reasons. First, it is clear that the policy has divided the PLO more completely than ever before and therefore may place in question some of the most basic underlying philosophies of the PLO—namely unity of the Palestinian movement. If this is so, one must ask if we have not really reached another breakpoint in the PLO's organizational history. It is yet too early to tell where this policy will lead, however, and therefore how enduring it is.[8]

PLO RELATIONS WITH SYRIA

Ambivalence has always characterized Syrian perceptions of its neighbors, especially Palestine and Lebanon. During the United Nations consultations in the fall of 1949, Syria advanced claims on eastern Galilee, and Palestine is still seen as "southern Syria" by many Syrians. President al-Asad reportedly said as much to Yasser Arafat in 1977.[9] In fact, this ambivalence about Syrian nationalism in its relationship to Arab nationalism and other local nationalisms, has been a consistent element of Syrian behavior and thought. While Syria maintained close and cooperative ties with the Arab Higher Committee and later with the PLO, Damascus has always supported its own "candidates" for Palestinian leadership. "It was never quite clear where fraternal support ended and where Syrian ambitions began."[10]

Syrian support for the original PLO was severely constrained by the fact that the Syrian government perceived the organization to be Egyptian-controlled in large measure. Consequently, Syria refused to allow al-Shuqairy to conscript Palestinian refugees, as he had proposed to the Arab League. However, Syria did provide training facilities to the Palestine Liberation Army (PLA) and allowed the formation of a Palestinian battalion within the Syrian army.[11] But the Syrian branch of the PLA had never the slightest independence. And the Syrian commander in chief of the PLA was a Syrian puppet who soon became an important part of the move to reduce al-Shuqairy's powers.[12].

Much more fulsome Syrian support flowed to Fatah,[13] which during this period must be looked upon as driven principally by Damascus. The Syrian government appears to have perceived Fatah as something of a counter, *its* counter, to the Egyptian-dominated Arab League's PLO.[14] Fatah (and other guerrilla groups) enjoyed Syrian authority to operate on Syrian territory but not from it. That is, after initial raids, Syria directed Fatah and other groups to enter Israeli territory not from Syria but from Jordan or, occasionally, Lebanon.[15] Moreover, although announcements of Fatah raids were customarily made in Damascus, Fatah headquarters were in Lebanon until mid-1965. Operations were limited in number, scope, and effect—not by the Syrians as much as by the limited human and material resources available to the guerrillas. Syria also provided some matériel to Fatah through Syrian military intelligence channels.[16]

Fatah's second year brought many developments. Improved security in Jordan and Lebanon prevented infiltration at the start of the year, and the Syrian government briefly opened the corridor to Israel through Syrian territory. The Ba'th coup of February 1966 brought to power in Syria a completely new group bent upon revolutionary change in Syria and much more fully committed to guerrilla action. Fatah received significantly greater support from Syrian military intelligence for a period after 1966,[17] but came under severe pressure to drop whatever independence remained from the earlier period.[18] During this phase, Fatah was used as much against other

Arab governments as against Israel.[19] But the imprisonment of Arafat and other Fatah leaders for an unauthorized raid was an object lesson for Fatah, which quietly transferred its command headquarters back to Lebanon.[20]

By late 1966, Fatah was no longer under complete Syrian domination, but was, instead, supported as well by Egypt. The Syrian Ba'th had created a new guerrilla organization, al-Sa'iqa, at its Ninth National Conference. Sa'iqa eventually became Syria's "house Palestinian" group.[21] As a function of the mutual defense agreement between Egypt and Syria, coordination of Fatah actions was divided between Egyptian and Syrian intelligence. Following Israel's reprisal raid against al-Samu in mid-November 1966, Syria and Egypt used both Fatah and the PLO in a blatant attempt to depose King Hussein. This use of the Palestinian resistance for inter-Arab politics was to become a characteristic of Syrian policy.

After the 1967 war, Syria was the first Arab state to provide training areas to Palestinian guerrillas but did not permit raids to be instigated from Syrian territory. Syria continued to support Fatah and remained an important influence over the organization. Some senior Fatah members have acted as Syrian agents inside the organization.[22] Nevertheless, Syrian support moved definitively to Sa'iqa after about 1968, as Fatah's support from other sources — and therefore the organization's independence from Syria — grew. Egypt and Syria also collaborated in 1967 and 1968 in supporting the takeover of the PLO by the guerrillas. Sa'iqa worked with Fatah to effect the coup and was rewarded with an appropriate number of seats in the PNC and other relevant committees. The Syrian-controlled PLA leadership staged a mutiny which contributed in its own way to the discrediting of the al-Shuqairy clique.[23]

The commando takeover of the PLO completed, the new leadership itself tried to exert control over the movement. One remaining outstanding issue was the "independence" of the PLA. Having failed in the past to bring the PLA to heel, Yasser Arafat had himself named head of the PLA at the Seventh Palestine National Council in 1970. Predictably, the Syrian-supported commander refused to recognize the decision. The change was finally effected on paper, but in reality 'Uthman Haddad, who was very close to the Syrian minister of defense, retained most of his power and, as a result of a facesaving compromise, was later renamed to the position of chief of staff.[24]

In the major PLO crisis of 1970 in Jordan, Syria was the only country to come to the physical aid of the PLO in Jordan. Iraqi forces based in Jordan did not intervene in the fighting, and only a limited Syrian intervention in fact occurred. Ground forces moved into northern Jordan, but al-Asad refused to allow his air force to participate, precipitating the defeat of the ground forces. In fact, this discontinuity between PLO policy and Syrian policy has been the rule rather than the exception.

In the period prior to al-Asad's "corrective movement" (coup) in 1970, Syria had achieved something of a reputation for instability. Syrian politics directly and significantly affected the PLO and its predecessors. For example, Salah Jadid, the Syrian strongman from 1966 to 1970 (while al-Asad was defense minister), looked to Sa'iqa for support *against the Syrian military forces* controlled by al-Asad. This placed Sa'iqa directly in the middle of the inevitable confrontation between Jadid and al-Asad. When al-Asad won control of Syria, Sa'iqa's leaders were imprisoned and a new set of leaders loyal to the new strongman installed.

After the first phase of the Jordanian civil war (September 1970), the Fatah/PLO leadership recognized that it needed the support of the Arab countries and needed as well to preserve what was left of its position in Jordan. The PLO chairman attempted to unify the PLO under Fatah's leadership—not, as was charged, to impose monolithic control, but instead to avoid further clashes with Jordan that could only further weaken the movement and increase Arab support to protect the PLO. However, the al-Asad government sought, for its part, to weaken Arafat, perhaps with the goal of installing a leadership more responsive to Syria or, at least, reducing the independence of the PLO from Syrian influence. To this end, Damascus sponsored several challenges to Arafat both from within the PLO and from the PLA.[25]

The intermittent friction between the PLO and Syria was evident in Lebanon, where Syria enjoyed a powerful influence because of its military resources and access to Palestinians. While Syrian power initially flowed to the support of the Palestinians through Sa'iqa and the PLA, nevertheless, Syria was forced to undertake military operations against the PLO in 1976 and periodically after that. The Syrian attack on Palestinian forces in Lebanon was costly to the al-Asad regime at home and in the field where large numbers of Palestinians in the Syrian-controlled PLA units and even in Sa'iqa defected to the Palestinian forces fighting Syria. Organizationally, only the PFLP—GC of all the Palestinian groups remained openly allied with Damascus during this period. Syrian advisors were present (with Israelis as well) as Tal al-Za'tar fell to the combined Christian militias in 1976. Following the Syrian intervention in Lebanon, a mini-Arab summit endorsed Syria's move by deciding to establish an Arab Deterrent Force (ADF). The follow-up meetings in Cairo saw the PLO endeavoring to secure greater Arab participation in the ADF to protect the PLO from Syrian forces.[26] Although the Syrian government often portrayed its role in Lebanon in terms of the conflict with Israel, the Syrians fought much more doggedly against the Palestinians in 1976[27] than they did against invading Israeli forces in 1982,[28] when they accepted each and every cease-fire as rapidly as possible, leaving the Palestinians isolated and exposed to Israeli firepower.

Nevertheless, the Sadat initiative and Camp David forced the PLO and Syria back into the same corner for some time. Indeed, the result of Camp David in some respects was to give Syria more influence and near-control over the PLO than it has ever enjoyed before. Both the fourteenth and fifteenth PNCs (1979, 1981) were held in Damascus, and some key PLO leaders allege that it may only have been Syrian pressure that prevented the PLO from endorsing the 1981 Fahd Plan.[29] As the 1980s began, Syrian cooperation with Fatah and the PLO was extensive, but conflicts were at least as noteworthy. The strong tie between elements of the Muslim Brotherhood and the Fatah leadership asserted themselves in the northern Lebanese city of Tripoli, where Syrian forces were allied with an 'Alawi population — most of which had been settled there from Syria during the previous five years — and allied against the majority of the city dwellers — Sunnis whose ties to the conservative Sunni areas of Homs and Hama in Syria were strong. It was by contrast to this element that Fatah lent its support. Thus, Fatah worked closely with and armed a local fundamentalist movement, Tawhid, that fought the 'Alawi militia.

Syria had also forced the PLO to boycott the Amman summit of 1980, very much against Arafat's will, and had exhausted all means to destroy the dialogue between the PLO and Jordan in 1979 and 1980 (ironically, a dialogue Syria had worked hard to initiate when Jordan was aligned with Syria). Syria was also a key factor in preventing a more forthcoming PLO posture in response to the Reagan initiative of 1 September 1982. In 1983, Syria supported a mutiny that became an open rebellion against established Fatah authority;[30] the leaders, longtime Fatah members, were Syrian agents, and the result was a full-scale internecine war between different Palestinian factions. Prior to this 1983 split, the determination to preserve consensus had been a prime force in Palestinian politics. Despite the Rejection Front and other episodes of disunity, the divisions that arose in 1983 appeared the most serious in the history of the movement. Moreover, rather than proceed on the basis of restoring consensus, the Fatah leadership determined to pursue its own course. Arafat, freed from the Syrian yoke, initiated the policy abruptly by stopping in Cairo even as he was forced out of Tripoli.

After 1983, Syria carried out or supported selected terrorist attacks against PLO human and other targets — endeavoring to disrupt the new peace strategy worked out by Yasser Arafat and King Hussein — and prevented a reconciliation among Palestinian factions. Indeed, when most factions of the PLO sought a new PNC in 1984, President al-Asad intervened to ensure Algeria, the desired site, would not host it. (This strategy backfired when the Seventeenth PNC met, instead, in Amman. Boycotted by Syrian-backed factions, the PNC adopted a new and moderate approach in keeping with the evolving Jordanian-Arafat alignment.)

The negotiation approach espoused by Fatah between the Seventeenth (1984) and Eighteenth (1987) PNCs and notably in a joint agreement with Jordan in February 1985, had long been sought by the Jordanians and others favoring a settlement. The strategy was defeated by a combination of factors discussed elsewhere in this chapter. However, from the onset its dangers were well understood by the Fatah leadership. A PLO shorn of Syrian support over a long period is a dangerously exposed PLO, in view of Syrian access to the Palestinians in Lebanon and Syria and increased PLO dependence upon Jordan and Egypt.[31] It should be noted that the PLO left three seats open on the PLO Executive Committee at the Amman PNC, symbolically demonstrating its readiness for reconciliation. But on whose terms? Skeptics questioned whether the PLO would abandon its inherent priority of unity; whether it could continue to defy Syria openly for a prolonged period; whether it would ever be prepared to make a fundamental decision as to the identity of its true constituency. Syria retained its access to the Palestinians in Lebanon and Syria, was the only Arab state prepared to confront Israel (even if it chose not to do so at specific times), and could bring pressure to bear upon the rest of the PLO and on Jordan, too.[32]

Throughout 1985 and 1986 Syria both took the disruptive measures already discussed and pursued its determined efforts to erode Yasser Arafat's constituency through support for Shi'i militia sieges of Palestinians in camps near Beirut, infiltration of anti-Arafat Palestinians, and execution of Arafat supporters in the camps near Beirut and Sidon. The bitterness of the feud between Asad and Arafat, which reflected personal antipathy as well as divergent interest, led many to conclude that reconciliation was impossible. Yet, fluid alignments and violence have characterized Syrian-Palestinian relations throughout recorded history, and there is little to indicate that this trait will change soon. Indeed, the PLO sent numerous envoys and delegations, both openly and secretly, to attempt to persuade al-Asad to abandon his boycott of and opposition to the Arafat group. When the Eighteenth PNC met in Algiers, some groups based in Syria did rejoin the PLO "mainstream"; Syria could certainly have prevented or at least increased the cost of such restored unity. But while a strengthened PLO could not be seen as in Syria's interest, the new unity was purchased at the expense of any freedom of action toward a settlement with Israel. In effect, al-Asad recognized he could not obliterate or control the PLO as long as Arafat was alive, but succeeded in paralyzing the organization and neutralizing its only significant threat to Syrian policy.

Pressures on Syria to relax its war on the PLO were powerful. The Soviet Union actively pursued a compromise at several secret negotiations on the issue. Arab Gulf states as well sought a reconciliation. The restored PLO position in Lebanon during and after 1986 and the PLO and Druze alignment with various factions in Lebanon put heavy pressure on Syria's increasingly isolated and weak Shi'i ally, AMAL, until finally direct Syrian intervention was required to shore up AMAL's position and that of Syria.

PLO RELATIONS WITH JORDAN

If Palestinian and hence PLO relations with Syria are complex and intimate, they are even more so with Jordan. The population of Jordan is over half Palestinian in origin, and the destiny of Jordan and Palestine—as many Jordanians and Palestinians alike are wont to point out—is indissolubly linked, and has been from the end of the Ottoman era.

During the mandate period, Emir 'AbdAllah of Transjordan advanced a Greater Syria concept that looked toward the uniting of the political components of geographical Syria under Hashemite leadership. The idea received little support. Perhaps the only realistic Arab political leader of his era, 'AbdAllah engaged in a number of negotiations with Jewish Agency leaders and, later, their Israeli successors. He understood where real power lay and did not confuse it with Arab rhetoric.

When Israeli independence was declared and fighting erupted, the Arab Legion moved into some areas allocated to the Arabs and was the only Arab fighting force to acquit itself with distinction in the 1948 Middle East war. The result of the legion's combat was preservation of eastern Jerusalem and the area usually referred to as the West Bank. Palestinian notables were gathered subsequently to "choose" to affiliate with Transjordan, which through this annexation of the West Bank (eastern Palestine) then became the Hashemite Kingdom of Jordan.[33]

The initial Egyptian, Syrian, and Iraqi proposals in 1959 to form a Palestine entity were opposed by Jordan since such an entity carried a strong potential for sedition and appeared clearly to be a foreign Arab plot. Egypt and Iraq continued to use the idea against each other: "To Jordan's relief, the Arab League never accepted the Palestine Entity plan because Egypt and Iraq kept vetoing each other's proposals. . . ."[34] The idea to construct a Palestinian entity gained popular support about 1963 after some years of turmoil in which the issue was disregarded. The First Arab Summit, meeting in Cairo at the end of 1963, decided to form a Palestine entity. Convening in the same city nine months later, the Second Summit recognized the PLO[35] (then under the direction of al-Shuqairy) as the Palestinians' spokesman and decided to create the Palestine Liberation Army under the Unified Arab Command. King Hussein was very concerned from the outset about the natural tension between the PLO and the kingdom over the loyalty and support of Jordan's Palestinian population. This distrust was not soothed by al-Shuqairy's behavior. In mid-1964, the PLO leader stated that all of Jordan (including the East Bank) was part of Palestine!

Jordan—in contravention of the decisions of the Second Arab Summit— did not allow the PLA to recruit Palestinians in Jordan, and did not establish purely Palestinian units within the Arab Legion. On the contrary, Palestinians in lands now Jordanian by Jordanian law continued to be drafted regularly into the national armed forces.

The opposition of the Jordanian government to the requests being made by the young PLO had placed it in the forefront of those opposing the organization. But in 1965 Nasser himself reversed course and cut the ground from under the PLO at the Third Arab Summit in Rabat. The king, sensing the moment, decried the dangers of the PLO's approach, but used his strength to arrange a compromise in which al-Shuqairy was to cease pressing for Palestinian fighting units, requesting PLA recruitment, and attacking publicly the Jordanian government; in return, the PLO was allowed to open an office in Amman to establish broadcast facilities there. Friction increased in early 1966, however, as Jordan's relations with Egypt deteriorated. Throughout the spring and summer, the PLO and Syria waged a propaganda war against the Hashemite monarchy, haranguing that the liberation of Jordan was a necessary step on the road to the liberation of Palestine.[36] While Nasser remained silent,[37] he encouraged PLO inflammatory rhetoric over its Cairo broadcast facilities. (Only in late 1966 did Egypt itself join in the attack.) Moreover, Nasser, who had until then condemned the guerrilla attacks of Fatah, suddenly became a leading advocate that the guerrillas be allowed to operate.

While the PLO did establish facilities in Jordan after the agreement between King Hussein and al-Shuqairy, the Jordanian government kept close watch over the movement and its members. Fatah—in these days prior to its inclusion in the PLO—appeared even more of a danger in view of the character of its activities, the nature of its relations with other Arab governments, and the militancy of its supporters.[38] Surveillance of members and suspected members was intensive, and Jordan even cooperated with Israel in monitoring the group.[39] In spite of intensive Jordanian intelligence efforts, most raids into Israel in 1965 and 1966 were mounted from Jordanian territory, and it was therefore Jordan that bore the brunt of Israeli reprisals.[40] Under mounting pressure, the Arab Legion clashed with Fatah several times in the summer of 1966, and with sufficient success that raids increased from Syria and decreased from Jordan. However, Israeli forces continued to attack Jordan for the raids, which, in any case, increased once again after the Egyptian change of position. Israeli reprisals culminated in the attack on the village of Samu in November 1966.

The aftermath of the Samu raid was one of the most tumultuous periods in the Middle East. The Jordanian government experienced demonstrations and riots which, while enjoying Palestinian support, were clearly incited by Syrian, Egyptian, and PLO agents. Fatah units entered the country from Syria—not the first or last time Syria was to intervene directly—to overthrow the monarchy. Ultimately, the regional crisis in the succeeding months led to the June War of 1967,[41] and with it the loss of the West Bank.

The Jordanian position after the war was significantly different from before June 1967. The strength of the army was reduced as a result of the losses sustained during the fighting and the shock and depression of the defeat. The popularity of the guerrillas increased even further. Moreover, the growing power of the guerrillas affected all groups, including those other than Fatah. Whereas the leadership group in Fatah took a public position against intervention in the domestic affairs of Arab countries, subordinating all other issues to the liberation of Palestine, other groups did not necessarily adhere to this policy. In particular, the PFLP and even more the DFLP propounded a strident ideological line that stressed the necessity of overthrowing "Arab reaction" prior to the recovery of Palestine. And the growth of Fatah itself was so rapid after the Battle of Karameh[42] that many elements entered the organization whose views on nonintervention, for example, differed from those of the leadership.[43]

Unable to resist the overwhelming popular support for the guerrillas, the Jordanian government worked with them.[44] This was particularly true after settlement hopes declined in 1968. Military cooperation between the guerrillas and Jordanian forces grew, and Jordan even permitted the Palestinian units of the Iraqi army in Jordan to provide covering fire for guerrillas attacking Israel.[45] Given their collaboration with the government, the guerrillas had moved their headquarters and units to the Jordan Valley where they remained until the Karameh battle. Afterwards, they were removed to the hills west of Amman overlooking the valley. Israel then used air raids against the positions, so they were moved again—this time to the cities. Now, the guerrillas were present in large numbers within Jordan's cities for the first time, lighting a fuse leading to an inevitable explosion.

Jordan tried to find a way out of the impasse. King Hussein evolved a modus vivendi with the guerrilla leadership that was posited on (1) Jordanian assistance to the guerrillas in movement and supply and (2) permission to operate in Jordan in return for (3) guerrilla rejection of Arab government control, (4) abnegation of any involvement in internal affairs, (5) control of the refugee camps, (6) pledges not to attack Israel from Jordan, (7) guarantees to avoid specific Israeli targets, (8) promises not to arm the civilian population, and (9) assurances that armed and uniformed guerrillas would be kept out of the cities.[46] No one expected the PLO to pay heed to the pledge not to attack Israel from Jordan.

The agreement failed for the same reason that the PLO-Jordan relationship was doomed from the start: the most fundamental requirements and values of the two parties were diametrically opposed. The fragmentation of the resistance movement prevented an agreement concluded with Fatah from being effective on all groups. Fatah eschewed attempts at control of the movement as a whole, even when they might have been successful. All the organizations depended upon support from Iraq or Syria, and could not exclude influence by them. The ideological groups, and those totally controlled by foreign governments, had no intention of honoring the accord. These issues led to the first major confrontation between the guerrillas and the Arab Legion.[47]

While the first clash was relatively minor, it set the tone for the multistage confrontation yet to come. At a moment when prospects for a settlement appeared unusually favorable, a Syrian oppositionist was kidnapped and returned to Syria. Later, the *Kataeb al-Nasr*, a small group led by Tahir Dablan, was to incite a riot against the US embassy. The Jordanian government led a serious crackdown on the guerrillas but blamed the problem on the *Kataeb al-Nasr*, endeavoring to isolate it from the other groups. Yasser Arafat and the Fatah leadership cooperated in this ploy—but only inside Jordan. Outside Jordan, however, the Voice of Fatah took the *Kataeb* side and urged the Jordanian and Palestinian people and the Arab Legion not to support the government. The king blamed Sa'iqa.[48] In November 1968 another accord was reached between the government and the resistance, laying out a series of restrictions on guerrilla behavior.

Despite the growing volcano in Jordan, 1969 was peaceful, in part because clashes in Lebanon precluded the PLO from allowing anything untoward in Jordan. However, the restrictions of the November 1968 accord were not enforced, and the concern over the passage of time after the 1967 war led the king to view guerrilla actions as preventing the freezing of the cease-fire lines. Another reason for avoiding a showdown from the government side was that any crackdown tended to reinforce the extremists at the cost of the more moderate groups, such as Fatah. Indeed, the government feared another clash might move Fatah toward the PFLP.

In December 1969, US Secretary of State William Rogers launched a US peace initiative. Fatah vehemently opposed the attempt, which both Egypt and Jordan supported. A major clash ensued in February. Israeli indications of support for the king weakened him, but pressure from Transjordanians on him led to a partnership in which it was up to the king to control the East Bankers, and up to Fatah to control the other groups.

Throughout 1970, a number of additional clashes occurred, the PFLP, DFLP, or PFLP—GC generally among the precipitators. The political interests and perspectives of the two sides led to the clashes, but they were also provoked by issues unrelated to guerrilla needs or Jordanian nationalism. The establishment of de facto *fida'i* autonomy meant the concomitant establishment of *fida'i* civil power. Such power is routinely abused by governments at all levels, but the abuse seems the more odious when carried out by governments that do not even purport to represent the citizenry. The guerrillas armed civilians; they disregarded Jordanian laws; they excluded themselves from Jordanian financial obligations and taxes; they established their own courts whose venue they insisted upon for trials of guerrillas accused of various crimes; they patrolled streets and parts of the city outside their areas; they rejected registration of their vehicles; they incited demonstrations and riots; they attacked government buildings; they abducted Jordanians and foreigners alike; they intimidated journalists. Among the most visible, most painful, and most counterproductive, although least damaging, of their activities was routine extortion of money from drivers, shopkeepers, and others — a minor cost in theory, but a loathsome symbol to Jordanians of the loss of their own country and of the absence of security, law, and order. While Fatah was forced at times to close ranks with the other groups,[49] Yasser Arafat attempted to work with the king to avoid violence. (However Fatah radio in Cairo consistently opposed the Jordanian government, calling for its overthrow.)[50]

The Jordanian civil war was the earthquake to which all the pressures building up in Jordan for years had finally and inevitably led.[51] To a very great extent, it was provoked by the PFLP and DFLP against the will of Fatah.[52] The war in fact took place over several stages lasting about a year, at the end of which the PLO was no longer in Jordan. The bitterness of many Palestinians over the Jordan fighting was reflected in the formation within Fatah of "Black September," a special operations organization intended for use against Israel and Arab regimes that were deemed to be anti-PLO. Jordan was high on Black September's list, and the organization did in fact assassinate Prime Minister Wasfi al-Tall.

Yet PLO-Jordanian relations could never be confined to issues of law and order, of military affairs, and of security strategy. From the outset, the rise of the PLO threatened the Jordanian claim to be the rightful heir to Arab Palestine, even if only a part of it. Throughout the years after 1949, when the West Bank became a part of Jordan and after 1950 when the West Bankers were granted Jordanian nationality, Jordan's claim remained intact. The capture of the West Bank in 1967 found Jordan in the forefront of the Arab states seeking a peaceful settlement. But the Fourth Arab Summit at Khartoum had insisted on the three "no's"—no recognition of, no peace with, and no negotiations with Israel—a policy that effectively deprived Jordan of diplomatic maneuver. As it gained strength, the Palestinian resistance demanded to be recognized as the representative of the Palestinians, a demand directly contrary to Jordan's own claim of representation of at least those Palestinians on or from the West Bank.[53] This was to become a central theme of the relationship after 1970. The attempted reconciliation between the government and the resistance in late 1971 also broke down on this difference. In 1972, King Hussein proposed joining the East and West Banks federally as a United Arab Kingdom[54]—another implicit indication of Jordan's maintaining its own responsibility for the Palestinians and for resolving the Palestinian problem.[55] The plan was rejected by the Arab world, and Jordan's isolation—already severe after 1970 and 1971—was heightened still further. Not until a decade later when the US president proposed a similar plan, or later still when, after rejecting both, the PLO advocated another joint peace plan with Jordan, did the ideas get a hearing.[56]

The PLO saw in the United Arab Kingdom proposals a direct challenge to the very raison d'etre of the organization and lobbied diligently—and in the end effectively—to prevent its delegitimization. Through a process of improved relations with Egypt, the PLO succeeded in having the Arab summits at Algiers (1973) and Rabat (1974) ordain that the PLO was the "sole legitimate representative" of the Palestinian people. King Hussein's acceptance of this dictum in Rabat meant that Jordan could no longer put itself forward as the *interlocuteur valable* for the West Bank. While Jordanian diplomacy continued to quietly seek openings to assert its own credentials as a representative of the Palestinians,[57] the PLO and Jordan continued to view each other with bitter antipathy.

In the period after Sinai II (1975), Jordan and Syria developed a very close alliance.[58] Jordan needed a protector in the Arab world, but Syria's objectives were more far-reaching. Asad sought to create an Eastern Front[59] against Israel to maintain the kind of strategic threat that might push Israel toward concessions. Preliminary to such an entente would be a reconciliation between Jordan and the PLO. Moreover, in the face of Israeli refusal to negotiate with the PLO, Jordan might prove a necessary interlocutor, at least at an early stage. Asad worked diligently to encourage the PLO to accept a reconciliation, and Sadat seemed to indicate that Jordanian-Palestinian confederation was the only feasible resolution to the core of the Arab-Israeli problem.[60]

Meanwhile, a parallel dynamic was underway within the PLO. Many of the same Palestinian leaders who believed in the desirability of a rapprochement with Jordan were also convinced that the emphasis of the PLO must change from armed struggle to diplomacy.

These currents matured in early 1977. In February, Arafat sent a PLO delegation to Amman, and later that month the chairman and the king met publicly (for the first time since the battles in Jordan) at the Afro-Arab summit conference in Cairo. At the Thirteenth PNC in Cairo immediately thereafter, the proposal to move forward with relations surfaced. No formal decision was reached, but the Fatah leaders within the PLO Executive Committee proceeded with the initiative anyway.[61]

The vehicle that propelled the reconciliation was the Sadat initiative with the subsequent Camp David accords. Jordan remained noncommittal in the early stages but rejected the accords when King Hussein reached the conclusion, after requesting US explication of a number of elements, that no real autonomy would ensue and that the accords could in no way lead to an acceptable end to the Palestinian problem. In September 1978, Yasser Arafat met the king in Jordan, and by October a PLO office was reopened. That the king could take such a step in the face of strong East Banker feelings reflected his absolute popular support in Jordan.[62]

The Ninth Arab summit in Baghdad (November 1978) saw Jordan join the most active group of leaders opposing Camp David. The summit agreed to increase aid to Jordan, the PLO, and the resistance in the Occupied Territories. Jordan's return to a position of prominence on the Palestinian issue was symbolized by the summit's decision to divide responsibility for the last category between Jordan and the PLO.[63]

During 1979, Jordan's long-strained relations with Iraq improved, and in fact a secret alliance developed between the two governments. Thus when Iraq and Syria, former arch-rivals that had reconciled at the Ninth Arab Summit, split once again in July 1979, Jordan quietly and gradually moved into the Iraqi camp. Bereft of Egypt, and with most Palestinian strongholds in Lebanon either occupied by Syria or subject to Syrian firepower-backed "influence," the autonomy of the PLO was eroding. The opening to Jordan, which Syria now no longer pushed,[64] was one means of retaining some flexibility.

The Israeli invasion of Lebanon fundamentally altered the PLO's perceptions, creating conditions that impelled many of the traditional Fatah leaders around Arafat even more toward the views of Amman. Consequently, following some tactical errors at the Arab summit in Fez, the king and these Fatah leaders attempted to capitalize on the Reagan initiative. However, Palestinian irreconcilables and others who felt that Israel was neither inclined to nor capable of making the kinds of concessions that would be necessary and acceptable, cooperated to scuttle attempts by Hussein and Arafat to respond to the American approach.

Syria's heavy-handed efforts to gain complete control of the PLO through rather than around Fatah led to a split both within Fatah and within the PLO. This split ironically strengthened Arafat's hand by providing him with the nonirreconcilable constituency required to move toward a settlement. Syria actively prevented the holding of another PNC, prevailing upon Algeria not to host it. When King Hussein offered Amman as the site, Arafat accepted. At this stage, King Hussein, prominent Palestinians close to the king, and Arafat's own group worked closely together to hold a program that aimed at a peaceful settlement based on Resolutions 242 and 338 and that assumed a Palestinian polity in the West Bank linked in some manner to Jordan. While the Seventeenth PNC held in Amman at the end of 1984 did not address this evolving plan directly nor explicitly accept King Hussein's opening challenge to deal with the realities, it did allow the process to go forward. The absence of most of the irreconcilables and Syrian-controlled groups established the permissive environment required.

In February 1985, the next and capital step in the cooperative path Jordan and the PLO were pioneering together took place in Amman, where King Hussein and Yasser Arafat agreed to a program envisaging the formation of a joint negotiating team to pursue negotiations with Israel over a peaceful settlement of the Palestinian problem. The costs of this approach, anticipated by both, were rapidly confirmed, as Syrian-sponsored terrorist attacks resulted in the assassination of prominent Jordanian diplomats and Palestinian leaders, sabotage of Jordanian facilities overseas, and the hijacking of Jordanian planes.

The essence of the February 11 initiative assumed that PLO participation was necessary and sufficient to secure moderate Arab support for a settlement.[65] Thus, the PLO participation would enable Jordan to take the lead in negotiations but conditioned on PLO approval. The initiative failed for several reasons. First, the reluctance of the United States to assume any burden of active participation or leadership left a vacuum. While US diplomats worked diligently to resolve specific issues, they were unable to sustain momentum. At several critical points the PLO leadership felt it had gone as far as it could and required "rewards" to show its own constituency that progress was in fact being made. Afraid of the domestic political costs, the United States government did not respond. Second, the political weakness of the Israeli government precluded the kind of response to constructive proposals for the resolution of differences that might have established the necessary momentum. When signals were forthcoming—such as the Israeli prime minister's acceptance of a Palestinian negotiator known to be close to the PLO—the US government (perhaps correctly) took the most conservative interpretation of this action. Third, the PLO leadership failed to or was unable to exercise control over even those constituents remaining under its umbrella. Dramatic incidents staged to disrupt the peace process and embarrass Arafat combined with internal struggles that required political retreats from commitments made by PLO leaders. Finally, the moderate Arab states delivered the coup de grace at the Casablanca Arab summit when as a result of direct Syrian pressure they failed at a critical juncture to endorse the joint PLO-Jordanian initiative. This action demonstrated that Syria was in a position to block resolution and that the underlying assumption of the PLO-Jordanian initiative—that PLO acceptance would produce a settlement most of the Arab world could accept—was fatally flawed.

After a year of effort, King Hussein publicly admitted that the initiative had failed. Jordan placed much of the blame on the PLO, undertook a highly publicized rapprochement with Syria that was more form than substance, and tried to encourage West Bank Palestinian leaders to come to the fore. However, the peace process with its attendant promotion of Yasser Arafat and the PLO had restored much of Arafat's position on the East Bank as well as reinforced it on the West Bank. Jordan's sudden reversal vis-a-vis the PLO was followed by reduction in the PLO offices in Jordan and by promotion of a "Palestinian" military officer long loyal to Jordan as a replacement for the traditional PLO. For its part, the PLO abandoned the February 11 agreement at the Eighteenth PNC. The organization's renewed unity immediately increased the (already growing) friction with Jordan, given the posture of the groups that rejoined the Executive Committee. None of these attempts appeared likely to reduce PLO support on the West Bank or its newly reestablished legitimacy on the East Bank.[66]

With or without a peace process, with or without a joint Jordan-PLO approach, the struggle between the PLO and Jordan for the political identity and loyalty of the Palestinians in both the East and West Banks will continue to shape the structures, processes, and behaviors that characterize Jordanian-PLO relations.

PLO RELATIONS WITH LEBANON

No country has suffered more from the Palestinian tragedy than Lebanon. No people, including the Palestinian people, has suffered more than the Lebanese. No phase of Palestinian history is less accurately painted than the Lebanese period.

Contrary to the suggestions of some recent Palestinian historiography, the Palestinians were generally welcomed by the Lebanese,[67] and by none more than the Christians.[68] The author has personally interviewed many Lebanese who were themselves or whose parents were actively engaged in setting up shelters, who donated land or belongings, and who committed themselves to the assistance to the refugees. The Palestinians encountered no resistance from the Lebanese—although many of the refugees disdained the under-developed south and its inhabitants;[69] quite the contrary. Even the Beirut Jewish community joined in anti-Israeli demonstrations in 1948 and 1949. The lands on which a number of Palestinian refugee camps were built were donated by the Maronite and Greek Orthodox churches.

It was long an article of faith in Lebanon that the country was a special case due to its tenuous sectarian balance. This delicate matter was seen to influence the nature of Lebanon's relations with its Arab neighbors and, *a fortiori*, the nature of its posture toward Israel. Specifically, Lebanon, though an Arab state bordering Israel, was never considered a "confrontation state." Its limited role in the 1948–1949 Palestine war[70] and nonparticipation in the Arab-Israeli wars of 1956, 1967, and 1973 were scarcely criticized by mainstream Arab governments or leaders.[71] However, Palestinians and certain other pan-Arabists (who were disproportionately represented among Lebanon's population in both Christian and Sunni Muslim communities) came increasingly to the position that the Palestinian cause eclipsed all others in importance, including the interests of the state. Indeed, despite apparent threats or costs to "parochial interests," as those of individual Arab states were seen in this concept, the interests of the "Arab nation" were to be realized, and were existentially threatened, first and foremost in the context of the Palestinian problem.[72]

For Lebanon this evolution represented a particular problem. Having proceeded on the premise that "our weakness is our strength,"[73] the Lebanese army was too weak to take part in the struggle with Israel without endangering the very existence of the state. Rhetoric replaced action. As one observer commented, "Palestine provided Lebanon a way of proving its dedication to Arabism and in so doing to stabilize and insulate its ethnic [sic: sectarian] heterogeneity."[74]

This is not to say that Lebanon was so different from other Arab Fertile Crescent societies that territorial ambitions in Palestine were unknown.[75] Still less is it to say the Palestinians were viewed as Lebanese or that Lebanese authorities were supremely indifferent to political organization among the refugees. Lebanese military intelligence (G-2) monitored political developments closely, particularly as a sense of Palestinian national identity grew and Palestinian political organization proceeded. In this respect, it would be accurate to say that G-2—whose presence in Lebanon, especially after 1958, was heavy and ubiquitous—was as wary of the Palestinians as it was of any organized political group of Lebanese, but enjoyed somewhat (and not all that much) more freedom of action as regards aliens than it did in respect of Lebanese nationals.[76]

The Palestinians were regrouped in refugee camps, several of them previously established for earlier generations of refugees that had come to Lebanon—Armenians, Kurds, and so forth. A number of the camps became small cities or quarters, and those around the larger cities, especially Beirut, tended to spawn entire quarters of the urban area that were ghettos in which Palestinians tended not only to live, but also to replicate in some measure their own traditions and values and indeed to Palestinize the communal value structure.[77] It would not be an exaggeration to say that the population of the camps, of the Palestinian quarters, and of Palestinians resident elsewhere in Lebanon, constituted a sort of country of Palestine, though located elsewhere. While the same could be said of other Palestinian refugee communities, it was always more true of Lebanon, if only because of the relative weakness of the central government and army.[78]

Lebanon's government shared Jordan's skeptical views about the formation of a Palestine national entity, as this idea, which had surfaced in the late 1950s, gained momentum in the mid-1960s. When the Arab states decided to proceed with the establishment of what became the PLO, Lebanon opposed the concept of a PLA. In the event, the PLA was prohibited from entering Lebanese territory. Palestinians resident in Lebanon could join the PLA outside, but they were informed that they would not be allowed to re-enter Lebanon if they did so.

As for Fatah, which came later to lead the PLO, its first operation was to be launched from Lebanon. Participants, however, "leaked" it to G-2, which prevented it and caused the arrest of the team members. News of their arrests was in turn intentionally "leaked" in order to discredit Fatah. When Fatah's next operation (from Jordan) was carried out, Yasser Arafat, whose headquarters were then in Beirut, was arrested, and he spent over a month in a Lebanese prison. At the end of 1965, Fatah was planning an important operation "to celebrate" its first year. The anniversary operation was to be led by Jalal Qa'ush. Qa'ush, however, was arrested by G-2 and subsequently died while in custody. Syria and Fatah both excoriated the Lebanese government for torturing Qa'ush, and it has been alleged that both sought to use the incident to demonstrate to the Lebanese government that the domestic political costs of opposition to Fatah activities were far higher than any Israeli military costs were likely to be.[79] Commando strikes into Israel were not publicized at all in Lebanon in the period prior to the 1967 war. Indeed, such raids were at times intercepted by the Lebanese army.[80]

There was little criticism of Lebanon's nonparticipation in the 1967 war, even from the Palestinians. However, the position of Lebanon was to change drastically after the war, as Palestinian fighters of Fatah and other groups, at Damascus' direction, began to infiltrate the country from Syria.[81] Lebanese opinion polarized: while many (especially among the Christian community, but also many Sunni merchants and other establishment figures) feared for Lebanon's safety, others (especially Sunnis, but also many Christians outside the area known as Mt. Lebanon) fervently advocated Lebanon's duty to provide the PLO (after 1968) a front to carry out its "armed struggle."[82] The fuse lit by this polarization (which gathered momentum in 1967 and 1968) led rapidly and ominously to the conflagration that ignited in 1975.[83]

With the growth of the Palestinian armed presence in the South, and the increasing armament available in the camps elsewhere, the Palestinian community took on the specter of a state within a state. More relevant to this review, Palestinian raids into Israel, whether from Jordan or Lebanon, increased rapidly. In Lebanon, skirmishes between the *fida'iyin* and the army occurred.[84] The first major Israeli retaliatory raid took place almost exactly one year after the June War. The pace of raid and counterattack heated up in the aftermath of the Karameh battle, which infused so much hope and enthusiasm into the Palestinian movement. At the end of 1968, in retaliation for an attack on an Israeli airliner,[85] Israeli heliported commandos attacked Beirut airport, destroying thirteen aircraft. In some respects, the Beirut raid can be seen as the end of an era. Many believed that Lebanon was the model for an eventual peace in the region, that a settlement could evolve slowly from a desire for peace based on tangible interests in peace. The December 1968 raid suggested that even a government, such as Lebanon's, that sought no part in the conflict, was to be compelled to choose sides. It brought an end to Lebanon's luxurious era as a bystander, an end to the only model of peaceful coexistence with Israel, and ultimately an end to the Palestinians' most comfortable refuge.

In the period after the airport raid, Palestinian guerrillas continued their rapid build-up in Lebanon. Syria is known to have indicated the use that could be made of the paralysis and fragmentation the Palestinian issue induced into Lebanese politics. And, predictably, when the Lebanese army began to crack down on infiltration, bases, and supply routes, Palestinian forces, almost exclusively Fatah and Sa'iqa, enjoyed substantial Syrian support.[86] The Lebanese government did try to control the situation. Lebanese officials even met with Israelis on the issue.[87] Army action, again predictably, produced political crisis which in turn limited the army attempts. An agreement reached between the guerrillas and the army in April 1969 limited the former to specified routes. However, it was never the PLO intention to live with this agreement indefinitely,[88] and as winter approached, threatening to cut off guerrilla forces in the Arkoub from their supply routes to Syria, a large PLO military operation was planned with substantial Syrian support.[89] The continuing political crisis was expected to paralyze the Lebanese army. In fact, the army inflicted a military defeat on the guerrillas in the South and was in a strong position.[90] By contrast, the political position of the Lebanese government was dire: the domestic problem continued unabated (indeed inflated), and Beirut was subjected to extraordinary pressure from virtually the entire Arab world. The result was an agreement between the PLO and the Lebanese government mediated by and reached in Cairo which was subsequently seen to have "legitimized" the PLO presence in Lebanon by spelling out PLO rights and obligations.[91] The "Cairo Accord" also delineated a number of specific limitations on the PLO's freedom of action. As one observer has noted, "The Cairo Agreement . . . tended to be looked upon [by the Palestinians] as an acquired extraterritorial right never to be abandoned but rather to be consolidated and expanded where possible."[92]

The 1969 crises in Lebanon merit study. As in Jordan, the Lebanese government generally supported Fatah and condemned Sa'iqa and Syria. As in Jordan, Fatah tried to avoid direct clashes with the Lebanese authorities except when attacked. As in Jordan, individual members of Fatah did not follow organizational orders. As in Jordan, Fatah did advance unwarranted and far-reaching demands on Lebanon. As in Jordan, the Voice of Asifa (Fatah) in Cairo was strongly anti-Lebanon and preached violence and revolution. As in Jordan, Israel took measures to support the Lebanese government.[93] Unlike the Jordanian case, when the guerrillas backed off, the Lebanese army did take the initiative.[94]

During the period between the airport raid and the Cairo Accord, large-scale smuggling of arms into the refugee camps made several of them quite literally "armed camps." The November crisis led to the ousting of Lebanese police and military (G-2) monitors, and for the first time the PLO, through the Palestine Armed Struggle Command (PASC),[95] was truly master of the camps.

The pace of raids and counterraids varied markedly between December 1969 and January 1972, with the exception of a single clear and consistent trend—the increasing severity and brazenness of Israeli reprisals. Air raids, mechanized infantry assaults, temporary occupations—all were used. Indeed, a military road *part of which actually ran through Lebanon* was built to monitor developments in the South. The Lebanese army was involved in some confrontations with the guerrillas and in some with the IDF. The crescendo of violence in the South began to drive large numbers of southern Lebanese to evacuate. Most of them were poor Shi'i villagers and farmers who ended up as refugees in a "belt of misery" around Beirut and close to the Palestinian refugee camps and quarters.

The exodus of guerrillas from Jordan in 1970 and 1971, as a result of the conflict there, inevitably fed the level of infiltration into Lebanon. As the development of an infrastructure near completion, the influx also led, just as inevitably, to a renewal of the growth of raids against Israel in 1972—and, in turn, of Israeli threats[96] and retaliation. While there was no direct collaboration between the two armies, the Lebanese army at one point reestablished its control in the Arkoub (Fatahland) after an Israeli attack and brief occupation. This and other similar events, including widespread public pressure on the government from the Christians and the residents of the South, led to a process throughout 1972 of increasing limitations on the PLO and a return of control by government forces over territory in the South. The PLO deferred to increasing government control and made concessions wherever necessary in order to prevent a major confrontation with the Lebanese government.[97]

Tragically, no one was satisfied with conditions in late 1972. The Palestinians, especially the extremists, sought to increase their ability to attack Israel. Having kept much of their infrastructure in the South, they struck intermittently and planned to change the trend of events. Israel sought to provoke a full-scale confrontation between the army and the PLO to drive the latter from Lebanon. Residents of the South and much of the Christian community sought greater restraints on the PLO and its disarming. Supporters of the Palestinians and many Muslims sought a more even-handed posture on the part of the army, wishing it to invest as heavily in protecting Lebanon against Israel as it invested in controlling the PLO.

Another turning point toward the Lebanese holocaust took place in April 1973 when Israel launched a daring commando raid into the heart of Beirut, killing several prominent Fatah leaders, as well of course as a number of Lebanese civilians. The raid produced riots and demonstrations calling for greater army protection and accusing the army of collaboration with Israel to eliminate the PLO. There followed a number of incidents, principally inside Lebanon, and the major confrontation between the army and the PLO that Israel had long sought. Once again, the army (and the tiny air force which was called into use briefly) carried the day on the battlefield[98] in the most difficult of conditions, combat in a built-up and densely fortified area. Once again, Syria provided help to the PLO, this time with moves of the PLA. Once again, the Lebanese government was forced by domestic and regional political pressures to stop the army and to compromise. The PLO concluded that a future and more telling confrontation was a certainty. Consequently, some PLO planners began to set out a systematic strategy for the continuation and even the growth of Palestinian power in Lebanon.[99] But the confrontations of the spring of 1973 persuaded all but the most insensitive Lebanese that a real showdown was inevitable—and that it would be violent. Militias of all sorts, but particularly that of the Kataeb party, began to arm seriously in preparation for "the next round" That round turned out to be the series of events in February and April 1975 that are generally considered to be the opening of the Lebanese conflict.

While the fighting in April 1975 was brief and limited, Lebanese fought Lebanese as well as Palestinians.[100] None could maintain this was merely another series of demonstrations. Renewed hostilities erupted in the late summer and autumn in Beirut, and fighting elsewhere (especially around Tripoli) occurred even earlier. Fatah tried to remain outside the battle, although individual members of Fatah joined with Rejection Front partisans, DFLP and Sa'iqa fighters, and Lebanese members of the National Movement in the battle against the Christian militias.[101] The PLO helped maintain cease-fires, and Yasser Arafat cooperated with President Frangieh to try to reestablish order. In the second stage, Fatah and especially Rejection Front Palestinians were much more active.

After a brief respite initiated by a reconciliation between the president and prime minister, fighting erupted again. Frangieh had turned to Syria for assistance. Syria played a peculiar game at this stage, on the one hand permitting the dispatch of PLA troops into southern Lebanon that allowed about eight thousand experienced PLO fighters to engage in the North, while Syrian observers and advisors were present in a major move by the Christian militias to eliminate all Palestinian and Muslim quarters in the Christian area.[102] The disintegration of the Lebanese army saw one element, the so-called Lebanese Arab Army (LAA), come under PLO influence. (The LAA was to fight side-by-side with the PLO thenceforth.) The PLO as a whole was forced into an alliance with the National Movement[103] (leftist and predominantly Muslim) that proved catastrophic to all. For the Syrian government— whatever it thought of Frangieh's views—was committed to him and to Syria's new role as protector of Lebanese legitimacy. Consequently, Syria quietly—but visibly—deployed armor inside Lebanon to blunt one National Movement offensive and sent PLA and Sa'iqa troops to protect the presidential palace.

At the end of March 1976, after talks between Kamal Jumblatt and Hafiz al-Asad broke down, Yasser Arafat took his own turn negotiating with Syria. Pursuant to the agreement reached with the PLO, Syrian forces were deployed even in Beirut along the Green Line, though in the uniforms of PLA.[104]

The PLO had been trapped in the internal politics of Lebanon, to the extent of planning and helping to execute a coup d'etat that fizzled,[105] and was soon enmeshed in an inter-Arab rivalry no less intense. The emerging Jordanian-

Syrian entente was perceived as a threat to the PLO. Amman and Damascus, it was thought, might be prepared to offer Israel a settlement on the West Bank in which Jordan would reassert its sovereignty and control, leaving the PLO out in the cold. Consequently, although Arafat met with Asad and tried to coordinate activities in Lebanon with Syria during the first year of fighting, the growing Syrian inclination to intervene raised the specter of a Syrian attempt to destroy the autonomy of the PLO. Despite Sinai II, Arafat reopened a dialogue with Sadat, and the latter dispatched Egyptian PLA units to assist the PLO. On 1 June, Syrian troops entered Lebanon and were committed against the PLO.

PLO constituents split. As the fighting grew on several axes, wholesale defections from Syrian PLA and from Sa'iqa units took place. The Syrian-sponsored PLO groups wavered, then most sided with the PLO against Syria. (Sa'iqa and the PFLP—GC were the principal exceptions, but defections also occurred within these groups).

The PLO was deeply divided over the decision to support the National Movement against Fatah's traditional ally, Syria. The momentum of Syrian military victories and the reluctance of the two allies the PLO had hoped might restrain Syria—Iraq and Egypt—shifted power within the PLO to the hands of those who favored aligning with Syria. The PLO/National Movement "fighting withdrawal" was in fact a PLO attempt to exit the conflict with Syria.[106] The brunt of the fighting in the North until 1977 was between Syrian forces and the PLO. Two Arab meetings produced an Arab Deterrent Force (ADF) for Lebanon, which was really a legitimization of Syria's paramountcy in the country.

The south of Lebanon had become rather quiet. In the period after 1973, PLO forces returned in large numbers to the South. However, Israel had developed a close relationship with the Christian villagers of the area and had armed and assisted them in the formation of local militias. (These formed the core of the militia that was to come under the command of Sa'ad Haddad.) As the PLO returned, the local militias engaged it. When Syria entered Lebanon, its forces were expressly forbidden to enter the area south of the Zahrani River by the terms of the unwritten agreement between Israel and Syria governing Syrian intervention. This proscription meant that only the small, ill-equipped local militias were available to limit the Palestinians and the LAA allies which returned with the PLO to the South. Raids continued but diminished in 1977 as a result of the sometimes-peaceful, sometimes-violent efforts of Lebanese President Elias Sarkis, PLO Chairman Arafat, and Syrian President Asad to bring surcease to the fighting in Lebanon.

When Sarkis became president, he attempted to establish a dialogue with the PLO. He urged Arafat to meet with Asad and Asad to meet with Arafat. Although some PLO-Syrian meetings did occur, the overall negative relations between Fatah and the PLO, on one hand, and Syria, on the other, and the interdependence of the PLO and the National Movement served to prevent enduring accords. The Syrians preferred the language of the gun to that of negotiations.[107]

The Lebanese government, now armed with its (Syrian) ADF, demanded the disarmament of the PLO and withdrawal of the PLA. Arafat, turning to Egypt and Saudi Arabia for diplomatic support, refused the former, raising the fear of massacres of Palestinians. He demanded in turn the disarmament of the Christian militias. A similar stalemate obtained in domestic Lebanese politics, where the familiar issue of reform-before-restoration of order versus restoration of order-before-reform continued to rage. The diplomacy of the PLO, recognizing that in the fragile state Lebanon found itself procrastination would probably lead to victory, succeeded. Sarkis' impressions:

> Arafat stalled in refusing to apply the provisions of the Cairo Accord. Any pretext was good, as far as he was concerned, whether it was the necessity to deal with the Rejection Front, the death of Kamal Jumblatt (which, to believe him, placed everything in question), Begin's election, or the invasion of the South. . . . Moreover, in each case Arafat was able to find an Arab ally to support and defend him, and he played constantly on the numerous differences in the Arab world.[108]

The stalemate inside Lebanon did not however paralyze regional developments, and Sadat's initiative and trip to Jerusalem expedited a rapprochement between the PLO and Syria. As the PLO's only remaining sanctuary, Lebanon became the Palestinian avenue for response to Sadat.[109] A PLO raid inside Israel led to the Israeli occupation of southern Lebanon, which in turn gave rise to the presence of U.N. forces and to the consolidation of Sa'ad Haddad's territory. At about the same time, Syrian guns were turned against the Christians in Beirut and Zahle.

By 1979, the South was a free-fire zone, Israel subjecting it to constant bombardment, battles raging between Haddad and the PLO, and squabbles with the United National Interim Force in Lebanon (UNIFIL) erupting as well. Sarkis tried in vain to get Syria to control the PLO and to prevent the organization from carrying out raids into Israel, preferably through a freeze on operations. Meeting with little response from Damascus, Sarkis turned to Saudi Arabia only to find equal resistance. From this dead-end, Sarkis turned toward the PLO, beginning direct discussions with Abu Iyad with a view toward meeting with Arafat.[11] The Arafat-Sarkis encounter clarified positions, but changed nothing. Neither the PLO nor the LAA nor the National Movement was prepared to accept the deployment of the Lebanese army to the South; nor was the PLO prepared for a freeze. Indeed, far from improving the diplomatic climate between the two, the meeting hardened positions, and Arafat worked diligently and effectively at the Tenth Arab summit (Tunis, November 1979) to isolate and defeat any Lebanese initiative.

In February 1980, Fatah carried out an attempted assassination of Bashir Gemayel (using Lebanese agents). Gemayel survived, but his daughter was killed.[111] Nor was the PLO alone in sensing the growing power of Gemayel. Damascus began a concerted courting of the Kataeb.

The development of the Zahle crisis took place in an unusual environment. The Lebanese government, which had depended upon Syria almost completely, saw itself increasingly at odds with Damascus. Syria was once again exerting strong pressure on the Christians, especially Gemayel's Lebanese Forces. At this juncture, Arafat took the initiative, sending an emissary to the Forces on 8 April 1981, as the Zahle crisis was peaking. Arafat warned that Syria intended to create a major explosion in Lebanon, an explosion that the PLO saw as contrary to its vital interests. Arafat suggested that the Forces stall as long as possible around Zahle and Beirut, and offered to open whatever doors he could in the Arab world to the Kataeb so that they could present the Lebanese dilemma.[112]

The missile crisis around Zahle introduced the American mediation, which, failing to resolve the missile crisis itself, effected a cease-fire in the South, bringing to a virtual—but, alas, temporary—end the state of unending violence to which that area had been subjected. Despite Israeli complaints to the contrary, the cease-fire held remarkably well. The cease-fire was uniformly popular on neither side of the border. Many Israelis saw it as a tacit recognition of the PLO and attempted to broaden the cease-fire's intent and terms to cover the entire world. Many Palestinians saw it as undermining the cherished fantasy of the "armed struggle." Indeed, when the PFLP—GC refused to accept the cease-fire, Fatah had to go to battle to enforce its terms. The record shows violations on both sides, but far fewer from the PLO than from Israel. Moreover, some Israeli military activities—probably by intelligence units—were designed to encourage PLO violations.

Israeli military leaders planned the destruction of the PLO infrastructure in Lebanon.[113] By the spring of 1982, PLO leaders and other observers were aware that Defense Minister Sharon and Chief of Staff Eytan were determined to invade Lebanon. The only questions were when, where, and how far. Despite intelligence and warnings, many PLO leaders were surprised when Israel pushed all the way to Beirut, destroying the PLO infrastructure in the South and in the camps. The 1982 war[114] led to the departure of all PLO forces (except some under cover) from Beirut and the South. The PLO remained behind Syrian lines in the Biqa' and in the camps of the North.

From 1982 to 1986, the PLO no longer interacted in any significant way with the Lebanese government. However, the PLO was far from past Lebanese history. Once the Lebanese crisis moved to its post-1982 phase,[115] Syria attempted to take over the PLO once again. The battles — as usual — were fought in Lebanon. The disintegration of Lebanon, which proceeded even faster and further than before, was accompanied by Palestinian problems of high visibility, but none could accuse the PLO this time of being the principal cause of the tragedy.

During the period of Palestinian military presence south of Beirut, the PLO had dominated the area from the Green Line to the Israeli border, excepting only certain localities where Sa'ad Haddad or UNIFIL or AMAL (the Shi'i movement) held sway. However, that dominance had expressed itself in countless transgressions against the Lebanese inhabitants of all social or sectarian groups. Because the PLO had served, in effect, as the Sunni militia in a country in which power truly came from the barrel of guns, there was little or no Sunni resistance against the PLO at any time. By contrast, Christian, Druze, and Shi'i resistance was pronounced. Since the Christian heartland was outside the area of PLO control, and only limited PLO forces were deployed later in the Shuf, the area in which local and Palestinian interests clashed most clearly was predominantly Shi'i, and the populous but lightly armed Shi'i community resorted to force against the PLO by the late 1970s and early 1980s.

It was for this reason that the Lebanese Shi'i community welcomed at the popular level its deliverance from the PLO at the hands of the invading Israeli army.[116] (That army's subsequent occupation produced a determined resistance as well.) When the IDF withdrew, the re-arming and reactivation of the Palestinian camps excited the fears of the Shi'i community, and major battles raged in the Palestinian camps, battles conducted by AMAL to establish Shi'i control over the camps in Lebanon. In this respect, too, the PLO paid dearly for Syria's attempt to take over the organization because Syrian leaders saw the camps as dominated by pro-Arafat sympathies and set out to destroy them. In fact, Syrian support for the Shi'a backfired, since all Palestinians united in the face of the Shi'i onslaught.

The AMAL-PLO battles continued from 1984 onward. However, typical of the conflicts in Lebanon, the passage of time complicated matters. By late

1985, the more militant elements of the Lebanese Shi'i community, taking their direction from Iran, entered into a tacit alliance with the PLO against Amal. The Druze also supported the Palestinians. Druze support was important both because of intermittent supporting fire from the Progressive Socialist Party (PSP) in 1984 and 1985 and, more significantly, because of the Druze willingness to allow PLO fighters to enter the camps. The government of Lebanon and later the Lebanese Forces also provided logistical and other support to the PLO, and the latter, in turn, provided significant sums to both its new Christian allies. A coalition of "leftist," Druze, and PLO forces than carried what had been the "camps war" to AMAL, taking over large areas of West Beirut. Syrian intervention constrained the PLO and its allies, but even afterwards PLO strength continued to grow both around Beirut and in the South, as Druze, Christian, and some Shi'i elements continued to work—each for different reasons—with the PLO. The PLO was back in Beirut and the South with thousands of fighters only partly and in some areas was constrained by the Syrian presence[118] that had restricted PLO freedom of action prior to June 1982. PLO political and military power in Lebanon, thought to be only a memory after 1982, was once again a major consideration.

PLO RELATIONS WITH IRAQ

Rhetorically, Iraq maintained the most consistently hard-line policy against Israel of any Arab country until the 1980s. However, Iraq's potent language has not generally been matched by action. Nevertheless, Iraq may justifiably claim some responsibility for the creation of the PLO. Private discussions among Egypt, Iraq, Syria, and Jordan over the creation of a "Palestine entity" impelled 'Abd al-Karim Qassim to publicly propose the creation of such an organization with its own armed forces to be manned by personnel recruited from among Palestinian refugees.

Qassim's purposes in promoting a "Palestine entity" must be traced much more to Iraq's Arab rivalries than to its untrammelled support for the Palestinian cause. The historic competition between Cairo and Baghdad for regional leadership was a primary reality in the 1950s.[119] The Qassim proposal, while anathema to Jordan, was designed to exploit and seize the initiative on the Palestinian issue, to serve as a platform to attack Egyptian policy, and to undercut Egypt's position.[120] Iraq's proposals, focusing on a Palestinian national entity, were fundamentally contrary to the pan-Arab polemic emanating from Cairo and Damascus. Ironically, the subsequent history of Iraqi relations with the PLO has been characterized by Baghdad's preoccupation with Arab, rather than Palestinian, issues, and the Ba'th government of Iraq has preached the kind of pan-Arab line the original proposals for a Palestine entity effectively undermined.

Following the Arab summit decision to create what became the PLO, Iraq, which had proposed a Palestinian army, became the first to contribute to it in 1960 by forming a battalion of soldiers for the PLA recruited from among Palestinian refugees in Iraq. Haj Amin al-Husaini, the former Grand Mufti of Jerusalem, who had been given refuge by the Iraqi government, personally assisted in the recruitment. Moreover, the Iraqi "government offered training facilities for aviation technicians and established some scholarships for Palestinians at the military academy."[121] Baghdad was unprepared for the seizure of the initiative by the guerrillas, however. Iraq did not have its own Palestinian guerrilla group and, lacking a front with Israel, was ill placed to establish and support one. The intermittent opposition of Jordan and control of their borders with Israel by Egypt, Lebanon, and Syria made such support impossible.

Aware of the growth of guerrilla power and popularity, the Iraqi government did encourage some Palestinians in Iraq to become affiliated with Sa'iqa. Iraq had not enjoyed close ties to the PLO, since the original organization was dominated by its rival, Egypt, and the post-1967 PLO was dominated by organizations whose linkages to "suspect" Arab governments concerned Iraq. Moreover, the fractious nature of relations with Damascus and bumpy relations with the PLO itself led to a decision to establish the Arab Liberation Front (ALF), nominally formed from Palestinian elements of the Iraqi Ba'th in April 1969. As its title suggests, the ALF emphasizes Palestine as a pan-Arab problem rather than a Palestinian one, quite in keeping with the pan-Arabist ideology of the Ba'th. Indeed, for all their differences, and in spite of inconsistencies in this regard, the rival Ba'th parties of both Iraq and Syria have often denied the legitimacy of a discrete Palestinian national people.[122] And the ALF has been composed of a majority of non-Palestinian Arab Ba'thists.

The ALF can be seen both as an attempt by Iraq to prevent the growth of independent guerrilla power in Iraq as it was emerging in Jordan (and was soon to emerge in Lebanon), on the one hand, and as a bid to limit rival Arab regimes' power or increase Iraqi options within the Arab political scene, on the other.[123] In fact, the objective conditions probably precluded any threat from autonomous Palestinian power in Iraq,[124] and the ALF has been but a marginal player in either Palestinian or regional terms.

The Iraqi government insisted that all guerrilla groups in Iraq coordinate movement through the government and its "house" commando group, and tried to force all based there into some affiliation with the ALF.[125] Relations with Sa'iqa were a reflection of the Iraqi-Syrian relationship[126] and those between Fatah and the Iraqi government continued to deteriorate. However, despite its strong rhetoric, Iraq remained largely inactive in the resistance. As the rapid growth of the guerrilla presence in southern Lebanon led to crises in 1969, Iraq urged the Lebanese people to side with the Palestinians and against the Lebanese government, which did little to smooth relations with either the Lebanese government or moderate elements in the resistance. Friction with Syria meant the ALF could never develop roots in that country. Some ALF were deployed in Jordan where they constituted an unruly element, but one that had little popular base in the camps.[127] Syria arrested or expelled ALF members and supporters, confiscating their equipment, on several occasions. However, the presence of regular Iraqi forces in Jordan did constitute an asset for the ALF. Correctly perceiving itself isolated and limited in its ability to use the Palestinian card, Iraq attempted to attract Fatah (and thus the PLO) from Syria or at least to reduce its degree of dependence on Damascus. It would be accurate to see this as much more of an inter-Arab conflict posture than an Arab-Israeli posture.

The crescendo of PLO-Jordan and PLO-Lebanon crises in 1969 and 1970 continued to confound Iraq's efforts to construct a coherent policy. The provocative stance taken by Baghdad in both instances was confined largely to rhetoric. In Lebanon, however, Iraqi ALF and other Palestinian elements designed to relieve PLO forces trapped in the South by the Lebanese army did enter the country (with Fatah and Sa'iqa units) and participate in the fighting there. But much more notoriety attended Iraqi behavior in Jordan.

Throughout the crisis leading to the decisive September 1970 confrontation, Iraq had supported the resistance politically and had vehemently opposed the Rogers Plan that Egypt and Jordan expressed interest in. The ALF took part in attacks in Jordan on a small Palestinian group led by Issam Sartawi, a group supporting the Egyptian position. (Iraq had also rejected Resolution 242.) In addition, as the crisis heated up, Iraq announced that it would place, then that it had placed, its forces under the command of the resistance, suggesting strongly that the substantial Iraqi forces (about fifteen thousand men) in Jordan would actively support the PLO. In the event, they did not. The failure of Iraqi forces to come to the aid of the PLO produced riots in Iraq, where the affair was used in the on-going power struggle between military and civilian leaders,[128] and as a result of the disrepute that followed put to rest any lingering hopes Iraqi might have entertained about taking a leading role in the resistance. By 1971, the government reached the point of refusing to pay the salaries of PLA stationed in Iraq; this was the nadir of Iraq's relations with the Palestinian movement.

The upturn in relations with the resistance began in 1972 as a result of a conscious effort by the Ba'th leadership. Iraq pushed hard for the conference of Arab forces supporting the resistance which was held in Beirut in November 1972. In addition, the government eased restrictions on the issuance of Iraqi passports to Palestinians and generally improved conditions of the Palestinians in Iraq. Similarly, Baghdad increased its economic aid to the PLO, facilitated the transshipment of arms to the PLO through Iraq, and worked to improve Soviet-PLO ties. The PLO, in turn, played a key role in mediating the Iraq-Kuwait border crisis of 1973. When renewed hostilities erupted in Lebanon, once again Iraq went out of its way to support—short of the use of military means—the PLO.

Throughout this period of active cooperation that began in 1972, Iraqi security personnel and elements of Fatah worked closely together behind the scenes on intelligence and terrorist planning. The Black September (Fatah) liaison with Iraqi intelligence was none other than Sabri al-Banna, known more commonly under his *nom de guerre*, Abu Nidal. The PLO's change in orientation toward a compromise of a two-state solution in Palestine once again alienated Iraq and antagonized Abu Nidal as well.[129] When the PLO decided as a part of its new posture that Black September's time was past and consequently disestablished the organization, Abu Nidal defected to Iraq. At about the same time, The PFLP, PFLP—GC, Palestine Popular Struggle Front, Iraqi Ba'th, and of course the ALF formed the Rejection Front to oppose the new Fatah line. Once again Iraq and the PLO were on opposite sides.

Iraqi relations with the PLO continued to vary throughout the next few year. On the one hand, the Iraqi Ba'th in Lebanon was part of the Lebanese National Movement and therefore supported the PLO; on the other, the Iraqi government periodically cautioned greater consideration of the needs of the Lebanese Christians, and Abu Nidal waged his own war against Fatah, using his own group, also called Fatah,[130] to do it. When this war heated up in 1977 and 1978, the PLO retaliated against Abu Nidal assassination attempts on PLO moderate leaders by attacking Iraqi diplomats. The war was terminated abruptly by the signing of the Camp David accords, which ushered in a period of improved Iraqi-Syrian and Iraqi-PLO relations.[131]

After 1979 and 1980, Iraqi relations with the PLO have continued to be a function of more salient problems confronting Iraq. Thus, as Iraqi-Jordanian relations improved in 1979, as Syrian-Iraqi relations deteriorated even further, and the Iran-Iraq war broke out in 1980, Iraq's orientation toward the PLO has been dominated by considerations related to these more important political developments. Although Iraq played a major role in lighting the fuse that led to the 1982 war in Lebanon, [132] the post-Lebanon war period, which has seen a more distinct step toward peaceful settlement by the PLO, has therefore not alienated Iraq. On the contrary, Iraq has itself for the first time begun issuing moderate statements on Arab-Israeli issues, has been closely behind Jordan in improving ties to previously-isolated Egypt, and appeared to support the initiative put forth by King Hussein and Yasser Arafat and codified in the 11 February 1985 agreement between the two. For the first time, Iraq and the PLO shared fundamentally similar views of political objectives in the region. As always, however, the PLO and the Palestinian issue generally remained a peripheral issue to Iraq.

The failure of the February 11 initiative had only minimal impact on Iraq, particularly since the PLO continued to support the February 11 agreement, and Iraq continued to moderate its stance toward Israel. Iraqis met secretly with representatives of Israel, and prominent members of the American Jewish community were invited to Iraq. In part the continuing evolution of Iraqi attitudes was intended to secure direct or indirect US assistance in the Gulf war. While Baghdad was disappointed with the US response, the erosion of Iraq's position did lead Washington to tilt more and more toward Iraq—quietly. US-PLO differences stood in stark contrast to the increasingly cooperative turn in US-Iraqi relations, and inevitably American officials queried Iraq about that country's intentions vis-a-vis the PLO, which was allowed to expand its operations in Iraq following Jordanian pressure to restrict PLO activities in Jordan. Iraq saw the PLO as a counter to Syria. More important, neither Iraq nor any other Arab state wanted the PLO to fall under Syrian control, a concern of much greater moment after King Hussein announced the failure of the February 11 agreement and placed principal responsibility for that failure upon the PLO. The alternative Iraq offered to the PLO was presented to others as necessary, reflecting primarily the necessity to prevent a PLO-Syrian rapprochement. This too was the reasoning behind the logistic and financial support Iraq provided to PLO forces in their Beirut camps in 1986: anything that complicated Syrian policy was, ipso facto, in Iraq's interest.

CONCLUSION

The PLO interactions with the Fertile Crescent states have been the organization's most intense relationships and little wonder. Syria claims all of

Palestine. Jordan has important interests in the West Bank. Both these countries and Lebanon border Israel and old Palestine. The confusion of nationalisms and overlapping of loyalties in the Arab world is nowhere more problematic than in this area and affects none more than it affects these peoples. An 'Alawi leader, who has launched more than one bloody war against Palestinians and whose policies have undermined Palestinian interests more than those of any other Arab state (an arguably more than Israel's), claims to be more sensitive to Palestinian nationalism than the PLO leadership because he simply does not recognize a distinct Palestinian identity, a phase even Israeli leaders have long since passed.

The creation of the PLO was a function of inter-Arab politics, and in many ways the organization has never ceased to be dominated by inter-Arab conflict. Divisions in the Arab world created the PLO, and it is true that some flexibility has accrued to the PLO as a result of continuing differences among the Arab states. However, the differences have hurt the PLO far more, as we have seen. In each case, the PLO has acted as a mirror of the Arab world, with its own divisions reflecting more or less verisimilarly the schisms in the larger region.

The PLO's immersion in the continuing problems of the Arab subsystem has crippled PLO diplomacy on the Palestinian problem (though not necessarily on others). Important, long-range decisions have been postponed and postponed again, or have been shunted aside while the leadership deals with the immediate crises at hand. In no small part this also reflects the power of non-Palestinian Arab governments, particularly that of Syria, inside the PLO. For the most part, not one of these governments has favored a truly independent PLO; and not one favors it today.

Is the PLO independent? Has it ever been? The organization has always been most powerful when it was an instrument of state policy, and weakest when it acted alone. Yet, this is far from saying it has been most effective in representing Palestinian interests when it was an instrument of state policy. When the PLO was an instrument, it survived. There are those who maintain that success in Middle East political terms can only be measured by survival. But survival is not leadership. Nor is survival progress toward objectives. And survival without progress while change takes place is usually retrogression.

While the Arab world created the PLO, it did so in an environment made possible by the selective intervention of the Western powers whose policies in Palestine followed no discernible course of reason prior to 1948 and have not discovered a more rational path in the period since. Political support to a minority nationalist movement that excluded the majority; peacekeeping that, as history has shown, neither kept the peace nor made one; intervention that was adequate to stop hostilities but never to force or allow a decision — these are the legacies of Western involvement, legacies shared generously among all the states of the Fertile Crescent, including the moderates who sought only surcease of the violence that threatened them.

Seduced by their powerful sponsoring governments, constituent members of the PLO fell for the state-within-a-state trap, and were victimized no less than their hosts. The shibboleths of Palestinian rights were used to cover Palestinian wrongs in Jordan and Lebanon, individual abuses of power, and group misconduct. Rhetoric is no substitute for sound policy. Blaming others will not bring justice nearer home. In Jordan and in Lebanon again, the PLO became accustomed to "playing revolution," an error that only rarely characterized the Algerians Fatah's leaders so admired.

And what happened to the extremists who so ardently defended the PLO and passed for its ideological allies? The pan-Arabist radicals have virtually all become subservient to one or another of the Arab governments that sponsored them.[133] From their mouths comes the same verbiage, but their actions — so slavishly faithful to their masters — speak far louder than their words.

Within the PLO and beside it, extremism is still in vogue, even if it does not carry the day. Yet their slogans of violence and fantasies of power have engendered a cost not only in missed opportunities and wasted time. They have also exacted a heavy toll in human lives. While they prefer to blame the Americans, the Israelis, or other Arabs for the "conspiracies" against them, who brought the confrontations between the PLO and the monarchy in Jordan to the breaking point? Who insisted on carrying the revolution to Lebanon? The preferred tactic in war is to fight on any soil but one's own. The extremists within and without the PLO preferred to do battle on the soil of the moderates and were profligate with Palestinian lives, lives the Palestinian extremists let themselves be led into spending.

The literature of the PLO reflects a passion for the word that is eminently Middle Eastern. Strong rhetoric has been the hallmark of the PLO. Even in the best of times in Jordan and Lebanon, PLO rhetoric was strong and seditious. This is hardly an indictment of the PLO; it is evidence that the PLO is an authentic actor in a region in which words that are used to defeat others typically make their speakers captive, a characteristic of both the Arab states and Israel.

And nowhere is the recoil of logomachy more apparent or more tragic than in the fantasy of the "armed struggle." In order to retain this fantasy, the

PLO has been compelled to adopt policies that have alienated the refugees' hosts in the very Arab states where they were most welcome and in which the most fundamental values were shared, policies that have even tended to make the word, "Palestinian," opprobrious within and beyond the region. Worse, the fantasy has caused those who pursued it to pass by the real opportunities to arrive much closer to their aspirations.

It is remarkable that the opportunities for settlement before 1948, those that were so heartily rejected by Palestinian leaders of the time, would have been immeasurably superior for Palestinian interests to even the most expansive goals today. The opportunities that surrounded King 'AbdAllah's negotiations with Israel immediately after 1949 and were so heartily rejected by Palestinian leaders of the time, would have been demonstrably superior to today's Palestinian aspirations as well. The proposals advanced by King 'AbdAllah's grandson in 1972, which were rejected then by the PLO in scabrous terms, envisaged a settlement with terms beyond what the PLO leadership can expect today. And it is safe to say that tomorrow's terms will be even less accommodating than those that may be available—if any are—today. The criticism of PLO leadership that Lebanese and Jordanian leaders have issued addresses this point: what is the direction in which the Palestinians are being led, other than to permanent exile? Flamboyant rhetoric and macho fantasies may soothe the psyche in the short term, but as substitutes for pragmatic, indeed opportunistic policies, they have been employed at the cost of Palestinian interests and aspirations.

The wise general bases his strategy on what he does well, not what he does poorly (or his enemy does better). The wise gambler does not throw good money after bad. PLO diplomacy in the Fertile Crescent has been characterized by poor strategy and bad gambles. The PLO deals from a position of weakness, and therefore one cannot expect the movement to score endless victories. Nevertheless, what victories the PLO has achieved have come from political pragmatism, not from the absurd "military solution." Extremism is an extravagance affordable only to the more powerful in a contest of strength. The only victories that can attend the Palestinian irreconcilables are rhetorical. There are more practical and far more important achievements that wait to be realized.

Ironically, from the time the PLO emerged as the representative of the identity and will of the vast majority of Palestinians, a time when the group around Yasser Arafat dominated Fatah which in turn dominated the PLO, the moderate governments supported Fatah and tried to work with it. For a time in Jordan, had the Fatah leadership chosen to do so, it could have cracked down on the extremist organizations and unified the mainstream of the movement, constituting an *interlocuteur valable*, an indispensable element of any negotiated settlement. In the period after 1968 and before September 1970, Fatah enjoyed Hashemite support. [134] Whatever their reservations, Lebanese leaders too supported Fatah. Yet, Fatah and the PLO allowed themselves in both cases to be manipulated—at their expense—by the extremists.

In part this anomaly may be a function of the "external leadership" of the PLO, for its historic base—and not just the leadership—has also been external. The externals have a different set of priorities. Many come from what is now Israel proper; they can never return. Many believe they have nothing to lose from extremism—though the recent past should amply demonstrate how wrong they are in that belief. By contrast, the internals, that is, the residents of the West Bank and Gaza, have a different set of priorities and have always been underrepresented in the PLO. While the long-term interests of the two groups are realistically not divergent, differences of perception have led to major variations in tactics and values.

The PLO movement toward peaceful settlement, an evolution over the last decade, brings the organization much closer to the internal Palestinian community, to Jordanian views, and to those of Jordan's ally, Iraq. The majority in Lebanese public attitude has for an even longer period favored a settlement, although Syrian domination of Lebanon muffles these views. Only Syria finds itself fundamentally at odds with the PLO's approach.

Will this moderating trend achieve success? The evolution of PLO presence in Jordan and Lebanon suggest that both countries are moving toward a reprise, with a few modifications, of the situations prior to 1970 in Jordan and 1982 in Lebanon. The level of arms in the camps will not be as great. Much history has already been played out. But it remains to see what the PLO will do with its second chances. Once again the changing circumstances of organized Palestinian presence cannot be considered without reference to inter-Arab struggles that are determining the rules and players of the game. And so the perennial conflict between Arab states continues and will continue to dominate the PLO and its relations with the Arab world states. And thus too will the role of the Arab states in the PLO impede the search for solution to the Palestinian problem.

NOTES

1. The claim that "Jordan is Palestine" is a particularly ironic one in view of the fact that the Jordan River has been an administrative or political boundary as far back as the era of Harun al-

Rashid. See Paul A. Jureidini and R. D. McLaurin, *Jordan: The Impact of Social Change on the Role of the Tribes* (New York: Praeger for the Center for Strategic and International Studies, Georgetown Univ., 1984), 10.

2. See the Syrian section, and specifically the interesting comments attributed to President al-Asad by Kamal Jumblatt below.

3. Syrian claims on Lebanon are longstanding. Syria has always refused to establish diplomatic relations on the basis that relations were too intimate for diplomacy, and numerous Syrian leaders have announced that Lebanon is really a part of Syria.

4. Barbara Anne Wilson, *Conflict in the Middle East: The Challenge of the Palestinian Movement* (Washington, DC: Center for Research in Social Systems, The American Univ., 1969), 22.

5. Al-Shuqairy was a well-known figure and had served other Arab governments, but in the period immediately prior to his being named, he had become completely dependent upon Egypt. Although serving as the chairman of the Saudi delegation to the United Nations, he refused to present a Saudi protest over alleged Egyptian subversion to the United Nations. As soon as he returned to the Middle East, the Arab League nominated Shuqairy to lead a Palestinian delegation to the U.N.

6. Malcolm Kerr, *The Arab Cold War*, 3d ed. (New York: Oxford Univ. Press, 1971), 115.

7. See, e.g., Helena Cobban, *The Palestinian Liberation Organisation* (New York: Cambridge Univ. Press, 1984); Abu Iyad with Eric Rouleau, *My Home, My Land,* trans. Linda Butler Koseoglu (New York: New York Times Books, 1981).

8. Cobban, *The Palestinian,* passim.

9. Kamal Jumblatt, *I Speak for Lebanon* (London: Zed Books, 1982), 78.

10. Barry Rubin, *The Arab States and the Palestine Conflict* (Syracuse: Syracuse Univ. Press, 1981), 16.

11. The battalion was permitted Palestinian officers and was also allowed to consider itself PLA. Wilson, *Conflict,* 28.

12. William B. Quandt, Fuad Jabber, and Ann Mosely Lesch, *The Politics of Palestinian Nationalism* (Berkeley: Univ. of Calif. Press, 1973), 68–70.

13. Indeed President Amin al-Hafiz approved the idea of support for Fatah in late 1964. Ehud Yaari, *Strike Terror: The Story of Fatah* (New York: Sabra, 1970), 57.

14. For a while in mid-1965, Nasser attempted to woo Fatah himself, presumably to wrest it from Syrian control. He failed.

15. After Jordan and Lebanon began to impose their own controls on Fatah operations, Syria did permit certain limited activities by Fatah, almost exclusively mine-laying near the frontier. Ze'ev Schiff and Raphael Rothstein, *Fedayeen: Guerrillas Against Israel* (New York: McKay, 1972), 68. Interestingly, Israel chose to retaliate not against the Syrian original source of the raids, but instead against the state from whose territory the guerrillas came. Schiff, *Fedayeen,* 71. Indeed, the al-Samu reprisal of November 1965 in Jordan was a response to a raid for which Syrian responsibility was not in doubt.

16. The head of Syrian military intelligence was deeply and directly involved in supporting Fatah. See Wilson, *Conflict,* nn.82ff., 39–40; John W. Amos II, *The Palestinian Resistance: Organization of a Nationalist Movement* (New York: Pergamon, 1980), 56–57; Edgar O'Ballance, *Arab Guerrilla Power: 1967–1972* (Hamden: Archon, 1974), 29–31; and John Cooley, *Green March, Black September: The Story of the Palestine Arabs* (London: Cass, 1973), 92.

17. Hafiz al-Asad had been one of the prime supporters of Fatah even in its earliest days in 1964. Abu Iyad relates that al-Asad secured weapons for Fatah without the knowledge of the Ba'th or of the Syrian government. (Abu Iyad, *My Home,* 42.) In the new government al-Asad became minister of defense.

18. Despite many concessions to the Syrian government, Fatah retained some autonomy. During this period the Syrian government tried to take Arafat's position and to replace him with a Palestinian officer who had served in the Syrian Army, but the usurper was killed by those loyal to Arafat.

19. Especially against Jordan. See Wilson, *Conflict,* 41.

20. Syria used many means to secure a more complete control over Fatah, including infiltrating Ba'thists into the organization's ranks. Abu Iyad, *My Home,* 45.

21. Helena Cobban correctly points out that in the aftermath of the 1967 war Sa'iqa's ability to depend upon the Ba'th party infrastructure enabled it to absorb large numbers of the suddenly plentiful volunteers and therefore to grow more rapidly than the other organizations. Cobban, *The Palestinian,* 157.

22. Cobban is more diplomatic, suggesting that some Fatah members took the alliance with Syria to be strategic, not tactical. Syrian policy in this regard was evident early when a young Palestinian officer in Saudi Arabia was inserted in Fatah at Syrian request in return for Syrian support for Fatah military operations. The officer later left Fatah, and, after several organizational peregrinations, established the Popular Front for the Liberation of Palestine—General Command. Ahmad Jibril has remained loyal to Syrian policy over the years and was one of the few Palestinian leaders to remain allied with Syria in Lebanon even during 1976. His group later played a lead role in the 1983 Fatah mutiny in Lebanon.

23. Cobban, *The Palestinian.*

24. Cobban, *The Palestinian,* 73. It is important to note that Haddad was more than a Syrian ally in inter-Arab politics; he was an ally of Hafiz al-Asad in the then-ongoing internal struggle in Syria, opposing Sa'iqa in that context.

25. PNC Chairman Hammuda called for a PNC meeting to demand Arafat's dismissal, and the PLA suggested that the *fida'iyin* should be placed under PLA control.

26. The most detailed treatment of the diplomacy and politics of this period is the fine book by Karim Pakradouni, *La Paix manquee: le mandat d'Elias Sarkis (1976–1982)* (Beirut: Fiches du Monde Arabe, 1984). His discussion of the perennial suspicions toward Syrian leadership harbored by the PLO and of the diplomatic steps the PLO engaged in as a result, is very useful.

27. See Paul A. Jureidini, R. D. McLaurin, and James M. Price, *Military Operations in Selected Lebanese Built-Up Areas, 1975–1978* (Aberdeen, MD: US Army Human Engineering Laboratory, 1979), for detailed discussions of some of the battles between Syrian and Palestinian forces.

28. The best treatment of Syrian combat in the 1982 war is in Trevor N. Dupuy and Paul Martell, *Flawed Victory* (Dunn Loring, VA: HERO Books, 1985). Cf. also Richard F. Gabriel, *Operation Peace for Galilee* (New York: Hill & Wang, 1984) and Ze'ev Schiff and Ehud Yaari, *Israel's Lebanon War* (New York: Simon and Schuster, 1984).

29. See Cobban, *The Palestinian,* 113–14.

30. See Barry Rubin, "Yasser Arafat's Tightrope in Arab Politics," in Shireen Hunter, ed., *The PLO After Tripoli, CSIS Significant Issues Series,* 6(10) (1984): 11–17; R. D. McLaurin, "Peace in Lebanon," in W. A. Beling, ed., *Middle East Peace Plans,* (London: Croom Helm, 1986), 179 and n. 52; and Adam Garfinkle, "Sources of the al-Fatah Mutiny," *Orbis* 27(3) (Fall 1983): 603–41.

31. Helena Cobban, "The 1983 Inter-Palestinian Fighting in Tripoli and the Future of the Palestinian Movement," in Hunter, ed., *The PLO,* 3–4.

32. See Aaron David Miller, "The PLO After Tripoli: Prospects for Reorganization," in Hunter, ed., *The PLO,* 7–8; also Miller, *The PLO and the Politics of Survival* (New York: Praeger for the Center for Strategic and International Studies, 1983), 76–81. Miller points to Syria's access to (and therefore leverage over) the same families in Lebanon that Arafat has been accused of abandoning; that Syria could support a rival leadership, which in fact is close to what has happened since the seventeenth PNC. *Politics of Survival,* 81.

33. Jordan granted citizenship to all Palestinian residents in Jordan in 1950 as a function of the annexation of the West Bank and remains the only Arab state to grant its blanket citizenship in this fashion to the Palestinians. We will not delve into the conflict arising from the Jordanian action except to note that other Arab states never recognized the legality of Jordan's annexation of the West Bank. Egypt never annexed the Gaza Strip, although it appeared for some time that this was the Egyptian government's intention.

34. Clinton Bailey, *Jordan's Palestinian Challenge, 1948–1983: A Political History* (Boulder, CO: Westview, 1984), 21.

35. The PLO had been officially proclaimed at a first Palestine National Congress convened by al-Shuqairy in Jerusalem, May 1964.

36. The emphasis on destroying the Jordanian government as a prerequisite to the liberation of Palestine may have been a Syrian innovation.

37. Egypt was endeavoring to maintain a moderate tone in its relations with Jordan during this period.

38. Fatah's second operation into Israel crossed from Jordan. On returning across the river, the unit encountered a Jordanian army unit that engaged it and killed the leader of the Fatah unit. These are indications that the king understood the danger of fida'i action—Israeli reprisals, subversion by hostile Arab regimes, and eventually loss of the West Bank.

39. Schiff and Rothstein, *Fedayeen,* 63. See also Cobban, *The Palestinian,* 37. Jordanian army intelligence liquidated a number of Fatah groups in May through September 1965, and the pressure led Fatah to begin mounting operations from Syria itself for a while. Yaari, *Fatah,* 168. See also Bard E. O'Neill, *Armed Struggle in Palestine: A Political-Military Analysis* (Boulder, CO: Westview, 1978), 164.

40. See, e.g., "Anti-Jordan Plot Alleged by King," *The New York Times,* 4 Dec. 1966.

41. Wilson, *Conflict,* 43.

42. The Battle of Karameh was a turning point in the guerrilla movement. While measured by ordinary military standards the battle was an Israeli military victory, the losses inflicted on the Israel Defense Force (IDF) and the powerful resistance put forth by the Arabs caused the battle to enter Palestinian mythology as a great Palestinian victory led by the guerrillas. In fact, although it was true that Karameh was a guerrilla base, the brunt of the Arab fighting was conducted by the Jordanian army which acquitted itself very well but received little credit. See Trevor N. Dupuy, *Elusive Victory: The Arab-Israeli Wars, 1947–1974* (New York: Harper & Row, 1978), 350–56; Brigadier S. A. el-Edroos, *The Hashemite Arab Army 1908–1979: An Appreciation and Analysis of Military Operations* (Amman: The Publishing Committee, 1980), 438–42.

43. Cobban, *The Palestinian,* 48–49.

44. In fact, the Jordanian government established its own short-lived guerrilla group under the command of none other than Sherif Nasir bin Jamil, King Hussein's uncle. The group disappeared after only a few months. Sherif Nasir was later to help force the September 1970 showdown.

45. Fuad Jabber, "The Arab Regimes and the Palestinian Revolution 1967–1971," *Journal of Palestine Studies* 2(2) (Winter 1973): 87; Bailey, *Jordan's,* 31–32.

46. Paul A. Jureidini and William E. Hazen, *Six Clashes: An Analysis of the Relationship Between the Palestinian Guerrilla Movement and the Governments of Jordan and Lebanon* (Kensington, MD: American Institutes for Research, 1971), 50.

47. Jureidini, *Six Clashes,* 51–52. This is the most detailed study of the events leading up to the civil war in Jordan.

48. Indeed, Yasser Arafat toured Amman in a police car to urge the citizens to avoid helping the *Kataeb.* Jureidini, *Six Clashes,* 53–57. Throughout this interesting study, each clash is considered not only in terms of the background and course of events, but also in terms of propaganda themes used by each side.

49. In order to maintain its own leadership in guerrilla ranks, to prevent the ideologists from taking control of the movement, and because the middle echelon of Fatah appears to have been much more hawkish than Arafat and his immediate leadership group.

50. This section borrows heavily from Jureidini, *Six Clashes.*

51. See Cooley, *Green March;* Jureidini, *Six Clashes;* Marvin Kalb and Bernard Kalb, *Kissinger* (Boston: Little, Brown, 1974), ch. 8; Henry Kissinger, *White House Years* (Boston: Little, Brown, 1979), ch. 15; William B. Quandt, *Decade of Decisions: American Policy Toward the Arab-Israeli Conflict, 1967–1976* (Berkeley: Univ. of Calif. Press, 1977), ch. 4. Military developments are treated in the greatest detail in Jureidini, *Six Clashes,* and El-Edroos, *The Hashemite,* 449–72.

52. Arafat spent much of his time as the confrontation neared in "putting out fires" in the relationship, fires often set by the provocative stance of these two organizations. In fact, George Habash and Nayif Hawatmeh made little secret of their desire to provoke such tensions that would lead to a final confrontation. Both organizations were close to the poor and deprived Palestinian refugees, especially those in the camps. (See Gerard Chaliand, *La Resistance palestinienne* [Paris: Seuil, 1970].) In 1969 and 1970, the DFLP went so far as to set up "Soviets" in Jordan. The DFLP also claimed, as do many Israelis, that Palestine had been unnaturally

divided between East and West Banks. (Nayif Hawatmeh is a Christian East Banker; his own leadership of a Palestinian movement would be illegitimate without such a claim. The DFLP continued to take a uniquely harsh stand on Jordan: see Paul A. Jureidini and R. D. McLaurin, *Revolutionary Perceptions of Harsh Realities: The Democratic Front Takes Stock* [Alexandria, VA: Abbott Associates, 1983].) Indeed, the emergency session of the PNC in Amman in August 1970 rejected the partition of Palestine. So, the extremist organizations succeeded in provoking a confrontation, but with results different from those they anticipated.

53. This paper will not delve extensively into the evolution of West Bank political attitudes and behaviors. Emile Sahliyeh, in a forthcoming book on the subject, analyzes the forces at work in the West Bank and suggests that a combination of these forces led to the reduction of the role of traditional political elites tied to Jordan. While some of these forces were primarily local in nature, some of the most powerful were produced by the interplay of Jordanian, Israeli, and PLO policies and actions.

54. The PLO (actually, PNC) reaction to the king's proposals was to call for a joint Palestinian-Jordanian national liberation front.

55. See Bailey's rather harsh assessment, *Jordan's,* 63. In fact, whatever King Hussein's motivation as far as Jordanian interests are concerned, subsequent history suggests that the Arab world might have been better off pursuing the approach at least as a trial balloon to secure return of the occupied territories. Cobban indicates that Jordanian influence in the West Bank declined after the events of 1970–1971, and that the territory was not particularly supportive of the UAK proposal. (*The Palestinian,* 172.) Bailey, while not disagreeing, notes that "[t]he occupied territories were perhaps the only Arab area in which the Federation Plan was not rejected out of hand." (*Jordan's,* 63.)

56. However, what might have been available in 1972 would certainly prove far more costly, if possible at all, after 1985.

57. King Hussein indicated that he did not deny to the PLO representation of the Palestinians, only that he did not see how the PLO could claim to be their sole representative. Since over half the population of the East Bank was now Palestinian and since these were Jordanian citizens, his position was that in that context if in no other the Jordanian government must certainly be a Palestinian representative.

58. See Paul A. Jureidini and R. D. McLaurin, *Beyond Camp David: Emerging Alignments and Leaders in the Middle East* (Syracuse: Syracuse Univ. Press, 1981), 39, 50–51, and "The Hashemite Kingdom of Jordan," in P. Edward Haley and Lewis W. Snider, eds., *Lebanon in Crisis: Participants and Issues* (Syracuse: Syracuse Univ. Press, 1979), 193, 298 (n. 26).

59. Cf. Fehmi Saddy, *The Eastern Front: Implications of the Syrian/Palestinian/Jordanian Entente and the Lebanese Civil War* (Alexandria, VA: Abbott Associates, 1976); R. D. McLaurin et al., *Foreign Policy Making in the Middle East,* (New York: Praeger, 1977), 256–57.

60. Bailey, *Jordan's,* 84–85. For a perceptive analysis of Sadat's intentions throughout this period, see Thomas W. Lippman, "Sadat's Strategy Emerges," *The Washington Post,* 4 Dec. 1977, A1.

61. See Cobban, *The Palestinian,* 85–86; and issues of the *Daily Report* of the Foreign Broadcast Information Service for the period of the PNC which covered debates on this subject quite intensively.

62. Indeed, many Palestinians resident in Jordan were concerned at the return of the PLO lest they once again be forced to make a choice of loyalties.

63. It is interesting to note that while the PLO objected to this allocation of responsibility as a derogation of its status as the "sole legitimate representative" of the Palestinians (a protest that went unheeded by the conference), there was little anti-Jordanian tenor to the PLO position nor was any such intent perceived by the Jordanian government.

64. Syria and the Palestinian groups responsive to Syrian control in fact reserved more vituperation for the Jordanian monarchy than for Israel. Most visible in this regard were the PFLP—GC and the DFLP. DFLP documents and statements of this era were characterized by stronger attacks on the United States and Jordan than on any other countries. Jureidini, *Revolutionary Perceptions.*

65. The key Arab regimes had all indicated that as far as the Palestinian element of a settlement was concerned they were prepared to accept what the PLO would accept.

66. The new political leadership on the West Bank derived much of its legitimacy from the PLO in the first place. PLO retribution against moderates who were "too moderate," the unwillingness of Israeli leaders to make any concessions, the Israeli refusal to permit the growth of an independent indigenous political leadership (such leaders had been expelled, imprisoned, or subjected to other forms of control), Israel's attempts to constrain Jordanian influence—these and other factors tended to reinforce the importance of the PLO as the principal legitimizing institution of West Bank political leadership.

67. Lebanon absorbed a much higher refugee burden (at least in the immediate period after the first war) relative to its size than any other Arab state, including Jordan. In view of the fragile sectarian balance in the country, this is remarkable because while many Christian Palestinian refugees entered Lebanon, the refugees as a group were overwhelmingly Muslim.

68. See Jean-Pierre Peroncel-Hugoz, *Une Croix sur le Liban* (Paris: Lieu Commun, 1984), 101–3.

69. See Rosemary Sayigh, *Palestinians: From Peasants to Revolutionaries* (London: Zed Books, 1979), who provides a litany of Palestinian comments about the backwardness of the Lebanese from the point of view of those Palestinians who trekked north from the Galilee.

70. The minuscule Lebanese army fought one battle in the war, a limited victory near the village of al-Malikiyya.

71. The prime minister did order the Lebanese army into action in 1967, but the army commander demurred, as was expected. Lebanon's adherence to the United Arab Command in 1967 was seen by Israel as the termination of the armistice agreement. Indeed when, in 1984, Lebanon sought to undertake talks with Israel on the latter's withdrawal, it did so under the auspices of the armistice agreements. Israel was adamant that the talks were quite independent of those agreements whose application, Israel insists, lapsed as a result of Lebanese behavior. Lebanon's role in 1973 was limited to the provision of some radar assistance to Syrian forces.

72. This is the conflict between *raison d'état* and *raison de la révoltion*. See Ghassan Tuéni, *Une Guerre Pour les Autres* (Paris: J C Lattès, 1985), 173.

73. In other words, by posing no threat to others, the Lebanese would not be attacked by others; but also, by avoiding a large military establishment they would escape the threat of military coups. R. D. McLaurin, "Peace in Lebanon," 165–66.

74. Rubin, *The Arab States*, 15. Rubin goes on to add that Lebanon's pan-Arab-oriented (Sunni) Muslim community understood that Lebanon's interests and its own were best served by keeping the Palestinian problem "at arms' length," and that Sunni leaders therefore were quite happy to substitute rhetoric for action. Rubin, *Arab States*, 15.

75. During consultations at the United Nations in the late 1940s, Lebanon advanced claims to western Galilee.

76. While Lebanon was the freest Arab country and anything but a police state, Lebanese G-2 was extremely powerful, especially after the commanding general of the Lebanese army, Fuad Shihab, became president in 1958. Not until the end of the Shihab era in 1970 was G-2 power reduced. (Shihab's successor, Charles Helou, president from 1964 to 1970, was never able to control the G-2.)

77. Tuèni, *Une Guerre*, 169.

78. Cf. the remarks, Tuèni, *Une Guerre*, 171–76. Tuèni also discusses succinctly but tellingly the issue of the conflict between *raisons d'état* and *raisons de la révolution*, a conflict that applied with particular relevance to Lebanon.

79. Yaari, *Strike*, 82.

80. O'Neill, *Armed Struggle*, 169–70.

81. The reports of the Lebanese Surete generale provide a detailed review of the progress of this infiltration. From the summer of 1968 on, when they catalogue the infiltration first in dozens then in hundred, the reports also show the support provided by Sa'iqa at the outset, and later directly by Syrian intelligence. However, the reports also show that this intervention, far from being opposed by the local populations, frequently received its active support. Antoine Basbous and Annie Laurent, "Le Liban et son voisinage," (Ph.D. diss., Université Paris 2, 1986).

82. Walid Khalidi's fine study, *Conflict and Violence in Lebanon: Confrontation in the Middle East* (Cambridge, MA: Harvard Univ. Center for International Affairs, 1979), 40–41, makes these and many other points with real sensitivity.

83. It would of course be a mistake to say that the fuse consisted only of this material. The conflicts in Lebanon are multi-faceted. Some believe in fact that the Palestinian element was incidental to them. We suggest instead that that element was the single most important contributor to the violent nature of the conflict in its several phases between 1976 and 1982. Cf. McLaurin, "Peace."

84. Riad N. el-Rayyes and Dunia Nahas, *Guerrillas for Palestine: A Study of the Palestinian Commando Organizations* (Beirut: Al-Nahar, 1974), 125.

85. The attack was in Athens, but the (PFLP) attackers had flown to Athens from Beirut and it was Lebanon therefore that was held responsible by the Israeli government.

86. Sa'iqa members were more active than Fatah in April. Syrian helicopters were even used.

87. O'Neill, *Armed Struggle*, 170.

88. Lebanese Surete generale reports predict an inevitable explosion between Lebanese and PLO forces that would prove more violent than the Internal Security Force (note this force is predominantly Sunni)-PLO confrontations of 1969. Surete generale report of 27 Apr. 1969, reprinted in Basbous, "Le Liban."

89. The support included a propaganda attack, the closing of Syrian borders (a strong move against Lebanon which was dependent upon Syrian trade routes), massing of Syrian troops along the border (to protect and cover the impending Palestinian invasion), intermittent artillery and mortar support, logistic support of PLO forces, and the presence of some Syrian soldiers among Sa'iqa units.

90. See O'Ballance, *Arab*, 99–104; Jureidini, *Six Clashes*, 212–20.

91. Actually, the agreements were general and were the subject of later negotiations between the PLO and senior political and military officials of the Lebanese government. However, in general, subsequent delineation of the specifics tended to be even more favorable to PLO interests and generally exceeded by far what the original negotiators thought they had concluded in Cairo. At each juncture, no Lebanese officials wanted to be held responsible for another series of confrontations; concessions were always the path of less resistance.

92. Khalidi, *Conflict*, 80.

93. A well-informed Israeli observer has indicated that "Damascus was warned indirectly by Israel that any further attempt to invade Lebanon or precipitate civil war in that country would be met by Israeli action to protect her border and that this might entail the seizure of Lebanese territory to preserve 'regional tranquillity.' " Schiff, *Fedayeen*, 237.

94. Jureidini, *Six Clashes*, 212–23.

95. One problem associated with the use of the PASC and with the agreement as a whole was the nonparticipation of the PFLP, which had considerable strength in several refugee camps, in the PLO and PASC at various points.

96. In late January 1972 the Israeli government warned Beirut that if the Lebanese government could not restrain the guerrillas, the IDF would permanently occupy portions of southern Lebanon. El-Rayyes, *Guerrillas*, 130.

97. The Black September attack on the Israeli Olympic team in Munich in September 1972 led to a major Israeli riposte against Lebanon, the first retaliatory raid in about two months. Although the army and the PLO fought together against the IDF, both taking heavy casualties, the raid was followed by an army demand that the PLO leave the southern part of Lebanon in its entirety. Over the objections of some PLO elements, the organization complied with the army order.

98. One of the curiosities of Lebanese historiography is the repeated myth that neither the army nor the PLO was strong enough to defeat the other. While this is literally true from a political standpoint, it is inaccurate to suggest, as do some of the best Lebanese historians (including Christian historians), that the army and PLO encountered a stand-off in 1969 and 1973. Army actions were effective and victorious from a military standpoint on both occasions, although (particularly in 1969) there were incidents (such as in Tripoli) to which the army did not commit substantial forces where the PLO reaped benefits. Could it be that only Israeli leaders recognized this phenomenon and that this explains their eagerness to provoke PLO-Lebanese army confrontations? Not if Israeli military writers, who have been extremely critical of the Lebanese army and its capabilities (even in the pre-1975 period) are any example.

99. E.g., a PLO committee prepared (25 May 1973) a written plan for a series of actions designed to reinforce the PLO position in the country. Taking into account the lessons of Jordan,

it involved continued growth of PLO armaments, harassment of the Lebanese army, more systematic mobilization of Palestinians in Lebanon, proliferation of training camps, tightening the links with friendly Lebanese elements, propaganda activities within and outside Lebanon, additional clandestine arms factories, and so forth. See Basbous, "Le Liban."

100. There is no simple way to characterize the sides. Cobban's description of the National Movement and its allies as "an untidy amalgam of Muslim traditionalists (Sunni and Shi'i), Muslim radicals (left and right), secularists (left and right), pan-Arabists of every brand, socialists, student activists, trade unionists, and . . . marxists" is certainly accurate, as is the comment that "One of the few things all . . . could agree on . . . was their support for the Palestinian resistance movement." (*The Palestinian*, 65.)

101. Cobban, *The Palestinian*, 66.

102. Indeed, both Israeli and Syrian observers were present during the siege and fall of the Palestinian camp of Tal al-Za'tar. Cobban, *The Palestinian*, 281; Jureidini, *Military*, 18; Minister of Defense Ariel Sharon's speech before Israeli Knesset, 22 Sept. 1982.

103. The PLO faced a major dilemma when the Lebanese president, with strong Syrian backing, promoted a formula to resolve the conflict. To choose Syria or to choose the National Movement; that was the question. See Iyad, *My Home*, 181.

104. Cobban, *The Palestinian*, 71.

105. The Aziz Ahdab coup. Ahdab was escorted to the presidential palace by Fatah. Cobban, *The Palestinian*, 71.

106. Cobban, *The Palestinian*, 74–76.

107. See Pakradouni, *La Paix*, 37–41, for a good example. This book provides a detailed account of the 1976–1982 period in Lebanon with countless revelations of aspects of the PLO situation and diplomatic activities that are otherwise undisclosed.

108. Pakradouni, *La Paix*, 168 (my translation).

109. Cobban, *The Palestinian*, 94.

110. Arafat put off the meeting as long as possible, hiding behind Abu Iyad as intermediary, because it was known that Sarkis wanted to request Arafat to freeze operations. Pakradouni, *La Paix*, 198.

111. Pakradouni, *La Paix*, 208.

112. Pakradouni, *La Paix*, 229.

113. Schiff and Yaari, *Israel's*, passim.

114. The war is discussed in the sources in note 26 above.

115. See Tuèni, *Une Guerre;* and Wadi Haddad, *Lebanon and the Politics of the Revolving Doors* (New York: Praeger for the Georgetown Univ. Center for Strategic and International Studies, 1985).

116. There was substantial Shi'i cooperation with the IDF in fact in the southern suburbs of Beirut where Shi'a helped identify the hiding places of Palestinian fighters. R. D. McLaurin and Paul Jureidini, *The Battle of Beirut, 1982* (Aberdeen Proving Ground, MD: US Army Human Engineering Laboratory, 1986), 26, 38.

117. In mid-1986, Lebanese President Amin Gemayel met secretly with PLO leaders and delivered documents facilitating their legal entry into Lebanon. Egypt and Iraq provided logistic and other support also as a means of complicating matters for Syria.

118. In July 1986, Syria deployed armed forces personnel in West Beirut "to improve security" there. Although some believed this deployment was designed to check the Palestinians, only a few hundred troops were actually sent, most of them intelligence and special operations personnel. The bulk of the manpower of this so-called "Syrian" force was in fact provided by Lebanese Shi'a of the Lebanese army's Sixth Brigade based in West Beirut. The limited size of the Syrian deployment suggests it was never intended for use against the camps, but rather was a political force designed to put sufficient pressure on the Beirut Sunni community to ensure support for Syrian policy lines.

119. It is interesting to note that Pakradouni, *La Paix*, 77, suggests that Syria has usurped Iraq's position of regional leadership. (Pakradouni later took the lead in forging an alliance between the Lebanese Forces and Iraq.) Indeed, while Iraq did enjoy a period of pronounced recrudescence in power, prestige, and attention in the late 1970s, the Iran-Iraq war returned Iraq to its secondary rank as an autonomous center of power in the Arab world. Meanwhile, Syria's

reputation increased apace, and widespread indeed was the circulation of the dictum, "no war without Egypt, no peace without Syria."

120. Iraqi publicists had been condemning Egypt for doing too little to support the Palestinians, indeed for participating in the rape of Palestine, a reference to Egyptian assumption of control in Gaza.

121. Wilson, *Conflict*, 28.

122. Of course, the conclusions differ. The Syrian Ba'th has suggested that since Palestine is only southern Syria it should rightfully be a part of Syria. The Iraqi Ba'th does not concur. It appears to see Palestine as an integral part of the Arab nation which should be led by Iraq.

123. Cobban, *The Palestinian*, 163–64, points out that the ALF was always seen as a tool of the Iraqi Ba'th and has been used primarily to counter Syria.

124. See El-Rayyes and Nahas, *Guerrillas*, 103, for a succinct explanation of Iraqi Ba'th paranoia concerning Palestinian guerrilla power.

125. In fact, local Fatah offices were closed for some time when the ALF was established. Jabber, "The Arab Regimes," 86.

126. Within months of the establishment of the ALF, Damascus arrested several hundred of the organization's supporters in Syria, expelling them to Jordan, and Syria continued to arrest ALF personnel and seize ALF arms thereafter. El Rayyes and Nahas, *Guerrillas*, 57.

127. This was not a function of ALF ideology, but of the predominantly non-Palestinian composition of the group.

128. Majid Khadduri, *Socialist Iraq: A Study in Iraqi Politics Since 1968* (Washington, DC: Middle East Institute, 1978), 58–59, discusses the affair. See also Hanna Batatu, *The Old Social Classes and the Revolutionary Movements of Iraq; A study of Iraq's Old Landed and Commercial Classes and of Its Communists, Ba'thists, and Free Officers* (Princeton: Princeton Univ. Press, 1978), 1096–97.

129. See Cobban, *The Palestinian*, 61–62.

130. This was not intended to confuse. Abu Nidal insisted that he represented the original orientation and essence of the Fatah movement. Thus, his group (which was quite small) was called Fatah; his *fida'iyin*, 'Asifa. And his terrorist group, modeled after Black September of which he had been a part, was called Black June.

131. Wadi' Haddad, the PFLP's principal organizer of terrorist attacks, especially airplane hijacking, was reported (by the PLO) murdered (poisoned) by Iraqi intelligence. (Voice of Palestine, 24 Aug. 1978.)

132. The unit that attacked the Israeli ambassador to Britain was part of Abu Nidal's group and was sent by Iraqi intelligence.

133. This point was made admirably by Walid Kazziha (*Palestine in the Arab Dilemma* [New York: Barnes & Noble, 1979], 103–4).

134. It is important to understand that the Hashemites do not and did not support the Fatah out of conviction but out of expediency. Ultimately, there is a conflict between any Palestinian organization, which must aim at the loyalty of Palestinians of both banks (and elsewhere), and the Hashemites who, given their Palestinian population, must promote their own bona fides as the repository of Palestinian identity. This does not suggest that Jordanian support for the moderates alters this fundamental reality, only that the inability of the Hashemites to destroy the PLO (and vice versa) has created de facto situations in which moderate governments are, whatever their views of most desired outcomes, prepared to accept and deal with Fatah in the short term.

3 THE PLO AS REPRESENTATIVE OF THE PALESTINIAN PEOPLE
RASHID KHALIDI

Palestinian nationalism became a significant political force in the early 1920s although there were signs of Palestinian protonationalism or local patriotism prior to 1914. By 1948 the nationalist movement that dominated Palestinian politics during the British mandate had been defeated by a combination of enemies: Britain, the Zionist movement, and Jordan. After a brief hiatus, a new phase of Palestinian nationalism began, one generally associated with the PLO. However, when the PLO was founded in 1964 by decision of the First Arab Summit, it was far from being an expression of autonomous Palestinian national feeling. Indeed, it was envisaged by many Arab governments as a device which would enable them to contain the growing influence among the Palestinians of various independent nationalist factions.

Two of the main trends among Palestinians in this period were represented by Fatah (which was founded in the 1950s but only emerged from clandestinity in the mid-1960s) and the Movement of Arab Nationalists (ANM). Out of these grew most of the politico-military organizations advocating armed struggle as the means to regain Palestine that took over the PLO in 1968 and 1969, turning it into an umbrella group for their own activities and for independent Palestinian nationalism. Since then, the mainstream of the PLO has been dominated without interruption by Fatah, by that group's Central Committee, and by its leader Yasser Arafat.

In assessing the PLO's representativeness today, two points relating to this earlier period are relevant: the first is that when the Arab states sponsored the formation of the PLO, Palestinian nationalism was a live and growing force. For over a decade after the defeat of 1948, much of the intense national feeling the Palestinians had displayed during the mandate period had been subsumed in larger transnational movements. These movements included Arab nationalist groups like the ANM and the Ba'th party; the Muslim

Brotherhood; several Arab Communist parties, including those of Jordan, Israel, and Egypt; and the Syrian Social Nationalist party (SSNP), which calls for the formation of a "Greater Syria" encompassing the Levant (including Palestine) and Cyprus. By the mid-1960s, however, Palestinians were increasingly returning to a primarily Palestinian focus for their political activity to liberate their homeland. The shock of the 1967 defeat of the leading Arab nationalist regimes decisively confirmed this trend.

A second point is that besides its anti-Israeli orientation, from the outset the PLO has embodied a longstanding contradiction between the Palestinians and many of the Arab regimes that dominate the environment in which most of them live. During their revolt of 1936 through 1939 and in the fighting of 1947 and 1948, the Palestinians were defeated primarily by Britain and the Zionist movement but faced as well the enmity—or at best malevolent neutrality—of Arab regimes more concerned for their relations with Britain (or with the Zionists) than with the interests of the Palestinians. This simultaneous conflict on more than one front has long been a feature of Palestinian nationalism. Nevertheless, it has become increasingly apparent in recent decades and has been a constant feature of the situation of the PLO since 1964. The fact that Palestinian nationalism has been in nearly constant conflict over the past few decades with both Israel and various Arab regimes is perceived as inevitable by most Palestinians. Many of them also see conflict with the policies of the United States as similarly inevitable, due to its support for Israel, as was conflict with Britain during the mandate period for similar reasons.

POLITICAL TRENDS WITHIN AND WITHOUT THE PLO

Although Palestinians share many perceptions, important differences also exist among them. These manifest themselves in different current political groupings and trends, which must be analyzed if the representativeness of the PLO is to be properly assessed.

Three main tendencies can be discerned within the framework of the PLO. In addition, there are notable tendencies outside of the PLO. The former include the great majority of Palestinians, while the latter constitute small minority factions at either end of the political spectrum. The broad framework of the PLO includes the following tendencies.

The mainstream within the PLO and indeed within Palestinian politics as a whole is represented by Fatah. From the early 1960s when it first began to challenge Egypt's Gamal 'Abd al-Nasir for leadership of the Palestinians, thus helping to precipitate the formation of the PLO, Fatah has been the most dynamic grouping in Palestinian politics. It has also been the largest—at least since 1969 when its dominance was recognized upon the election of its leader, Yasser Arafat, as chairman of the PLO's Executive Committee. He has held this post ever since. Fatah's diffuse nationalist ideology, its loose organization, and its ability to attract unaffiliated independents as supporters have helped it maintain its predominance. This has been reinforced by its financial independence—based on a vast support network among prosperous Palestinians in the Gulf and elsewhere—and the judicious management of the funds thus collected.

The second major trend is composed of several groups and a number of independent intellectuals whose programs are relatively close to those of Fatah and who have been politically associated with it throughout most of the history of the PLO. This trend includes the Democratic Front for the Liberation of Palestine (DFLP) and a newer formation, the Palestine Communist party (PCP). The DFLP was the first to advocate publicly the idea of a Palestinian state in the West Bank and Gaza Strip in 1972 and 1973, in close coordination with the Fatah leadership. In 1974 this concept became central to the PLO's provisional program. There have been differences with Fatah, generally tactical rather than over long-term objectives or ideology—although this is a nominally Marxist tendency, unlike Fatah. However, the groups within this trend have never broken totally with Fatah. Since 1969 they have always been careful to remain within the framework of the PLO, even when disapproving of its political line, as for example at the Seventeenth session of the Palestine National Council (PNC) held in Amman in November 1984 when the DFLP stayed away from the meeting but accepted its legality.

The third tendency, and the one most loosely associated with the PLO, is made up of a number of groups. The most notable of them is the Popular Front for the Liberation of Palestine (PFLP), which is the primary heir of the legacy of the ANM and is still led by that movement's founder, Dr. George Habash. At several key points in the PLO's history, this group has withdrawn from the leading organs of the PLO in opposition to its policies, notably for three years (beginning in 1974), when the Rejection Front was formed to oppose the idea of a West Bank-Gaza Strip state and again after 1984 when the National Salvation Front was formed in Damascus in order to oppose mainstream PLO policies. The PFLP has historical and organizational significance and is supported by a number of influential individuals, but the other groups within this tendency have hardly any following. This entire tendency is deeply divided internally, and has recently lost popular support due to the perception among Palestinians that it has served as a pawn for hostile Arab regimes, most recently that of Syria.

Discontinuous with the spectrum of views within the broad framework of the PLO are two further groupings, both small minorities: (1) extreme underground elements opposed to any compromise with Israel and advocating violence as the sole means of achieving a solution and (2) the partisans of King Hussein as representative of the Palestinians, who call for a negotiated "Jordanian solution" to the Palestine question.

The position of both groupings outside the PLO framework is determined by their rejection of the political objectives which represent a consensus within the PLO. This consensus can be defined as working by political and military means for an end to occupation and for Palestinian self-determination within part of Palestine (essentially the occupied West Bank and Gaza Strip) under the leadership of the PLO. It is clearly understood and has often been declared by PLO leaders that such a state would exist alongside Israel, although such an implication has never been formally spelled out. And the PLO has consistently refused to recognize Israel unilaterally—even implicitly—without a concomitant recognition by Israel of the Palestinian peoples' rights to national self-determination.

It is possible to discern positions at the margins of the PLO spectrum which seem to contradict elements of this consensus and which border on these two extreme minority positions. Some Fatah leaders have accepted apparent limits on Palestinian self-determination in the context of a confederation with Jordan; and there is a disinclination to accept the idea of a West Bank-Gaza Strip state as even an interim solution among important factions of the coalition led by the PFLP. Strong skepticism among most Palestinians as to whether Israel would even or under any circumstances accept such a solution reinforces this disinclination.

Moreover, whereas the PLO consensus by and large eschews attacks outside Israel and the occupied territories, the PFLP carried out several airplane hijackings before this tactic was condemned by its 1972 congress (after the issue of hijacking had played a major role in the separation of the DFLP from the PFLP in 1969). In addition, several major operations—including the Munich attack—were carried out in Europe by Black September, which was linked to Fatah; and a shadowy war of assassinations and counterassassinations has been fought largely in Europe between Israeli intelligence and Palestinians of various factions. Nevertheless, the PLO consensus can easily be delineated from the two groupings which stand outside of it. A fuller description of both groupings will show why.

The first is made up of a number of shadowy underground factions which reject any form of compromise with Israel or Zionism, condemn diplomacy and other political means, and advocate use of military means only, including indiscriminate acts of violence against civilian as well as military and economic targets both inside the occupied territories and Israel and abroad. The stated goal of these factions is the complete liberation of Palestine via the extirpation of the entire infrastructure of the state of Israel. Among groups which fall into this category are the Wadi' Haddad faction of the PFLP and the Fatah splinter group led in the early 1970s by Abu Mahmoud, both now defunct. Another is the so-called "Fatah Revolutionary Council," which split from Fatah in 1972 and 1973 under the leadership of Sabri al-Banna (Abu Nidal) and has been associated with his name ever since.

Aside from the striking contrasts with all the trends within the PLO in terms of means and ends, these factions can be easily distinguished from it by their lack of a mass base and indeed of an ideology calling for such a mass base; their lack of a public infrastructure providing social and other services and propagating their political line; their attacks on civilian targets worldwide; and their reliance on an Arab regime for protection and support. This has often meant that they have served as witting or unwitting fronts for Arab (and possibly other) intelligence services. Furthermore, some of these factions have assassinated leaders and envoys of the PLO (or of Arab regimes with which their Arab patrons were in conflict at the time). This frequent use of violence against elements within the PLO consensus is contrary to a basic PLO practice and is a distinguishing characteristic of some of these fringe factions.

The second grouping has no institutional framework. It is composed of those Palestinians, primarily in the occupied territories and Jordan, who look to King Hussein for leadership, would prefer a form of government similar to that in Jordan if the Israeli occupation could be ended, and believe that Jordan is best suited to end the occupation due to its acceptability to the United States and to elements in the Israeli political establishment. Those who follow this line are opposed to violence and to the PLO, do not support the idea of an independent Palestinian state in any part of Palestine, and are generally advocates of a traditional, nondemocratic, elite-dominated political process. The status of this group is in question in view of King Hussein's renunciation of responsibility for the West Bank and his severance of most of Jordan's links with it.

This grouping is made up primarily of members of the notable class through whom the Hashemite regime ruled the West Bank from 1949 until

1967 — in many cases the same individuals who played key roles during this period and members of their families. Also in this category are some teachers and other officials in the West Bank who formerly received salaries from Amman and others in the West Bank and the Gaza Strip whose interests are closely tied to the transit trade which moves via Jordan to the rest of the Arab world. This grouping includes as well Palestinians on the East Bank who have prospered in the service of the Jordanian regime or thanks to the material prosperity which the oil boom, the Lebanese conflict, and the Iran-Iraq War brought Jordan for about a decade after 1973.

Not surprisingly this is a narrow social stratum, and one which is getting ever-narrower as employment in Israel undercuts the economic basis for the domination of the traditional elites. It excludes most of the student sector, which is extremely active politically and forms a large proportion of the population of the occupied territories, 45 percent of which is under 18, and 60 percent under 30 (groups for which the Hashemite pre-1967 period can have but little meaning). It excludes as well the bulk of the professional and middle classes, most of whose members have nationalist, democratic, or radical leanings. They are naturally alienated by the monarchical autocracy which prevails in Jordan, via a system characterized by the pervasive presence of security services staffed largely by East Bankers. Finally this stratum does not include the many Palestinian professionals and clerical and skilled workers from both occupied territories and Jordan who for the past decade and more have made their living in the oil-producing countries, where they have met Palestinians from elsewhere, have been exposed to organized Palestinian nationalism, and have come to support the PLO.

Although there are no statistics from Jordan to support this assessment — the closed nature of the political process makes it impossible to do more than hazard guesses about political tendencies there — several sets of data can be adduced to confirm the above propositions with regard to the West Bank and Gaza Strip. These include trade union and university student body elections, in which pro-Jordanian candidates as a rule fail to win any seats while PLO-supported slates generally obtain large majorities;[1] the West Bank municipality elections held under the auspices of the Israeli occupation in 1976, in which candidates who ran on a pro-PLO platform won virtually all the seats contested, defeating others identified with the Hashemites; and recent polling data.

The most significant results emerge from a poll conducted in July and August 1986 of 1024 people in the West Bank and Gaza Strip chosen as a random sample to reflect their population in terms of place of residence, age, sex, occupation, place of work, educational level, and income. The poll was conducted for the *al-Fajr* newspaper, *Newsday,* and the Australian Broadcasting Corporation by Dr. Muhammad Shedid, a Palestinian academic at al-Najah National University in Nablus, with the advice of Dr. Richard Seltzer, Professor of Political Science at Howard University, and the Israeli scholar Meron Benvenisti.[2] According to an article in the Israeli paper, *Ma'ariv,* similar results were obtained in a study carried out in the occupied territories at about the same time by Professor Ephraim Ya'ar of Tel Aviv University with the aid of researcher from the Hebrew University.[3]

Less than 1% of those questioned in the *al-Fajr* poll said that Jordan represented the Palestinians, while 93.5% chose the PLO. Further, only 3.4% of those polled picked King Hussein as their preferred leader, as against 78.6% whose chose Yasser Arafat. Asked about their preferred final resolution of the Palestine question, 3.7% chose a Palestinian entity in the West Bank and Gaza Strip linked to Jordan, while a Palestinian state in all or part of Palestine was the choice of 94.8% (77.9% were for a state in all of Palestine and 16.9% for one in the West Bank and Gaza Strip alone). Even as a provisional solution, only 6.3% of those questioned chose a Jordanian solution, with 49.7% preferring a West Bank-Gaza Strip state and 43.2% opting for continuing to struggle for a Palestinian state in all of Palestine. These results demonstrate the isolation of the proponents of Jordan.[4] And this isolation has only been confirmed by the Palestinian uprising of 1987–88.

The *al-Fajr* poll results also demonstrate the limited support among Palestinians for the most radical tendencies: leaders identified with violence against innocent civilians such as Abu al-Abbas scored extremely low (.4%), as did others identified with a rejection of compromise or political means to achieve Palestinian objectives, such as Abu Musa (1.2%); Ahmad Jibril (.5%); and 'Isam al-Qadi (1.2%). Even a major radical leader like Habash received only 5.6%, as against Arafat's 78.6%. Asked whether bomb attacks on civilian airliners were justified, 79.3% replied negatively, and 63.1% said the same regarding the Rome and Vienna airport attacks of December 1985, although 60.5% expressed the opinion that armed struggle was the most effective means to solve the Palestine problem.

One other tendency which can be discerned from this poll is an Islamic trend of some importance. Its strength can be gauged from the response to a question regarding the preferred form of a future Palestinian state: 26.5% called for a state based on Islamic law. While smaller than the numbers calling for a democratic or secular or western model state (33.5%) or those preferring some form of Arab state (31.7%), it is still a large proportion of those polled. (Similarly large percentages were won by Islamic candidates in some recent student elections; see note 1). It should be noted that although the Islamic tendency has at times been encouraged by both the occupation authorities and Jordan as a means of fostering alternate authority structures to the PLO, in recent years Fatah has generally succeeded in harnessing important elements within that tendency into a loose anti-occupation coalition in student politics in the occupied territories. This has been reflected in the leadership of the uprising in most areas of the occupied territories. While there is no guarantee that such a tendency will not challenge the PLO in the future, it can be assumed that the Fatah leaders who have so far used the common threat of the occupation to put together a coalition between Islamic militants and their archenemies, the communists, will be able to continue to do so.

CHARACTERISTICS OF THE PALESTINIAN POLITY

If these are the political forces and tendencies among the Palestinians, what can be said of them as a group, and how can we assess the differences among them?

The Palestinian people are a relatively weak and fragmented transnational actor, in large part due to their unique situation of dispersion. There are about 4.5 million Palestinians, split into two main groups, each including several subgroups: (1) About 2 million Palestinians live within geographical Palestine (in Arabic al-dakhil, "the inside"), either under occupation in the West Bank and Gaza Strip or inside pre-1967 Israel. These are further divided into the over 700,000 living in Israel with Israeli citizenship; and the 800,000 in the West Bank and about 500,000 living in the Gaza Strip. (2) There are more than 2.5 million Palestinians living in the diaspora (al-kharij, "the outside"). Over 1.2 million live in Jordan, perhaps 400,000 in Lebanon, about 300,000 in Syria, over 250,000 in Kuwait, and over 200,000 in the rest of the Gulf, Iraq, and Egypt. There are many others in Europe and North and South America, perhaps as many as 200,000, although no reliable figures exist.

Among Palestinians both inside geographical Palestine and in exile, many distinctions exist. One involves those living in camps (about 800,000 according to 1986 United Nations Relief and Works Agency, UNRWA, figures) as against those who do not. Of all the subgroups mentioned above, only in the Gaza Strip are camp-dwellers a majority, but significant proportions of camp dwellers exist in the West Bank, Jordan, Syria, and Lebanon. The relevance of place of residence lies in its direct impact on political activism and radicalism. Not surprisingly, the *al-Fajr* poll shows an even higher number of supporters of Arafat in the camps than among the general population (the number of those choosing him as their preferred leader is 88.4% among camp residents against 78.6% among the West Bank and Gaza Strip population as a whole).

The fact that the Gaza Strip has a majority of camp residents and was administered by Egypt from 1948 to 1967 are among the factors which differentiate it from the West Bank. Perhaps the most important is the overcrowding of the Gaza Strip, one of the most heavily populated areas in the world. These factors seem to have had little impact on the extent of PLO support there, although in the early years of the occupation the radical PFLP had strong support in the Gaza region, where more recently the Islamic trend has witnessed its greatest growth. Little or no residual sentiment for Egypt appears to remain, and the Gaza Strip is thus comparable to the West Bank in many respects.

Far more significant are the distinctions between West Bank and Gaza Strip residents on the one hand and Palestinians who carry Israeli citizenship on the other. The former are in a sort of limbo, carrying Jordanian passports for the most part and having lived for two decades under a military occupation with no rights—whether political, legal, or human—and with the threat of absorption into an alien entity which covets their land but would like to rid itself of them.[5] Although the latter are Arabs in a Jewish state, one which has been at war with Arab states since its foundation, and although for these reasons they do not have all the privileges of Jewish Israelis and indeed are grossly underprivileged in relation to them,[6] they are nevertheless citizens of the state of Israel with explicit political and legal rights which put them in a very different position from their fellow-Palestinians across the green line in the West Bank and Gaza Strip. However, Palestinian nationalism has grown among them since 1967, reinforced by the renewal of contacts since then with their relatives and fellow-countrymen across the green line after nearly two decades of isolation in a predominantly Jewish environment.

There are other equally important differences between the exile populations. Palestinians in Jordan are citizens of that country and are thus spared the humiliations and trials of statelessness which afflict many other exiles. At the same time, Jordan is an autocracy governed by the Hashemites whose key retainers, especially in the powerful security forces and armed forces, are mostly from the East Bank. Its Palestinian citizens are in some cases quite prosperous but have no more chance than other Jordanians to participate in an open political process. Added to the decades-long history of conflict between Palestinian nationalism and the Hashemite dynasty, this helps to explain the continuing appeal of this ideology and of the PLO for Palestinians in Jordan.

Palestinians in other countries face very different problems. In Syria it is that of a regime which wants to appropriate the symbols of Palestinian nationalism for its own purposes, with very meager results so far; in Lebanon it is that of the deep involvement of the politically highly-mobilized and militarily formidable Palestinian refugee community in the politics of the country; in other countries such as those of the Gulf, it is that of a highly skilled group regarded suspiciously because of its high degree of politiciza-tion. In every case, it can be seen how the very problems of the diaspora testify to, and simultaneously serve to strengthen, Palestinian nationalism currently incarnated by the PLO. Palestinians are at home in these Arab countries, but for all the commonality of Arab culture, language, and history, they are not Syrians, Lebanese, or Kuwaitis, and do not want to become such any more than their hosts want them to do so. Palestinian nationalism is thus reinforced by the experience of the diaspora, even as it sometimes serves as a reason or a pretext for the hostility of host regimes and populations.

Nevertheless, the physical division just surveyed cannot fail to have a negative effect on the capabilities of the PLO. The different situations of so many disparate groupings of the Palestinian people necessarily impose on them different perceptions and sometimes differing interests. To this must be added the differences in interests between the various constituent groups which make up the PLO. (These differences are not class-based: Fatah is considered more "moderate" and the PFLP and DFLP more "radical," but there would seem to be little difference in the social background or educa-tional level of the leaders, rank and file, or supporters of these and other PLO groups). Although it is possible to compromise between these differing interests, this can take place at the cost of consistency, or of decisiveness. Furthermore, the leadership of all the groups is made up of individuals living in exile and thus cut off from the day-to-day reality under occupation of over 40 percent of their total constituency. When these problems are compounded by those arising from the direct interference of various Arab regimes in the PLO's internal affairs—not to speak of their opposition to its policies on broader strategic questions—the difficulty it faces in making policy can be appreciated.[7]

It should be stressed that while the PLO's resulting image and policy problems are not unimportant to Palestinians, they understand its narrow margin of maneuver and continue to support it notwithstanding them. This is not to say that there is not a perception that the current PLO leadership could perhaps do better: its performance received a 71.2 percent positive rating in the *al-Fajr* poll, which marks a noticeable drop from the 93.5 percent who stated that the PLO is the sole legitimate representative of the Palestinian people.

It would seem from these figures and from the tenacity of the PLO in maintaining its status as the leading force among the Palestinians for nearly two decades in spite of grave setbacks and the determined opposition of powerful enemies, that its "historic" leadership led by Arafat, his colleagues in Fatah, and their DFLP and PFLP rivals have succeeded in one thing at least: the cementing of a sense of Palestinian identity and national consciousness among nearly all segments of the Palestinian people. In doing so, they have provided a focus made up of an integrated sense of national unity and relatively highly articulated national institutions that were lacking not only in the difficult decades after 1948, but even during the mandate period when Palestinian nationalism first developed fully.

While it is easy to understand how this process might have taken place in the Palestinian diaspora where this generation of leaders and the PLO institutions they created were able to affect directly most segments of the population, it is both harder to explain and would seem to be a more striking achievement in regard to the occupied territories. Explanations for this phenomenon differ.

In view of the lack of direct contact between the PLO and the West Bank-Gaza Strip population, it has been argued (essentially by apologists for the Israeli occupation) that the overwhelming support expressed for the PLO there in polls and elections is more likely based on coercion than on genuine political commitment. A subsidiary argument along these lines is that such results are in effect concocted by pro-PLO researchers, a claim made by the head of the Judea and Samaria Civil Administration, Ephraim Sneh, regarding the *al-Fajr* poll.[8]

Careful consideration reveals the ludicrousness of such assertions on several counts. The first is that while it may be possible to coerce people into expressing lukewarm support in a carefully contrived situation, what level of coercion could bring large numbers of people of all walks of life to risk imprisonment, ill-treatment, and sometimes death at the hands of the occupation authorities in support of the PLO, not once, but repeatedly over the course of two decades? Furthermore, the developments in the occupied territories since December 1987 only underline the validity of this argument. No other conclusion is possible except that a higher level of commitment than could possibly be provided by coercion must be at work here.

Another consideration has to do with the fact that by its very nature, an occupation is based on coercion (the term "liberal occupation" is an Orwellian one which does violence to the meaning of the word itself: it is rather akin to the idea of benign rape). In addition to a full range of liberally used means of coercion, the Israeli occupation has had access to the normal panoply of bribes, inducements, and promises employed by any arbitrary authority. Yet with all this at its disposal, it has failed to produce its own supporters to match those allegedly coerced by the PLO. The most recent attempt to do so was the "Village Leagues," which in 1983 diminished into an embarrassing failure for its Israeli initiators, notably Professor Menahem Milson, after an unsuccessful attempt over two years to create alternate authority structures to the PLO in the countryside of the West Bank.

There is another response to the specious claim of coercion: if coercion could sway the Palestinians, why have they not been swayed by the coercion of Abu Nidal and other extremists who have sworn to kill their more moderate Palestinian opponents and have repeatedly demonstrated their willingness to do so by their murder of PLO leaders and envoys? The original coercion argument is based on the undoubted coercion by the nationalist Palestinian majority of the tiny minority of quislings and collaborators perceived to be aiding and abetting a hated, alien military occupation. However, it founders on its lack of distinction between strongly opposed trends in Palestinian politics, lumping them all together as "terrorists." It thus cannot explain the effectiveness of violence directed against collaborators with the occupation, backed as it is by a massive popular consensus, as compared to the inability of either the Israeli occupation authorities or the extremist Palestinian minority to shift the population from their loyalty to the PLO, in spite of the much more frequent use of violence by both.

Surely it is much easier to believe that more than two decades of occupation, of denial of rights, and of various forms of oppression and dispossession have produced an even more powerful nationalist impulse than originally existed in the occupied territories. According to the *al-Fajr* poll taken before the uprising began in December 1987, 47.5% of those questioned had been subject to administrative detention (that is without trial), 50.7% had been beaten or threatened by the authorities, 57.7% had been maltreated by Israeli soldiers, 22.8% had had property confiscated, and 37.6% had been fined or punished by military courts. In view of these statistics, it follows logically that the nationalist impulse has focused on the PLO, which advocates armed struggle to end the occupation and calls for the self-determination of the Palestinian people. This would seem to be the best, and indeed is the only plausible, explanation of popular support for the PLO in the occupied territories. This is particularly the case given the absence there of the broad range of services extended to Palestinians elsewhere by PLO institutions. In Lebanon, for example, these range from the provision of funds for the reconstruction of homes to defense of the camps in a hostile environment. Over a period of many years, these vital services together with the provision of jobs and other forms of routine political patronage have cemented the loyalties of the camp population in Lebanon, enabling the PLO to reestablish itself there only a few years after the crushing defeat of 1982.[9] In Lebanon, in addition to the direct pressure of Israel over many years, the PLO has had to contend with several hostile Lebanese factions and with the potent opposition of neighboring Syria, especially during the past four years. None of this appears to have diminished the loyalty of the bulk of the camp population to the mainstream PLO leadership. Paradoxically this opposition may well have reinforced loyalty to the PLO, convincing waverers that its suspicions of Syria and its allies in Lebanon were well founded. At times, events in Lebanon have helped to build support for the PLO in the occupied territories, as was evidenced by weeks of sporadic West Bank demonstrations in support of the PLO in Lebanon during the bitter "war of the camps" of the winter of 1986 to 1987.

The Lebanese case is an extreme one, but it is also revealing in showing the tenacity of Palestinian nationalism under the most adverse circumstances. Here too, extreme coercion—whether in the form of repeated massacres, or intense official oppression by the Lebanese state, or sieges of Palestinian camps by hostile sectarian militias—has not shaken the attachment of Palestinians to the PLO. As such, this case perhaps helps to explain how the adversity of occupation has provided an analogous environment for Palestinian national feeling and for loyalty to the PLO.

While the organizational forms which Palestinian nationalism has taken over many decades have changed, many of the essential conditions which produced it have remained relatively constant. As long as that continues to be the case and as long as the most basic forms of political empowerment continue to be denied the Palestinians, it is exceedingly likely that this sentiment will find a form to embody it. That form is currently the PLO, which for all its weaknesses remains the sole credible representative of the large majority of the Palestinian people.

NOTES

1. Student elections are a key barometer of political trends in the occupied territories. In a recent one, held at the Qalandia Vocational Institute on 6 Nov. 1986, a bloc representing a Fatah-DFLP coalition obtained 54.1% of the vote, a PFLP-backed slate 11.3%, and an Islamic bloc 34.5%; as a result the coalition obtained all 11 seats on the student council (WAFA [Palestinian News Agency; Wikalat al-Anba al-Filastiniyya], 7 Nov. 1986). Only at the Islamic University in Gaza does the Islamic tendency normally obtain a majority of the vote, although Islamic candidates did win the latest election at Hebron University, and in recent Bir Zeit University student elections the Islamic bloc got over 36% against 63% for the secular nationalist groups (they were divided into two slates, and Fatah and the DFLP thus took over the student government with a plurality of barely 40% of the vote).
2. There are many accounts of the poll (results of which were published in the al-Fajr English edition on 12 Sept. 1986), some providing apparently contradictory details of its findings partly because it included several questions of a similar nature. The most useful ones are: Thomas L. Freidman, "Poll in West Bank Finds Palestinians Strongly Favor Arafat," The New York Times, 9 Sept. 1986, A6; Avinoam Bar-Yosef, "Poll in Territories Shows Little Readiness for Compromise," Ma'ariv, 8 Sept. 1986; "Palestinian Opinion: New Public Opinion Survey in the West Bank and Gaza," Palestine Perspectives, (Sept./Oct. 1986): 8; "In Brief," Israel & Palestine, (Sept. 1986): 10; and by far the best account, including a breakdown on the nature of the sample and full responses to most of the questions, in Joseph Samaha, "A Political Reading into the West Bank Gaza Poll: Reaffirmation of the Stubborn Reality," Al-Yawm al-Sabe, (6 Oct. 1986): 10–12.
3. Avinoam Bar-Yosef, "Most Don't see Kahane as Representing Israel," Ma'ariv, Sept. 9, 1986, who also quotes Meron Benvenisti in support of the poll's validity. The same issue of Ma'ariv published an interview by Bar-Yosef with Bethlehem Mayor Elias Freij, a prominent supporter of Jordan, under the title: "Freij: Poll Doesn't Give True Picture." The interview is revealing of Freij's thinking and of his affirmation that "The PLO is the sole body authorized to represent the Palestinians and Arafat is the organization's leader."
4. The poll results did not bode well for a Jordanian development plan intended, among other things, to wean West Bankers away from their loyalty to the PLO. This pessimistic conclusion is confirmed by John Kifner, "Hussein Said to Act, With Israeli Aid, To Undercut P.L.O. in the West Bank," The New York Times, 23 Oct. 1986, A10; and "Hussein Plan in West Bank Lacks Money," The New York Times, 2 Nov. 1986, 15. In fact, the plan was scrapped by the king when he dissolved the bonds between Jordan and the West Bank.
5. Ann M. Lesch, Political Perceptions of the Palestinians on the West Bank and the Gaza Strip (Wash. DC: The Middle East Institute, 1980).
6. Ian Lustick, Arabs in the Jewish State: Israel's Control of a National Minority (Austin: Univ. of Texas Press, 1983) is the best analysis of the situation of Palestinians who live inside Israel.
7. For analyses of PLO decisionmaking until 1982; its functioning after the 1982 war; and the role of Yasser Arafat and the Fatah leadership in the process see R. Khalidi, Under Siege: P.L.O. Decisionmaking during the 1982 War (New York: Columbia Univ. Press, 1986); "Palestinian Politics after the Exodus from Beirut," in The Middle East after the Israeli Invasion of Lebanon, ed. Robert O. Freedman, (Syracuse: Syracuse Univ. Press, 1986), 233–53; and "Leadership and Negotiation during the 1982 War: Yasser Arafat and the PLO," in Leadership and Negotiation: A New Look at the Middle East, eds. Barbara Kellerman and Jeffrey Rubin, (New York: Praeger, forthcoming).
8. The Ma'ariv article cited in note 3 above stated that "Security officials strongly denied the poll had any validity," adding that Shadid was one of the most radical Fatah activists at al-Najah and that the members of the polling team were students "known for their violence and extremism."

9. Evidence of a revival of PLO fortunes in Lebanon in 1986 can be found in the following sampling of *New York Times* coverage for a key period of fighting involving the PLO in Lebanon, which followed soon after the shooting down of an Israel F-4 Phantom by PLO forces near Sidon during an air raid: Thomas L. Friedman, "Mixed Israeli Feelings over Lebanon," 31 Oct. 1986, A8; Ihsan A. Hijazi, "PLO Decides to Shift Priority to Armed Struggle" 2 Nov. 1986, 14; and Ihsan A. Hijazi, "Foes See PLO Gain in Lebanon," 29 Oct. 1986, A10. Friedman stresses the inability of Amal to stand up to the PLO forces and the role of the new fighting in unifying Palestinian groups, quoting a senior Israeli official as saying the PLO was once again building up an independent base in Lebanon and citing Israeli confirmation of PLO assertions that large PLO forces had returned to Lebanon. These are confirmed in his 2 Nov. article by Hijazi, who cites "Arab analysts." Syria reacted strongly to this PLO resurgence, acting through Palestinian proxies in mid-1988 to eliminate the PLO presence in Beirut.

4 THE PLO AND THE ISLAMIC REVOLUTION IN IRAN
CHRIS P. IOANNIDES

O n 17 February 1979, barely five days after the triumph of the Iranian revolution, PLO chief Yasser Arafat arrived unannounced in Tehran, leading a fifty-nine-member Palestinian delegation. The delegation included only Fatah leaders and cadres. The Marxist Popular Front for the Liberation of Palestine (PFLP) and the Democratic Front for the Liberation of Palestine (DFLP), whose leaders are Christian, were not represented in the PLO delegation. Upon arrival in Tehran, Arafat proclaimed:

> When one comes to one's own home, one does not need permission. Today is a day of major victory for Muslims as well as a day of victory for Palestine. When I approached Mahrabad airport, I felt as if I was landing in Jerusalem. The Iranian revolution proved that Islam and the Muslims will not bow to oppression. The pressure surrounding the Palestinian brothers was released with the Iranian revolution.[1]

Arafat's companions, who carried Khomeini's picture, shouted: "Today Iran, tomorrow Palestine." From Mahrabad airport, Arafat went directly to Qom and embraced Khomeini.

Two days later, on 19 February, the former Israeli consulate in Tehran was delivered to Arafat, who raised the Palestinian flag over it and thus inaugurated the first PLO office in Iran. Hanni al-Hassan, of Fatah's Muslim wing and a close Arafat aide, was appointed the Palestinian "ambassador" to Iran. These highly symbolic gestures illustrated the sudden and spectacular reversal of Iran's relations with Israel, for the Shah had granted de facto diplomatic recognition to the Jewish state since the early 1960s, and over the years Iran and Israel forged strong economic ties while SAVAK and Mossad cooperated in the intelligence and security fields. At the inauguration ceremony a euphoric Arafat declared to the crowd, which included several thousands of Mujahedin supporters: "I pledge myself, that under the leadership of Imam Khomeini, we will liberate the Palestinian homeland together."[2] For the next three days Arafat traveled throughout Iran receiving a tumultuous welcome wherever he went. In Khomeini's Iran, the Palestinian spring had begun.

The Iranian revolution could not have come at a more propitious historical juncture for the PLO. The Palestinian movement was faced with a great political (and military) challenge in the struggle against Israel: Egypt was about to sign the Camp David peace accords with Israel. The Egyptian-Israeli peace treaty was seen as a most severe blow to the Palestinian movement, for it removed the most important Arab country from the line of confrontation with Israel. But the Iranian revolution compensated for the loss of Egypt and boosted Palestinian morale. As Arafat put it: "The [Iranian] revolution has reversed the strategic balance in the Middle East against Israel and the United States. The Camp David document will be merely ink on paper following the basic changes brought by the Iranian revolution, both in the region and our Islamic nation and in world strategy."[3]

During the spring and summer of 1979, it looked as if the PLO had found a staunch ally in revolutionary Iran. The PLO had been recognized by Iran, and its representative in Tehran was granted ambassadorial status; oil shipments to Israel stopped, and Tehran broke off relations with Cairo, both actions costing Iran about $700 million in yearly revenue. It also appeared to the PLO that revolutionary Iran was supporting the Palestinian cause more out of idealism and conviction rather than self interest.

Overall, it appeared for a while that Arafat's gamble to go to Tehran and embrace the Imam was paying off. By the fall of 1979, however, ominous signs clouded PLO-Iranian relations. Following takeover of the embassy in November 1979 and the PLO attempt to mediate for the hostages' release, these relations took a downturn. The convergence of a score of other developments, such as the power struggle in Tehran, the Iran-Iraq War and the Lebanese crisis, all contributed to placing the PLO and the Iranian revolution on a collision course.[4]

THE IDEOLOGICAL DIMENSION

The embrace of Khomeini by Arafat was not enough to bridge the ideological cleavages and the divergent objectives of the PLO and the Islamic revolution. In ideological terms, the Palestinian movement, while by no means monolithic in its social and political programs, is nonetheless a nationalist movement *par excellence*. As in the case of Arab nationalism, Islam provided the cultural context in which the Palestinian movement grew. Yet, the movement developed a distinct secular orientation with a leftist ambience, especially during the last twenty years. The objective of the PLO is to secure the right of self-determination for the Palestinians and subsequently to establish national authority over the territory that was formerly Palestine. The PLO envisions the Palestinian state to be democratic and nonsectarian. Thus the recovery of territory and the establishment of national authority over it constitute the quintessence of the PLO struggle.

Following the decline of Nasserism in the wake of the Arab defeat in 1967, Palestinian nationalism became the strongest contemporary symbol of Arabism in the Middle East. Historically, however, Arabism had an uneasy relationship with Shi'ism. The Shi'i communities in the Arab East, especially in Iraq, have since the beginning of the century had antagonistic relations with the Arab nationalist movement. A major reason for this antagonism is that Iraqi Shi'a feared that Arab nationalism could be used as a means of discrimination, precisely because of their longstanding association with Persia, where the largest concentration of Shi'a in the world resides.[5]

Indicative perhaps of this uneasy relationship between Arabism and Shi'ism, is the fact that in the aftermath of the revolution, even secularly minded Iranian leaders did not appear to be comfortable with Arab nationalism and Ba'thism. Among the leaders who did not hide their negative view of Arab nationalism were Bani Sadr and Ibrahim Yazdi.[6] Sadeq Ghotbzadeh was somewhat more evasive on the subject, perhaps because of his earlier ties with the PLO and the Syrians. "The Iranian revolution is absolutely relevant for the Arab world," he stated and continued: "But we cannot be monolithic in dealing with it. The revolution has to deal with a diversified and even antagonistic Arab world, and, therefore, the formulation of our policy toward our Arab brothers becomes a rather complicated matter."[7]

Khomeini's objections to Arab nationalism are quite clear and they determine the way he perceives Palestinian nationalism as well. His hostility toward Israel is longstanding and beyond dispute. Such hostility, however, does not imply that Khomeini agrees with PLO objectives. His interest in the Palestinian cause emanates from religious rather than national concern.[8]

According to Khomeini, the establishment of nation-states in the Middle East has resulted from the introduction of nationalism into the region by the "lackeys of imperialist West." For Khomeini and his followers, Arab nationalism and its by-product, the nation-state, were a western plot to ensure that the colonial power continued their domination "over the lands and peoples of Islam. The *umma* [Islamic community] has been parcelled into small nation-states. . . . It is no exaggeration to say that the post-colonial 'independent' nation-states of today are more dependent on the West than they were in the heyday of colonialism."[9]

Given that Arab nationalism is considered a western import into the Middle East, all its mutations—Pan-Arabism, Arab socialism, Ba'thism and Palestinian nationalism (as expressed by the PLO)—are "corrupt ideologies" linked to the West or the East (Marxism). Therefore, Muslims should reject all of them.

A logical consequence of Khomeini's rejection of Arab nationalism is that he sees the Palestinian cause as going beyond the recovery of territory. Certainly, Muslims should recover what is theirs, he argues. But he believes that the logic of Arab-Palestinian nationalism reduces the issue of Palestine into the establishment of yet another nation-state in the territory of a fragmented *umma*. "I remind you," he says," that for us language and territory make no sense. . . . Nationalism is this: Pan-Iranism, Pan-Arabism, Pan-Turkism. This is contrary to God's will and the words of the Quran."[10]

The next logical step for Khomeini is to reject the casting of the conflict over Palestine in nationalist terms. He objects the use of the terms "Arab-Israeli conflict." Instead, he describes the conflict as one between "Islam and Kufr" (western polytheism, falsehood). He believes that Israel has been planted in the Middle East by the West in order to keep Muslims divided. Therefore, the struggle to liberate Palestine and Jerusalem, the site of Mohammed's ascent to Heaven, should be an Islamic one. It should be anchored in Islamic ideology and be waged by a united Islamic front.[11]

There are two major political implications in Khomeini's thesis, the necessity to transform the campaign against Israel into an Islamic struggle. First, Khomeini expects that such a struggle against Israel will "unite one billion Muslims" who are now divided because of their "corrupt rulers who depend on the *jahan-kharan* [the world eaters, the superpowers]." More important, cast in Islamic terms, this struggle cannot lead to compromise, for "Islam and un-Islam, truth and falsehood" cannot possibly compromise. Here Khomeini reminds Muslims that it was through an uncompromising Islamic struggle that he led the Iranian people to victory—the overthrow of the *taguti* [idolatrous] regime of the Shah, "an enemy of Islam, an agent of America and Israel."

On the other hand, an Arab-Palestinian nationalist campaign against Israel is bound, according to Khomeini, to lead to compromise with the "enemies of Islam." He points to the repeated Arab defeats at the hands of Israel and to what he considers the compromising policies of Arab leaders. Most notable

examples of these compromises are the Camp David accords; the Fahd Peace
Plan; the embrace of Mubarak by Arafat in December 1983 and the subsequent PLO-Egyptian rapprochement; the increasingly close ties of the PLO
with Jordan and the February 1985 Hussein-Arafat agreement for a settlement of the Palestinian question. All these moves were denounced by
Khomeini as "treacherous acts."

Finally, the Iranian leader also rejects the ultimate objective of Palestinian
nationalism: The establishment of a democratic, nonsectarian state. For
Khomeini, self-determination means the right of Muslims to establish an
Islamic government, as they did in Iran after they defeated the *taguti* regime.
Therefore, it would be tantamount to blasphemy should Palestinian self-
determination lead to the establishment of Jerusalem as the capital of a
Palestinian secular state. In this vein, Tehran reminded Arafat that "Palestine
is not only for the Palestinians but for Muslims as a whole because of the
religious importance of the Holy Qods [Jerusalem]."[12]

Leaving aside for a moment other critical considerations—such as time
and inter-Arab politics—the metamorphosis of the PLO from an umbrella
organization with a secularly oriented ideology into an Islamic movement
will automatically raise the sectarian question. Crudely stated, in an Islamic
PLO the Palestinian Christians, who have historically been a driving force in
the movement, will be left out in the cold. In "liberated Islamic Palestine"
they will be accorded,along with the Jews, the same rights prescribed in the
Quran for the "people of the Book."

Arafat has been acutely aware that the sectarian question could cause the
disintegration of the PLO. So, when he was asked, following his embrace of
Khomeini in Iran, whether the dream of a secular democratic Palestine had
given way to an Islamic Palestine, he answered angrily: "Stop that; it is
laughable and stupid. . . . I consider the imputation that I have been
stressing Islam (in Iran) as a distortion of facts."[13]

In the end, Arafat's utterances in Iran about liberating Jerusalem "under a
united Islamic flag," did not go beyond the realm of symbolism and rhetoric.
The PLO refused to adopt the Islamic path prescribed by Khomeini, and the
question of ideology and strategy to liberate Jerusalem became a litmus test
in PLO-Iranian relations. It was a matter of time, then, before the ideological
contradictions between the two revolutionary movements surfaced and the
PLO-Iranian alliance collapsed. But in addition to the ideological imperative, there was an equally important reason that precluded the joining of
forces between the PLO and the Iranian revolution. It had to do with the PLO
dependence on the Arab regimes.

THE OPPORTUNITY AND THE CHALLENGE

The Iranian revolution offered the PLO a great opportunity and a grave challenge at the same time. It was an opportunity because the PLO thought, for a while, that through its alliance with Iran a new power alignment in the Fertile Crescent could keep the military option open for the Arab rejectionist front. It was a challenge, both because Arafat had to deal with a leader unlike any other in the Middle East and because Khomeini's bent on exporting his revolution threatened Arab regimes which provided the PLO with critical support. Following the Egyptian-Israeli peace treaty, the PLO main objective was to prevent any other Arab regime from joining the Camp David peace process. The PLO saw in the Palestinian-Iranian alliance the opportunity to strengthen its hand in dealing with the Arab regimes that might be tempted to follow Egypt's path.

The Iranian revolution caused grave concern in Saudi Arabia and among the other Gulf states. They were all doubly disturbed, however, by the PLO-Khomeini alliance, for such an alliance could threaten even more their internal stability. Throughout 1979 it was thought that the Palestinian-Iranian alliance had the potential of being transformed into a Shi'i-Palestinian alliance encompassing the whole Gulf region.[14] Given the population composition of the region, a Shi'i-Palestinian alliance would render the Gulf regimes extremely vulnerable to domestic subversion. The Gulf Shi'a, who had welcomed the revolution in Iran, constitute majorities or sizable minorities in the Gulf states, while about 450,000 Palestinians are dispersed throughout the Gulf.[15]

The PLO-Iranian alliance and its disruptive potential in the Gulf provided the PLO with added political leverage in the region, and this has been one of the reasons behind Saudi and Kuwaiti decisions to reject the Camp David accords. The Saudis had been skeptical about the accords from the very beginning. As soon as the Camp David summit was concluded, the Saudi cabinet issued a statement on 19 September 1978, criticizing the accords because they did not call for full Israeli withdrawal and did not provide for Palestinian self-determination. In addition, the Saudis were reluctant to endorse Camp David because it ignored the question of the status of Jerusalem, an issue for which they are quite sensitive since they are the custodians of Islam's holiest places. The ensuing Islamic revolution in Iran and the PLO-Iranian alliance increased these Saudi sensitivities over the status of Jerusalem.

The Gulf regimes, as well as their populace, did not fail to see the symbolism in the Palestinian-Iranian alliance. It was a symbolism reflected in Arafat's statement while he was in Tehran. "We are all Muslims," the PLO chief proclaimed, "and we will march to Jerusalem under a united Islamic flag." What the PLO-Iranian alliance did to Gulf politics for a short period of time was forge a link between concerns over domestic stability and the Palestinian issue. Under these circumstances, and in addition to their other objections to a separate Egyptian-Israeli treaty, the Gulf rulers felt that they could not possibly endorse an American-sponsored peace agreement which ignored the question of Jerusalem and was denounced by the PLO and by a triumphant Islamic revolution in Iran. The menacing prospects of the PLO-Iranian alliance were reflected in a subtle warning that the PLO gave to the Saudis. It is said that shortly after the opening of the PLO office in Tehran, Faruq Qaddumi, the PLO "foreign minister," warned Prince Saud al-Faisal of the "vulnerability of Saudi oil-fields and also of the Islamic Holy Places."[16]

In addition to increased political leverage that the PLO expected to exercise in the Gulf region, a significant change in the overall Arab-Israeli strategic balance was expected by PLO leadership. Following Camp David, this balance had shifted decisively to Israel's favor.

In the spring and summer of 1979, the PLO worked for the establishment of a new front against Israel. For this purpose, Arafat paid repeated visits to Iraq and Syria. The axis of this front was to be Iraq, Syria, and Lebanon with Iran becoming its strategic rear. This Fertile Crescent front was to be supported from the south by the political and economic resources of the Gulf states, particularly Saudi Arabia. In the PLO calculations, Jordan had no other option but to join this front. Overall, the PLO had concluded that the fall of the Shah put an end to Persian pressure on the Gulf states who could now dedicate all their attention and resources to the struggle against Israel. Even Turkey was expected to soon join the new anti-Israeli alignment. According to Hanni al-Hassan, the Iranian revolution made possible the creation of a belt around Israel. This belt could lead to Israel's defeat if it was supported "by a basic change in Turkey which is inevitably coming."[17]

Thus, in the spring of 1979, the PLO saw an opportunity emerging for the creation of a new anti-Israeli front as a response to Camp David. The removal of Egypt from the confrontation with Israel seemed to have deprived the Arabs of a military option. In the eyes of the PLO, however, the Iranian revolution came along to make possible the restoration of the military option. Arafat envisaged a grand Arab-Iranian alliance evolving as follows:

> The Americans and the Israelis assigned the Shah a special role to enforce the results of Camp David. The Shah was to control Iraq, Saudi Arabia and the Gulf

States so that the Iraqi army, above all, remained tied to the Persians. . . . Since the revolution in Iran, Iraq can now throw its army fully into the battle against the Zionist enemy. And there is no Persian pressure anymore on Saudi Arabia and the Gulf states. On the contrary, Iran's new Chief of Staff regards his country now a confrontation state against Israel. . . . Yes indeed we lost the western front of Egypt, yet we gained instead a strategic depth from Beirut to Eastern Persia. [18]

Not since the times of Nasser's Pan-Arab struggle against Israel had the Palestinian movement seen the potential of the emergence of such a potent anti-Israeli front. But unlike all previous fronts, alliances, and alignments against Israel, the catalyst of the grand alliance of 1979 was—in the PLO eyes—a non-Arab force, the Iran of Ayatollah Khomeini.

In early April 1979, Hanni al-Hassan, the PLO representative in Tehran, gave a long interview to the Beirut magazine *Monday Morning*. The focus of the interview was the PLO-Iranian alliance and Arab-Iranian relations. Responding to a question about the fears that several Arab countries had of the Iranian revolution and whether the PLO was trying to allay those fears, Hanni al-Hassan said that these fears were irrational. Khomeini's revolution should not worry the Arab regimes, he argued, and added:

Our mission is to leave no room for Arab-Iranian conflict, because the days of Arab-Iranian conflict had gone with the Shah who believed in Persian domination of the Arabs. The Iranian revolution does not believe in Iranian domination of the Arabs but in Iranian obligations to the Arabs. Arab-Iranian conflict is what Zionism and the enemies of Iran and the Arabs want, and the Palestinian revolution will do a great deal to see that that conflict does not develop. [19]

Indeed, throughout 1979, the PLO exerted considerable effort to convince the Gulf rulers that the Iranian revolution was not directed against them. Unless they were convinced of that, the Arab-Iranian alliance the PLO was envisaging had no prospect of materializing.

While the PLO-Iranian alliance had strengthened Arafat's hand in dealing with the Gulf regimes, the PLO chief did not want to cause alarm among the Gulf rulers. In fact, some of these rulers thought for a while that the PLO might be the broker between them and revolutionary Iran. On its part, the PLO could use its close ties with Iran in order to pressure Arab regimes. But it could not appear to be threatening their survival. The PLO had learned in Jordan in 1970 that to cross the line separating the two might be suicidal. Wary not to jeopardize relations with the Gulf regimes and at the same time carried away by its vision of an Arab-Iranian alliance, the PLO failed to see that the Iranian revolution did threaten these regimes and that Khomeini's pledge to export the revolution was not just rhetoric. As a consequence of this gross misjudgment, Arafat appeared annoyed whenever he was asked whether the Iranian revolution posed a threat to the Gulf states. Characteristically, when he was asked in March 1979 if Saudi Arabia was threatened by the Iranian revolution he responded: "Come on now; that is nonsense. America tries to stir up the matter after the revolution, to make the states in that region feel insecure. And then it [US] sent ships from the Philippines to the Gulf of Arabia. . . . After my stay in Iran, I visited these states, telling them that they had nothing to fear from the Iranian revolution." [20]

Following this angry statement, Arafat visited Baghdad (27–31 March), where he held extensive deliberations with the Ba'thist leadership and with Saddam Hussein. Their meeting assumed special significance because the Camp David accords had just been signed in Washington.

Following the PLO-Iraqi meeting, the two parties issued a joint declaration which treated the Iranian revolution as a nonevent. It was ignored completely. Instead, the declaration repeated emphatically, five times in all, that the struggle to liberate Palestine was a "progressive, nationalist, and Pan-Arab struggle." [21] Apparently Arafat not only failed to convince Saddam Hussein that the Iranian revolution was a blessing for the Arabs, but he felt compelled to reaffirm his faith in Arab nationalism as the only path to liberate Palestine.

On the same day of the Baghdad communiqué, a Kuwaiti newspaper published an interview with Fatah's Abu Iyad (Salah Khalaf) who was with Arafat in Baghdad. He hailed the Iranian revolution as a victory for all Arabs and especially for the Palestinians. Still on the same day, Hanni al-Hassan stated that the Iranian revolution was becoming a pivotal force in the struggle against Israel. [22]

The contradictory positions advanced by top PLO leaders illustrated the pressures and counterpressures to which the PLO had been subjected. It was attempting to ride the wave of the Iranian revolution and to stay close to all the Gulf regimes as well. That this was a Sisyphian task was demonstrated by the PLO endeavor to find a modus vivendi between Khomeini's Iran and Saddam Hussein's Iraq.

The PLO position in Iran was, to a large extent, contingent upon the state of Palestinian relations primarily with Iraq and secondarily with Saudi Arabia. For the Ba'thist regime in Iraq, the Iranian revolution constituted a mortal threat. Among others, Iraq's Shi'ite majority had found inspiration in the Iranian revolution. Fearing an Iranian-sponsored Shi'i insurrection, Saddam Hussein dealt forcefully with Shi'i opposition. [23]

On its part, the Tehran regime saw in Iraq not only a promising opportunity to export the revolution, but it attributed domestic unrest in the provinces of Khuzestan and Kurdestan to Iraqi subversion. Khomeini was convinced that Saddam Hussein was the instrument of both the United States and the Soviet Union to bring down the revolution. In late September 1979, Iranian Foreign Minister Ibrahim Yazdi met Saddam Hussein at the Non-aligned conference in Havana. The meeting only confirmed the gap separating the two regimes.

Thus, the PLO had to overcome deep-seated mistrust between Iran and Iraq if it was to avert a crisis in their relations. Adding to the problem, pro-Khomeini demonstrations in Bahrain in August had increased the Gulf regimes' fear of Iran.

It was in the midst of this atmosphere of deteriorating relations between Iran and the Gulf states that a high-powered Palestinian delegation headed by Abu Jihad (Khalil al-Wazir) and Abu Walid (Sa'ad Sayil) arrived in Tehran. The PLO objective was to patch up relations between Iran and its neighbors. Soon, the PLO leaders discovered that relations between Iran and Iraq, particularly, were beyond repair. When they met with Khomeini, he denounced the Arab regimes that "act treacherously." When they met with Ayatollah Mohammed Montazeri they heard his scathing attack against Saddam Hussein. Shortly afterwards they met with Ibrahim Yazdi, the Iranian Foreign Minister, who stated that Arab nationalism and Ba'thism were bankrupt ideologies. "Revolution by Arabs can never triumph unless it is through Islam," Yazdi declared. [24] While the Palestinian delegation was still in Tehran, Iraqi President Saddam Hussein, accused Iran of expansionist designs, ridiculed its support for the Palestinians and called the PLO to follow the path of the "Arab nation." [25]

On 18 October, the Palestinian delegation left Tehran emptyhanded and faced with a worse dilemma than before. Tehran and Baghdad were demanding that the PLO take sides in their dispute. For awhile, the PLO resisted taking sides; doing so would automatically alienate one of its allies. Yet, as the PLO discovered, if it did not take sides it would probably succeed in alienating both of its allies. Less than two weeks after the departure of the Palestinian delegation, the hostage crisis erupted. Among its unforeseen casualties were PLO-Iranian relations.

THE EMBASSY IMBROGLIO

Contrary to a variety of accounts in the American media and elsewhere, there is little to suggest that the PLO had engineered the embassy takeover. The American Embassy was attacked and occupied by a group called *Danesjuan*

Peyrove Khat-e Imam (Students Following the Line of the Imam). The mentors of this group were the top leadership of the Islamic Republican party (IRP). It was they who decided to capture the embassy, and the PLO had little influence over them, if any.[26]

Four days after the embassy takeover, Abu Walid was back in Tehran heading another Palestinian delegation. His mission was to mediate for the release of the hostages. President Carter had decided to turn to the PLO for help through its U.N. mission and also through Illinois Congressman Paul Findley and former Attorney General Ramsey Clark. The United States contacted Arafat and asked him to use the good offices of the PLO to mediate for the hostages' release. The PLO chief agreed to mediate, hoping that a successful Palestinian mediation with Khomeini might lead to the long-sought American recognition of the PLO. So a top Palestinian leader, Abu Walid, was urgently sent to Tehran to meet with Khomeini. But neither Khomeini nor the embassy militants were about to allow the PLO to have a say in their "Second Revolution."

Khomeini refused to receive the PLO delegation, even Abu Walid. As for the embassy militants, they did not hesitate to denounce the PLO mediation attempt. When the Palestinians went to the embassy to try to persuade the militants to release the hostages, they were told blatantly that their presence was not welcome. "We told them that we knew how to make a revolution and succeed. We knew how to defeat American imperialism. The Imam showed us the way. We did not need their advice how to conduct our revolutionary struggle."[27]

Both Khomeini and the militants were incensed, the more so when Hani al-Hassan claimed credit for the 17 November release of blacks and females among the hostages. Immediately Khomeini denounced the PLO for "telling lies in order to get close to the United States."[28]

The PLO attempt to mediate the hostages' release backfired. Not only did it anger the Iranians, it also caused friction within the PLO. The PFLP, the DFLP, Sa'iqa, and even part of Arafat's own Fatah declared their solidarity with Khomeini and supported the embassy takeover. Like the Iranian communist Tudeh party, they saw "American imperialism burning in the Islamic world" thanks to Khomeini. And the weakening of the American position in the Middle East meant the weakening of Israel as well. Tactically, therefore, Khomeini deserved the support of "all revolutionary and anti-imperialist forces in the Middle East."[29] But here was Arafat appearing willing and ready to aid the United States in recovering from Khomeini's humiliating blow by seeking the release of the hostages.

Realizing that his rebuff by Khomeini might hurt his image as revolutionary leader "waging war against imperialism and Zionism," Arafat and his top aides were quick to perform an about-face. They went out of their way to emphasize that the PLO never attempted to mediate the hostages' release but rather was supporting the takeover and was ready to aid Iran to face the threat of a US military intervention. In early December, Arafat declared at a Beirut rally: "Tell our great Imam to give the order and we will all obey and move to strike imperialism at any time and in any place. The day will come when we will all say along with Imam Khomeini: Join the *jihad* to liberate Jerusalem. Join the *jihad* to liberate Jerusalem." [30]

Arafat's maneuvering could not work with Khomeini. Following the PLO attempt to mediate, and despite its subsequent support of the embassy takeover, PLO-Iranian relations took a steady downturn. Arafat returned to Tehran on 11 February 1980 to attend the celebrations of the first anniversary of the revolution. Khomeini was in a Tehran hospital at the time, recovering from a mild heart ailment. He received the PLO chief but the euphoria of 1979 had evaporated. The Iranian media downplayed Arafat's visit, an unmistakable sign of the declining PLO fortunes in Iran.

Yet, there were Iranian groups who were eager to appear as close as possible to Arafat and the PLO. They included the leftist guerrilla organizations, especially the most popular among them, the Mujahedin-i Khalq.

THE LEFTIST ALLIES

More than any other political group that had opposed the Shah, the leftist guerrilla organizations—the Mujahedin-i Khalq and the Feda'iyan-i Khalq— had developed the closest ties with the PLO. Since the late sixties, leftist Iranian guerrillas had been undergoing training in PLO camps in Lebanon. The Islamo-Marxist Mujahedin forged closer ties with Fatah while the Marxist Feda'iyan developed stronger ties with George Habash's PFLP. Both Iranian guerrilla groups patterned their armed struggle against the Shah on the leftist model of "national liberation wars." By the early seventies, though, it became evident that the guerrillas were not in position to pose a serious threat to the regime. [31]

Still, the Mujahedin and the Feda'iyan participated actively in the revolution, especially in its last phase. This, and the fact that they had close ties with the PLO, prompted many to suggest that through the leftist guerrillas the PLO had played a primary role in the revolution. [32] In reality, the role of the Mujahedin and the Feda'iyan in the revolution had been secondary and that of the PLO marginal. The Iranian opposition movement under Khomeini had waged a struggle which bore little resemblance to the guerrilla-type struggle that the leftists had waged against the Shah. Khomeini's struggle was carried out through a mass movement whose ideology, organization, and tactics were *sui generis,* not copied from any liberation struggle model, Palestinian or other.

This notwithstanding, as far as PLO relations with the Iranian opposition movement were concerned, the historical allies of the PLO in Iran were the leftist guerrilla organizations. As a consequence, when these organizations found themselves on collision course with Khomeini, the PLO was faced with yet another painful dilemma: choosing sides between its natural allies and Khomeini, the Imam, the leader and symbol of the revolution.

When Arafat visited Tehran in February 1980, the Khomeini forces, mainly represented by the Islamic Republican Party, the Revolutionary Guards, and the Revolutionary *Komitehs* (Committees) were engaged in open propaganda warfare with the Mujahedin. The organization's leader, PLO-trained Massoud Rajavi, had been banned by Khomeini from running in the presidential elections of January 1980. At the same time, the Mujahedin were subject to increased harassment by the hizbollahis—the supporters of the Islamic Republican party (IRP) also known as *Hizbollah* (Party of God). Thus, when Arafat met Rajavi twice, on 12 and 14 February 1980, he was embracing the Iranian leader who, in the eyes of the IRP, could pose the most serious challenge to the clerical drive for political domination. Top IRP leaders, such as Hojatoleslam Mohammed Bahonar, had already suspected that the Mujahedin were involved in a "plot against the revolution."[33] (Bahonar became prime minister in July 1981, only to be assassinated by the Mujahedin a month later.)

The Mujahedin gave wide publicity to their leader's meeting with Arafat. Their official publication came out with a front page picture of Rajavi offering a gratified Arafat a submachine gun while proclaiming: "We will always consider ourselves the apprentices of Palestine's revolutionary camps." On his part, Arafat expressed his gratitude and invited Rajavi to visit Beirut.[34]

However, the more the Mujahedin and the PLO advertised their historical ties and the closer they appeared to be drawing, the more precarious the PLO position in Iran was becoming. In the midst of a power struggle, the PLO appeared dangerously close with the *monafeqin* (hypocrites), as Khomeini branded his leftist opponents.

THE CRUCIBLE OF WAR

The Iran-Iraq war, which began with the 23 September 1980 Iraqi invasion of Iran, dynamited the already tenuous position of the PLO in Iran. The war forced the PLO to side eventually, although reluctantly, with Iraq. More important, it caused a profound inter-Arab schism which in turn gave Israel far greater room to maneuver regionally and internationally. This schism was one of the elements which precipitated the June 1982 Israeli invasion of Lebanon.

Realizing the negative consequences of the Iran-Iraq war for the Arab struggle against Israel, Arafat made a desperate mediation effort. As soon as the war started, he rushed to Baghdad. There, Saddam Hussein, who expected a quick victory over Iran, asked Arafat to side with "the Arab nation." The PLO chief responded that he was siding with the immediate end of hostilities. Then Arafat flew to Tehran, but Khomeini refused to see him. The Iranian leader has reportedly said of Arafat's visit: "Why did he come to Tehran? He should go to the devastated towns and villages at the front and see what Saddam is doing to the Muslims."[35] Still, Arafat was able to meet with President Bani Sadr and other Iranian leaders. They all demanded that he denounce openly "Saddam and the Iraqi aggression." While sympathetic to Iran, Arafat could not go so far as to denounce a brother Arab nation at war with a non-Arab country. He left Tehran emptyhanded.

Following Arafat's departure, the Iranian broadcast media were purged of all pro-Palestinian themes, which were replaced by Persian patriotic songs. The Palestinian cause was becoming a casualty of the historical Persian-Arab rivalry.

For a few months Arafat appeared to be adopting a pro-Iranian stand. The PLO was split over the war and pro-Iraqi groups clashed repeatedly with pro-Khomeini groups in Beirut. At the same time, Arafat came under intense pressure from his own Fatah, the PFLP, the DFLP, Sa'iqa, and also from Syria and Libya to side with Iran. They all saw the Iraqi invasion of Iran as diverting attention from the struggle against Israel. They also considered it an act toward weakening the anti-imperialist front since Iran was a major force fighting American imperialism in the Middle East. As a consequence of these pressures, the PLO, along with Syria, Libya, Algeria, South Yemen, and Lebanon, boycotted the Arab summit which took place in Amman 25–27 November 1980. The summit, attended by Saddam Hussein, adopted a pro-Iraqi stand, but the boycott confirmed the deep divisions that the Gulf war was already causing in the Arab world.

By the spring of 1981, though, the PLO started abandoning its pro-Iranian stand and leaning toward Iraq. This shift was prompted mainly by the convergence of two factors: the intransigence of Khomeini and the emergence of a new alignment in the Arab world.

Throughout the winter and spring of 1981, the PLO worked diligently to bring about a cease-fire in the war through the mediation of the Nonaligned Movement and the Islamic Conference Organization. On 1 March 1981, Arafat, along with the heads of five Islamic states—Pakistan, Bangladesh, Turkey, Guinea, and Gambia—visited Baghdad and then Tehran. In Baghdad, Saddam Hussein appeared willing to accept the mediation of the Islamic states to end the war. It was a different story in Tehran, where Khomeini received the delegation and gave it a sermon-lecture. He denounced Saddam Hussein as "a stooge of America and Russia," and demanded that any mediation should first determine who is the aggressor.[36] Following this ill-fated mediation attempt, Arafat was persuaded that Khomeini's intransigence was the most serious obstacle to end the war.

The other factor behind PLO's shift toward Iraq was related to realignment that has been taking place in the Arab world in the wake of the Gulf war. The catalyst for this new alignment was the common concern of monarchical, republican, and socialist Arab regimes that the Iranian revolution was undermining the legitimacy of their ruling elites. The first Arab regime to side openly with radical-socialist Iraq was the kingdom of Jordan. Its example was followed by all the conservative regimes in the Gulf. In this way, a new Arab alignment was formed around the Riyadh-Amman-Baghdad axis, and the PLO could not possibly ignore it, especially because this axis had the overwhelming support of the Arab regimes, leaving Syria relatively isolated at the time.

EGYPT RETURNS TO THE ARAB FOLD

During 1983 and 1984 Egypt and Iraq moved cautiously towards a rapprochement. By 1985 Cairo and Baghdad had established de facto relations. An important but little publicized aspect of these relations has been the Egyptian military assistance to Iraq which amounted to an estimated one billion dollars yearly. In this way Egypt joined informally the anti-Iranian axis. The search for a united Arab front against Khomeini continued in 1986 and 1987. King Hussein of Jordan has been particularly active in this respect, apparent in his attempts to bring about an Iraqi-Syrian reconciliation. The movement toward a pan-Arab coalition against Iran culminated in the Arab summit meeting held in Amman between 8–11 November 1987.

This has been an extraordinary summit for the Arab world as a whole and for the PLO in particular. For the first time since Arab summit meetings were initiated in 1948, the Palestinian question and the Arab-Israeli conflict were not the dominant concern of Arab leaders. By all accounts, the issue which dominated the November 1987 summit was the Gulf war and how the Arabs could confront the "Iranian threat." The Iran-Iraq war has, as King Hussein declared at the summit's conclusion, created "new confrontation states" (Iraq, Kuwait, and Saudi Arabia).[37] In the jargon of Arab nationalism until 1981, there could be only one type of "confrontation state"—the state which is confronting Israel. By definition, therefore, the confrontation states since 1948 have been Egypt, Jordan, Syria, and Lebanon. A redefinition or broadening of the term "confrontation state"—in the context of the Middle East regional subsystem—can only be made at the expense of the PLO. For such a redefinition implies that the Palestinian issue should share the attention and the resources of the Arab world with other Arab concerns. That is precisely what transpired in the Amman summit when the Palestinian issue became subordinate, momentarily, to the elevated Arab concerns about the Gulf war.[38]

Yasser Arafat did participate in the Amman summit, but unlike earlier summits, he was not among the protagonists. The PLO chairman was forced to listen to the Arab leaders' calling for a united Arab front against Khomeini's Iran, while the summit was taking place twenty-five miles from the Israeli-occupied West Bank and forty-five miles from Jerusalem.

Within a week of the summit, Iraq, Kuwait, the United Arab Emirates, Morocco, and Saudi Arabia had restored formal diplomatic relations with Cairo. Egypt's return to the Arab fold consolidated the realignment of the major Arab power which has been developing since the outbreak of the Gulf war.

What all this meant for the PLO, was that the Iranian revolution and its continuing aftershocks have had the opposite effect than the one Arafat had strived and hoped for. Instead of the creation of a new Arab front against Israel, there has been a gradual shifting of the strategic priorities of the Arab world—except Syria and Libya—from Israel and the Mediterranean toward Iran and the Persian Gulf. As for the PLO, it was left with no choice but to join the Arab coalition against Iran.

All this was to change, however, in the course of a few months. First, there was a historic development in the occupied territories. Barely a month had passed since the Amman summit—a summit of frustration for the Palestinians—when a full-fledged uprising erupted in the West Bank and Gaza. Second, there was a UN sponsored cease-fire in the Iran-Iraq war. The cease-fire followed a series of Iranian setbacks in the war. It took effect on 20 August 1988 amidst wild celebrations in Baghdad and a depressed atmosphere in Tehran. Iran's retreat seemed to vindicate Arafat's decision to side with Iraq and the Arab coalition against Khomeini's Iran. The combination of the Palestinian uprising and the cease-fire in the Gulf war contributed to bringing the Palestinian issue to the forefront of Arab concerns.

THE FAHD PLAN

The Gulf war was not the only factor that forced the PLO to join the anti-Iranian coalition. While the war was still at its initial phase, two of Tehran's Arab opponents, Amman and Riyadh, were becoming, in the summer of 1981, the point around which a settlement of the Arab-Israeli conflict might revolve.

King Hussein of Jordan, had re-entered the mainstream of Arab politics and by mid-1981 was enjoying considerable respect and prestige in the Arab world. This, along with the realization by Arafat that the king had a role to play in the determination of the West Bank's future, drew the PLO chief closer to Jordan. The Hussein-Arafat rapprochement culminated in the agreement they signed in Amman in February 1985. This agreement provided for a joint Jordanian-PLO stand aimed at a settlement with Israel on the basis of UN resolutions. The Hussein-Arafat agreement was short-lived. It was met with opposition from within Fatah's Executive Committee and it was also denounced by Syria and the anti-Arafat Palestinian groups. In February 1986, King Hussein announced the collapse of the agreement and for this collapse, blamed the PLO.[39]

At the same time, Saudi Arabia was attempting to promote a peace plan, the Fahd Plan, which contained a clause that could be construed as implicit recognition of Israel. The plan was endorsed by the six-nation Gulf Cooperation Council and, more significantly, Arafat appeared willing to discuss it. He felt that the plan was bringing the Palestinian issue to the forefront of Arab concerns, and he tried to convince other Arab leaders to consider it. Opposition to the Fahd Plan, however, proved decisive. Despite Arafat's posturing, it was opposed mainly from within the PLO, as well as by Syria and Libya, and the combined opposition to the plan was the primary cause of the collapse of the November 1981 Arab summit at Fez.

Arafat's setback at Fez was accompanied by Tehran's vehement reactions to the Fahd Plan. A week before the opening of the Fez conference, Khomeini unleashed a scathing attack against Saudi Arabia and stigmatized all those who supported the Fahd Plan, including Arafat. "They are traitors of Islam," he proclaimed. Thus, by branding Arafat a "traitor," he put a formal end to the faltering PLO-Iranian alliance.[40] The Tehran regime was even more incensed because the PLO failed to keep a distance from the Mujahedin, who had been engaged since June 1981 in a violent campaign against the regime. The regime saw the PLO siding with the anti-Iranian front externally while maintaining its ties with Khomeini's number one enemy internally. It was more than Tehran could tolerate.[41]

As for Arafat's PLO, by the winter of 1981, it had lost most of its faith in or good will toward the Khomeini regime. The PLO had to witness the systematic elimination of its allies, the Mujahedin guerrillas. It was also shocked by the reports that Tehran had been receiving shipments of Israeli arms. And finally it considered Khomeini responsible for the continuation of the Gulf war. PLO leaders warned repeatedly that inter-Arab divisions caused by the war would encourage a major Israeli move against the PLO in Lebanon. That move came in June 1982, when Israel invaded Lebanon. Out of that political and military labyrinth, the PLO emerged a loser, while the pro-Khomeini forces emerged stronger than ever.

KHOMEINI'S LEBANON

Lebanon had special significance for Khomeini long before the revolution. An apparent reason for his interest was that about one million of his coreligionists lived there. Lebanese Shi'a were a group with which Khomeini had established ties in the early sixties.[42] Their leader (until his mysterious disappearance in Libya in 1978) was al-Sayyid Musa al-Sadr, a cleric from Qom with close ties to Khomeini. Other associates of Khomeini, including Sadeq Tabataba'i, Mustafa Chamran and Sadeq Ghotbzadeh, assisted Musa al-Sadr in the seventies to organize the Shi'i paramilitary organization, AMAL, an acronym for Afwaj al-Muqawamah al-Lubnaniyya (Lebanese Resistance Detachments). AMAL also means "hope" in Arabic. All these ties were bound following Khomeini's victory in Iran and the emergence of the Shi'a of Lebanon as an important force in the country's politico-religious landscape.[43]

Lebanon was also important to Khomeini because he considered it the battle ground *par excellence* for Islamic confrontation of western cultural, political, and military encroachment in the Middle East. To him it was an Islamic duty for the Iranian revolutionaries to assist fellow Muslims against the United States and Israel on the battlefield of Lebanon. As a result of Israel's massive invasion, aimed at destroying the PLO as an organized fighting force, Khomeini and his supporters in Lebanon found an opportunity to propagate two important ideas: (1) not only were the established Arab regimes "proven bankrupt," but the PLO was as well; and (2) the "Imam's line," Islamic ideology and desire for martyrdom, offers the only promise of defeating American imperialism and Zionism.

With regard to the first point, there is a consensus that all Arab regimes had been discredited given their inability to confront Israel in Lebanon. Khomeini, however, carried this argument a step further by pointing out that the PLO represented a bankrupt ideology and a movement defeated militarily, like the rest of the Arab regimes.

As long as the PLO was under siege in Beirut, Tehran not only avoided criticizing it, but a week after the Israeli invasion, announced that it was dispatching a unit of Revolutionary Guards to Lebanon to fight the Israelis "along with the Lebanese and Palestinian combatants." This was a highly symbolic gesture which was contrasted to the passivity exhibited by the Arab regimes throughout the Israeli invasion.

It should be noted that the Israeli invasion of Lebanon came at a time when Iraq was under great military pressure due to an Iranian offensive which had started earlier in March. Hence Tehran's utmost priority in June 1982 was to bring its offensive to a successful conclusion. It is for this reason that Khomeini saw the Israeli invasion of Lebanon as an "American conspiracy to divert Iran's attention from the war to Lebanon for which Iran is sensitive."[44]

While Khomeini never lost sight of his highest priority—the war—he did not fail to see that developments in Lebanon in the summer and fall of 1982 were offering Iran an opportunity to advance the cause of the Islamic revolution. Subsequently, Islamic Iran appeared as the true champion of Palestinian rights and as the only genuine revolutionary force in the Middle East that can stand up to the "onslaught of American imperialism and Zionism."

Soon after Arafat agreed to the introduction of the western Multinational Force (MNF) to oversee and protect the PLO withdrawal from Beirut, Tehran initiated a new anti-PLO campaign. Arafat was denounced for leading the Palestinians to "a spectacular defeat," for "choosing disgrace," and for "inviting imperialism back to the Middle East." Tehran gave the following advice to the PLO: "What is necessary now is that the Palestinians revise their ideology and strategy to utilize the mounting wave of Islam."[45]

The next step for the Iranian revolution and its followers and sympathizers in Lebanon, was to prove the superiority of the "Imam's line in fighting imperialism and Zionism" in the propitious environment of Lebanon. The tactics of the pro-Khomeini forces in Lebanon—which ranged from the shadowy Islamic Jihad to the openly active Hizbollah and Islamic AMAL—was to do what the PLO had not considered doing in Lebanon: to attack the symbols of American political, military, and cultural presence in the country.

In the course of 1983, while Tehran and Damascus intensified their campaign against the presence of the US marines in Beirut, the main symbols of American presence in Lebanon became targets of terrorist attacks by Islamic fundamentalists. On 18 April a suicide truck-bomber attacked the US Embassy, killing fifty, including seventeen Americans. Throughout the Lebanese civil war and until its departure from Beirut, Fatah had effectively protected the US Embassy against any attack. On 23 October 1983 another suicide truck-bomber attacked the headquarters of the US marines who were stationed at the Beirut airport, killing 241. The marines had been invited and indeed welcomed by Arafat as part of the MNF.

On 19 January 1985 Malcolm Kerr, the president of the American University of Beirut, was assassinated in his office. The university, including its American officials, had been always respected by Arab nationalists, if only because it was a center which had produced prominent Arab and Palestinian intellectuals and leaders.

The United States appeared determined not to retreat from Lebanon under such pressure. Yet that is precisely what transpired when President Reagan, contradicting his earlier pronouncements, announced that the marines would be withdrawn from Lebanon by the end of February. The presidential announcement was made on 7 February 1984, two days after the collapse of the Lebanese army which was routed by the combined forces of the Shi'i and Druze militias. The Lebanese army had been trained and equipped by the United States and since September 1983 had been backed by the firepower of the Sixth Fleet. Its collapse made the US military presence untenable.

The last marines left Beirut on 26 February 1984. Moments later, Shi'i militiamen carrying pictures of Musa al-Sadr and Khomeini, raised the green flag of Islam over the abandoned marine camp.

Despite the US military retreat from Lebanon, the pro-Khomeini forces continued their campaign to destroy any vestiges of American presence in the once pro-western country. On 20 September 1984, the new American Embassy in East Beirut was attacked by a suicide truck-bomber. As in the previous suicide attacks against American targets, responsibility was claimed by the Islamic Jihad. Coming eighteen months after the attack on the US Embassy in West Beirut and eleven months after the devastating attack on the US marines at the Beirut airport, the spectacle of the American Embassy in Beirut once more in ruins, was particularly embarrassing for the Reagan administration. This embarrassment was increased when President Reagan had to face his own hostage crisis. On 14 June 1985, a TWA plane was highjacked from Athens to Beirut by two Lebanese Shi'i gunmen. For the next two weeks, Hizbollah—and possibly AMAL—held forty American passengers hostage.[46] Reagan, who had earlier capitalized politically on Jimmy Carter's "irresolution" during the Tehran hostage crisis, opted for the Carter approach—the peaceful resolution of the crisis—instead of the "prompt and swift retaliation against terrorists" that he had promised. Accordingly, the American hostages were released following lengthy negotiations between the White House and the highjackers, with AMAL's Nabih Berri serving as a key interlocutor.

The litany of attacks by the pro-Khomeini forces against the United States in Lebanon and the subsequent American retreat, represents a major foreign policy setback for the Reagan administration in the Middle East and for the last five years American influence in Lebanon has been at an all time low.

Developments which followed the American retreat from Lebanon reinforced even further the Khomeini line that only an Islamic struggle can enable the Arabs to confront successfully the "enemies of Islam, imperialism and Zionism." By 1984, Lebanese resistance against the Israeli occupation of the South grew dramatically, and by the winter and spring of 1985, Israel was searching for a path out of the Lebanese quagmire. The pro-Khomeini forces in the South played a major role in the anti-Israeli resistance.

When Israel invaded Lebanon in June 1982, many Shi'a welcomed the Israelis. The Shi'a in south Lebanon especially, had resented the presence of Palestinian Fida'iyin who were stationed in the area. The arrogant and often cruel behavior of the Fida'iyin was a source of constant friction and occasional clashes between the local Shi'i population and AMAL on one hand and the PLO on the other. It was mainly for this reason that many Shi'a were content to see the expulsion of the Palestinian Fida'iyin from their towns and villages. The Shi'a in the South, however, soon realized that the Israelis were digging in for a prolonged occupation, and by the fall of 1982 there were signs of growing Shi'i opposition to the Israeli army.[47] The sporadic attacks against the Israelis in 1983, escalated into full-scale guerrilla warfare by 1984.

The axis of Lebanese resistance in the South revolved around two loose coalitions, the Islamic Resistance Movement (IRM) and the Lebanese National Resistance Front (LNRF). The IRM incorporated the more militant Shi'i groups such as the Hizbollah and the Islamic AMAL. The LNRF represented a broader coalition resembling a popular front which transcended religious or party affiliations.[48] Secularist and leftist groups such as the Syrian Social Nationalist party (SSNP), the Organization for Communist Action, and the Lebanese Communist party constituted the membership of the front, which began its operations in 1982.

The Shi'i groups which opposed Israel and particularly the IRM had found inspiration and support in Islamic Iran and had followed Khomeini's exhortation to wage an "Islamic struggle against Israel and America and seek martyrdom." From June 1982 to June 1985, 650 Israeli soldiers died in Lebanon. Over half of them were killed in attacks by Shi'i guerrillas. Eighty-three Israeli soldiers died in suicide attacks perpetrated by young Shi'a. Suicide attacks against the Israelis have also been carried out by the SSNP, the pro-Syrian wing of the Ba'th party, and the Lebanese Communist party, especially during the last phase of the Israeli withdrawal.

What is significant in all this is that for the second time in a year, the pro-Khomeini forces in alliance with Syria could claim another major victory in Lebanon: first they forced the United States into retreat and obliged the Gemayel government to nullify the American-mediated Lebanese-Israeli agreement of 17 May 1983; then they forced the Israelis into an accelerated withdrawal from most of southern Lebanon by June 1985. Since then, Israel has been providing multifaceted support to the South Lebanon Army (SLA) which is controlling a "security zone" along the Lebanese-Israeli border.

Since the American and Israeli retreat from Lebanon, Khomeini has been contrasting the actions of "committed Lebanese Muslims who tellingly defeated America" to the "dishonorable conciliation" of Yasser Arafat. The latter's rapprochement with King Hussein and President Mubarak was seen by Tehran as yet "another disgrace against the ideas of the Palestinians and the Islamic world."[49]

For Khomeini and his followers in Lebanon and throughout the Middle East, this new Shi'i victory in Lebanon provided one more opportunity to propagate that it is the Khomeini line of Islamic struggle and not a PLO formula which offers the Arabs a viable course to confront Israel successfully. It is no coincidence that since Israel's retreat from Lebanon, Islamic militancy and attacks against the Israelis in the West Bank and Gaza have been on the rise.

PLO: BETWEEN DAMASCUS AND TEHRAN

Notwithstanding Israel's misadventure in Lebanon, the PLO expulsion from that country has dealt the Palestinian movement a critical strategic defeat: the deprivation of its only autonomous—more or less—politico-military base in the Arab world. As a consequence of the removal of the bulk of the Fida'i forces far away from Israel's borders and their dispersal throughout the Arab world, the PLO has been forced to depend more than before on the good will of the Arab regimes. Furthermore, the expulsion from Lebanon precipitated a PLO split into a pro-Arafat faction and an anti-Arafat faction. And at the same time, the shifting politico-military alliances in Lebanon also affected the PLO. These developments were bound to affect PLO-Iranian relations as well. Accordingly, while some of these developments pushed Arafat's PLO further away from Iran at one level, the two drew closer at another level. Therefore, PLO-Iranian relations will be briefly examined at three levels: the intra-PLO, the regional, and the Lebanese levels.

No other development has shaken the Palestinian movement more, since 1982, than the internal split of the PLO. Eight months after the PLO departure from Lebanon, a rebellion against Arafat took place among the Palestinian forces which stayed behind the Syrain-controlled Biqa' Valley. The rebellion was led by the veteran Fatah commander Sa'id Musa Muragha known as Abu Musa. The Fatah rebels were joined by the pro-Syrian Sa'iqa, the PFLP-General Command of Ahmad Jibril, the Popular Struggle Front (PSF), and Abu Nidal's Fatah Revolutionary Council. Damascus on its part, threw its weight behind the rebels and, on 24 June 1983, Yasser Arafat was expelled from Syria. In addition to Syrian support, Libya's Mu'ammar al-Qadhdhafi also aided the rebels.[50]

The rebel leader Abu Musa, named his group the Fatah Uprising and along with Sa'iqa, the PFLP-GC and the PSF formed an alliance called the Palestinian National Salvation Front (PNSF). George Habash's PFLP, which has been moving closer to Damascus since 1981, also joined the PNSF.

From the very beginning of the PLO-split, Iran sided with the anti-Arafat faction. The Khomeini regime, which has critical need for Arab allies in its war with Iraq, has, for the last five years, forged a close alliance with Syria primarily and with Libya as well, both of which happen to be the Arab states supporting the anti-Arafat faction. It is within this broader context of Iranian-Arab relations that Tehran's expression of support for the Abu Musa faction should be viewed. Since the PLO split, the Iranian media have been giving wide publicity to the activities of the Damascus-based PNSF and to its criticisms of the "compromising stand" of Yasser Arafat.

In the summer of 1985, the Iranian regime made a more tangible gesture of rebuffing Arafat's PLO by inviting the leaders of the Salvation Front to pay an official visit to Tehran. Indeed, Abu Musa, Ahmad Jibril, and other dissident Palestinian leaders of the PNSF paid a highly publicized visit to Iran between 3–11 August 1985 and while the extraordinary Arab summit in Morocco was taking place. The dissident PLO leaders, who denounced the Morocco summit, were received by President Khamenei and Prime Minister Mussavi and were hailed throughout their eight-day stay in Iran as the true representatives of the Palestinian people.[51]

The Palestinian movement's split has also affected the PLO's regional standing. The feuding Palestinian factions have been forced to increase their dependence on the Arab regimes. Arafat's PLO has found itself more dependent on those Arab regimes that are anathema for Khomeini. Since Arafat's expulsion from Syria, Fatah has moved closer to Khomeini's archenemy, Saddam Hussein. In this respect, the Fatah-dominated Palestine National Council (PNC) came out clearly on Iraq's side in the Gulf war. During the Seventeenth PNC session in Amman in November 1984, the Council hailed "fraternal Iraq and its valiant army," which was fighting Khomeini's Iran. In his concluding speech to the PNC, Arafat delivered an encomium for the Iraqi leader Saddam Hussein by stating:

> I send my gratitude to my brother the knight Saddam Hussein. I tell him that this war will end with the efforts of the Muslims and the non-aligned states so that we will move together with the Iraqi army, God willing, to Jerusalem. I thank him because when I went to him in Baghdad before coming here to H. M. King Hussein, and told him that we wanted to hold our PNC, he said: 'Baghdad, Iraq and the Iraqi people, are the Palestinian people's brothers. Decide and impose on us, on our people, brother Abu Ammar.[52]

This solid PLO stand in support of Iraq, was repeated during the Eighteenth PNC session which was held in Algiers between 23–27 April 1987. Overall, the PNC decisions in Algiers, represented a wider spectrum of opinions in the Palestinian movement since several guerrilla groups, such as the PFLP and the DFLP, agreed to work with Arafat under the PLO umbrella. With regard to the continuing Iran-Iraq War, the Algiers meeting determined that the "PNC stands at fraternal Iraq's side in defending its land and any Arab land that is the target of foreign aggression and invasion. The PNC condemns the occupation of Iraqi territory."[53]

Arafat's close ties with Baghdad are also illustrated by the fact that while officially the PLO headquarters are in Tunis, a very large number of PLO affairs are conducted by the PLO chief and his Executive Committee from Baghdad. This has been particularly the case, following the Israeli raid on the PLO headquarters in Tunis, on 1 October 1985. Indeed, during the mid-eighties, the PLO appeared to be closer to Baghdad than anytime since the fall of 1978, when Fatah and the Iraqis reconciled. The Khomeini regime perceives the Arafat-Saddam alliance as unholy, one that simply confirms Arafat's joining the ranks of the "treacherous" Arab leaders.

Despite the PLO-Iranian rift due to the war, Arafat keeps the door wide open for future reconciliation with Tehran. Characteristically, the PLO Chairman had this to say in January 1987, when he was asked to give an evaluation of Palestinian-Iranian relations: "These relations are normal." Pressed to clarify his statement, Arafat responded: "They are normal. For some time we have been a member of the Islamic Good Offices Committee. We have spared no effort to end the war."[54]

The labyrinth of Lebanese politics and violence seemed to have opened a channel for Arafat, through which he could reestablish some contact with Iran. Accordingly, the convergence of several developments in Lebanon, placed the pro-Arafat and the pro-Khomeini forces on the same side. First there was the "war on the camps." Since May 1985, the AMAL militia has been waging an especially violent and ruthless campaign against Palestinians in Lebanon.[55] There have been repeated clashes between AMAL and Palestinian forces in and around the refugee camps of south Beirut, Sidon, and Tyre. Despite the fact that AMAL is a Shi'i group, Iran distanced itself from it and tried to put an end to the AMAL attacks, as well as to provide food to starving Palestinians inside these camps. While AMAL carried out its intermittent attacks on the camps, there has been a parallel deterioration of its relations with the pro-Khomeini Hizbollah which refused to participate in the "war of the camps." In this particular juncture, this Hizbollah stand was beneficial to the Palestinians. Thus, as a consequence of AMAL's actions and in the context of Lebanon's ever shifting alliances, the PLO found itself on the same side with Iran and in the same trenches with the pro-Khomeini forces. (In Spring 1988, AMAL and Hizbollah were engaged in open warfare. Only Syrian intervention saved the AMAL forces from total defeat in South Beirut.)

In addition to the "war of the camps" and the AMAL-Hizbollah clashes, there has been a simultaneous development which, once more, placed the pro-Khomeini and the pro-Arafat forces in the same camp. Since the summer of 1985, there have been signs of friction between Hizbollah and the Syrians, mainly because the Syrian army has been attempting to place under its control Hizbollah's activities in the Biqa' Valley as well as in south Beirut. As a consequence, there have been serious clashes in the Biqa' Valley town of Mishgara between Hizbollah and the SSNP. The Iranians denounced the pro-Syrian SSNP and were indirectly critical of Syria as well because it allowed its supporters to attack "the Islamic forces of Hizbollah, the greatest revolutionary force in Lebanon."[56] yet, Tehran downplayed the SSNP-Hizbollah clashes in order to avoid antagonizing Damascus. The tension in Syrian-Hizbollah relations, however, was an additional reason to bring even closer the pro-Khomeini and the pro-Arafat forces in Lebanon. A very important consequence of this has been evident since the fall of 1985, when Palestinian Fida'iyin and Hizbollah guerrillas started launching joint operations against Israeli forces in Lebanon as well as on the Israeli-backed South Lebanon Army. If this ad hoc Palestinian-Hizbollah cooperation on the ground solidified, Israel's northern border would once more become a battlefield.

For a moment, and while all these concurrent developments were taking place in Lebanon, it appeared that Tehran had softened somewhat its tone toward Yasser Arafat. Consequently, the Iranian deputy foreign minister Javad Larijani, stated that Arafat had been trying to solicit an invitation to visit Tehran, but he had been rebuffed because his purpose was to mediate between Iraq and Iran. If, however, as Larijani put it, "Arafat changes his policy based on compromise with the reactionaries and imperialists, he is welcome and we will greet him at the Mahrabad airport."[57]

Soon thereafter, however, Tehran resumed its public denunciations of the PLO chief. The main reason for this, was that on 2 July 1986, Arafat met at length in Baghdad with the leader of the Mujahedin, Massoud Rajavi. The latter had moved his headquarters from Paris to Baghdad a month earlier and vowed to launch attacks against the Khomeini regime from Iraqi soil. During their meeting, Arafat and Rajavi discussed the Iraq-Iran War and the Iranian reiterated his support for the PLO. On his part, Arafat stated that "the war was part of an imperialist and Zionist conspiracy against the revolutionary centers in the Arab homeland."[58]

Tehran saw Arafat's meeting with Rajavi as well as his statement on the war as a provocative and hostile gesture against the Islamic Republic. Subsequently, the Iranian media labeled Arafat "a deviate, false, hypocrite and treacherous leader" and called the Palestinians to disassociate themselves from the PLO chief and "take independent decisions about their own future."[59]

The resumption of vehement Iranian attacks against the person of Yasser Arafat and his inclusion among the enemies of the Islamic Republic seem to render a PLO-Iranian reconciliation a difficult proposition, at least as long as the Iran-Iraq War continued.

The Irangate scandal—the revelations that the United States and Israel have been selling arms to Iran—did not make a PLO-Iranian reconciliation any easier. On several occasions, as in the latest PNC session in Algiers, the PLO denounced the sale of US and Israeli arms to Iran.[60] Yet, two major considerations dictated the downplaying of Tehran's secret deals with the United States. First, the PLO was unwilling to jeopardize its de facto alliance with Hizbollah in Lebanon. Second, Iran was standing up and confronting the superior American naval forces in the Gulf. For years, Arafat has been warning that "US imperialism was looking for an opportunity to build up its naval forces in the Gulf and reintroduce military bases in the area, a development that could only benefit US imperialism and Zionism."[61] Under these circumstances, the PLO saw no benefit in antagonizing Khomeini. After all, Iran had received only a limited amount of US arms while the Arab states in the Gulf had invited a US armada—over 36 ships—in the region.

In the final analysis, the Irangate revelations had little effect on PLO-Iranian affairs. This was so because at the time, it was Khomeini and his allies in Lebanon who exercised the most decisive influence on the course of these affairs rather than Arafat and his PLO.

THE ISLAMIC CHALLENGE IN THE WEST BANK AND GAZA

Since the revolution in Iran, Islamic fundamentalism has been gaining ground in the occupied territories.[62] The seeds of the Islamic resurgence of the 1980s have been sown in the aftermath of the humiliating Arab defeat in the 1967 six-day war. But there is little doubt that the Iranian revolution and Khomeini's militant message have come to provide great inspiration and encouragement to many Palestinian Muslims in the occupied territories. As a consequence of the growing influence of Islamic fundamentalism, both the Israelis and the PLO have been faced with an unprecedented challenge.

The first challenge is directed against Israel. Up until the early 1980s, resistance in the West Bank and Gaza has been dominated by the PLO. For the last few years, however, there have been growing acts of civil disobedience couched in Islamic slogans. A pervasive feature of recent demonstrations, rallies, and strikes has been the picture of the Dome of the Rock and such slogans as "Allah-o Akhbar" and "I am a Muslim-An Arab-A Palestinian." A more serious and violent challenge to the Israelis, has come from a newly established fundamentalist group, the Islamic Jihad Organization. The group should not be confused with the shadowy Islamic Jihad in Lebanon.[63] Since 1985, members of the Islamic Jihad have carried out a series of attacks against Israeli military as well as civilian targets in the West Bank and Gaza.

The rise of Islamic militancy in the occupied territories has been matched by multiplying signs of an Islamic resurgence among Israeli Muslim Arabs.[64] This trend, however, has not been translated, for the time being, into sustained violence against the state or terrorism. Nonetheless, the combination of a militant Islamic movement in the occupied territories with nonviolent Islamic activism in Israel proper, do pose a new challenge to the Jewish state.

The gravity of this challenge has been demonstrated in the *intifada*—the uprising of Palestinians in the West Bank and Gaza which erupted on 9 December 1987. While the *intifada* represented a spontaneous mass protest movement against occupation, Muslim fundamentalists emerged as a major force behind it. Despite the use of force and a variety of measures of collective punishment, Israeli security forces have been unable to suppress the *intifada* which continued throughout the spring and summer of 1988.

It is only too ironic that Muslim fundamentalism is posing a challenge — of a different kind albeit—to Israel's archenemy, the PLO. For the last quarter of a century, Palestinian nationalist and Marxist guerrilla groups operating under the PLO umbrella, have been waging a relentless campaign against Israel. These groups, through the PLO, have also dominated Palestinian society and politics. Since the Iranian revolution, however, a variety of Islamic fundamentalist groups have been undermining the PLO's hegemony in the West Bank and especially in Gaza.

Several Muslim leaders speaking for the *al-Ikhwan al-Muslimun* (Muslim Brotherhood), the *Jama'at Islami* (Islamic Society), and the *Mujama'a al-Islami* (The Islamic Charitable League) have made it clear that the secular line of the PLO does not represent the "Palestinian Muslim militants." Their reasoning for this, echoes the reasoning of the Egyptian Ikhwan leader Sayyid al-Qutb, as well as the Khomeini line that "there can be no liberation outside Islam and the divine path of God's Prophet."

Accordingly, and in veiled criticism of corruption in the PLO, Ahmad Yassin, an Ikhwan leader, has stated:

Those in the Palestinian movement, have no commitment to Islamic values. . . . I do not believe that a person who joins Fatah is a Muslim militant when at the same time he does not pray. He is like a Muslim who drinks wine and eats pork. Loyalty is acceptable only when it is devotion to God. [65]

Another Islamic leader, Khalil al-Quka, who leads the *Jama'at Islami* in Gaza, had this to say about the PLO while the PNC was meeting in Algiers in April 1987: "Since the PLO has no religion or Quran, it is no different from any other liberation movement." And al-Quka proceeded to dispute that the PLO represented "the Palestinian devotees of Islam." [66]

Regarding the objectives of the Palestinian struggle, another well known Islamic leader with ties to Islamic Jihad, Sheikh Abd al-Aziz Udeh of Gaza, reflected Khomeini's exhortation when he recently stated that resistance in the occupied territories should have one and only one objective: "The establishment of an Islamic state from the sea [Mediterranean] to the river [Jordan]." [67]

In the final analysis, and while Khomeini's personal appeal has diminished since 1982, his call for an Islamic struggle as the only means to liberation, has stricken a sensitive cord in the hearts of many Palestinian Muslims who have often felt betrayed by fellow Arabs. And while the PLO, especially its Christian and Marxist components, cannot accept this prescription for an "Islamic struggle," they cannot ignore it either, for it carries political weight among those who matter the most in the Palestinian movement: the Palestinians living under occupation. This has been amply demonstrated during the *intifada*, a development of historic significance for the Palestinian-Israeli conflict.

When the *intifada* broke out in December 1987, it took the PLO as well as Israel by surprise. As the uprising gained momentum in January, it became evident that a major force behind it has been that of Islam and Muslim fundamentalists. Gradually the PLO asserted its role in the *intifada*, and a secret committee — the Unified National Command (UNC) — was established to coordinate the uprising. Five Palestinian groups were represented in the UNC: Fatah, the PFLP, the DFLP, the Communist party and the Islamic Jihad Organization. The inclusion of the Islamic Jihad in the UNC was a clear sign that the PLO needed the cooperation of Muslim fundamentalists for they had won the right to have a say in Palestinian national affairs in the battlefield — the streets and mosques of Gaza and the West Bank.

Common opposition to Israeli occupation has drawn closer the PLO and Muslim fundamentalists while the PLO continued to represent the national aspirations of the Palestinian people as a whole. Yet, the basic contradictions between the nationalist, secular and leftist oriented Palestinian movement and the Islamic fundamentalist movement remained unresolved. In fact, an underlying tension has characterized their relations in the 1980s.[68] It is an open question, therefore, whether the PLO-Muslim fundamentalist coalition is a temporary phenomenon dictated by the needs of the *intifada* or whether it foreshadows a trend toward the formation of a more solid political alliance.

The resurgent Islamic movement in the occupied territories and the major role played by Muslim fundamentalists in the *intifada,* should not be seen as an exclusive by-product of the Iranian revolution. Still, it is the Islamic revolution in Iran under Khomeini's leadership that has served as a catalyst for the Islamic resurgence among Palestinian Muslims. Moreover, while Islamic militancy poses a new challenge to Israel, it also carries the potential of sharpening the ideological contradictions within Palestinian society in the occupied territories and beyond.

CONCLUSION

Since the victory of the Islamic revolution in Iran, Khomeini has been exhorting Arabs and Muslims to form a united Islamic front against Israel. Still, the uniting of Muslims has not been brought any closer by the Iranian revolution. Cases in point are the ongoing Iran-Iraq War, which has exacerbated inter-Arab divisions to the great detriment of the PLO, and the collapse of the PLO-Iranian alliance. Even the Syrian-Iranian alliance could disintegrate given the ideological incompatibility between Islamic Iran and Ba'thist Syria, the diverging political agendas of the two regimes vis-à-vis Lebanon, and the possibility of a Syrian-Iraqi rapprochement.

In retrospect, what has transpired in Arab-Iranian relations in general and in Iran's relations with the PLO in particular, demonstrates that the PLO had assigned itself an impossible task. By embracing Khomeini so tightly at the beginning, the Palestinian nationalist movement placed itself in the midst of the most ferocious ideological, political, and military struggle that the contemporary Middle East has seen. It is a struggle between the forces advocating an Islamic revolution and the overwhelming majority of the Arab regimes. It is a conflict comparable in intensity and depth to Arab-Israeli hostilities — only more bloody if one considers the carnage of the Iran-Iraq War.

The PLO has been able to exploit confrontation in the Arab arena to its advantage most of the time. Yasser Arafat is perhaps at his best when he is performing a balancing act in the maze of inter-Arab politics. He can do so because, as he puts it, he is able to "bring into the forefront of Arab concerns the Palestinian common denominator, the difficult factor in the Middle East equation."

For the last quarter of a century, this Palestinian factor has been a major focus of revolutionary activism and radicalization in Middle East politics. Since the Iranian revolution in 1979, there is a competing revolutionary force throughout the region, that of Islamic radicalism-fundamentalism. The leader of this messianic movement, Ayatollah Ruhollah Khomeini, is unlike any other in the Middle East. Truly, like Arafat, Khomeini is a revolutionary leader, but he is much more than that. He is the Iman, the "idol smasher," and the avenging archangel who can direct his divine-like wrath even at Yasser Arafat. But more important than the differences in style and symbolism between Arafat and Khomeini remains the fact that the Islamic revolution in Iran has unleashed formidable forces that are beyond anyone's ability to control or manipulate. It was precisely these forces which threatened the Arab allies of the PLO the most.

In the end, the PLO had to uphold its faith to its own Arab nationalist tradition. In turn, through this umbilical cord of Arabism, the PLO had to remain tied to the Arab regimes which provide it with indispensable political, diplomatic, financial, and logistical support. It was because of this Arab predicament of the PLO that is strategic alliance with the Islamic revolution in Iran was precarious from its very inception. Yet, the PLO could not remain oblivious to the role that Islamic fundamentalist forces could play in its struggle against Israel. It is precisely for this reason that the PLO started cooperating—tactically at least—with Hizbollah in Lebanon and Islamic fundamentalist groups in the West Bank and Gaza. Concurrently the PLO-Iranian rivalry has persisted.

Overall, the Islamic revolution in Iran and its cataclysmic repercussions in the Middle East, have undermined the complex network of PLO-Arab relationships which Yasser Arafat has worked so diligently to build and maintain. As a consequence, the delicate political balances which have allowed the PLO to pursue its own objectives within the wider context of Arab nationalism have been upset.

NOTES

1. *Tehran Domestic Service (TDS)*, 17 Feb. 1979, trans. in *Foreign Broadcast Information Service* (hereafter *FBIS*).
2. TDS, 19 Feb. 1979.
3. TDS, 19 Feb. 1979; *Voice of Palestine*, Beirut, 23 Feb. 1979, trans. in *FBIS*.

4. On the repercussions of the Iranian revolution on the Arab world as a whole, see James Bill, "The Arab World and the Challenge of Iran," *Journal of Arab Affairs* 2(1) (Oct. 1982): 29–45; Mohammed Ayoub, "Between Khomeini and Begin: The Arab Dilemma," *The World Today* (July-Aug. 1983): 254–63; Mohammed Anvari, "Implications of the Iranian Political Change on the Arab World," *Middle East Review* 3(3) (Spring 1984): 17–29.

5. On the subject of relations between the Shi'a of Iraq and the Arab nationalist movement, see Abbas Kelidar, "The Shi'i Imami Community and Politics in the Arab East," *Middle East Studies* 19(1) (Jan. 1983): 3–16.

6. See Bani Sadr's interview in *Middle East Reporter*, Beirut, 29 Dec. 1979; for Yazdi's views see his interviews in *An-Nahar*, Beirut, 1 Oct. 1979, and with *Tehran Domestic Service*, trans. in *FBIS* 5 Oct. 1979.

7. Personal interview with Ghotbzateh, Tehran, Mar. 1980.

8. For an extensive treatment of Khomeini's views on nationalism in general and Arab nationalism in particular, see Farhang Rajaee, *Islamic Values and World View: Khomeini on Man, the State and International Politics* (Lanham, Univ. Press of America), 1983, 73–92. See also Ayatollah Ruhollah Khomeini, *Islam and Revolution: Writings and Declarations of Imam Khomeini*. Trans. and ann. by Hamid Algar (Berkeley: Mizan Press, 1981), 332–33. For a more recent criticism of Arab nationalism by Tehran, see "Kuwait Harnessing Arab Nationalism to Counteract Islam," *Tehran Times*, 13 Aug. 1984.

9. See the article of one of the theoreticians of the Islamic Republic, Dr. Kalim Siddiqui, "Primary Goals and Achievements of the Islamic Revolution in Iran," *Kayhan International*, Tehran, 19 Aug. 1984.

10. Quoted in Rajaee, *Islamic Values*, 72.

11. On the need to transform the struggle against Israel into an Islamic one, see Khomeini's speeches in "Vital Messages of Imam Khomeini on the Occasion of Qods Day," *Tehran Times*, 28 June 1984; "Unified and Total Islamic Struggle to Liberade Qods," Statement by Dr. Ali Akbar Velayeti, Foreign Minister of the Islamic Republic of Iran, in *Jumhuriye Islami*, 27 June 1984; Ayatollah Janati, "Defense and Jihad in the Quran," *Tawhid*, 1(3) (Apr. 1984): 39–54, esp. 52; "Qods Day: A Pragmatic Approach," in *Imam*, Embassy of the Islamic Republic of Iran, London, June-July 1984, 8–10.

12. See the editorial "Another Plot against the Palestinians," *Tehran Times*, 14 Mar. 1985.

13. See Arafat's interview in *Der Spiegel*, 19 Mar. 1979, 132–37. The secular and leftist ideologies of the PLO have drawn criticism from some Arab quarters who also maintain that "the greatest betrayal of the PLO was its denial of its Islamic character." See Abdulwahab el Affendi, "PLO: National War or Jihad," *Arabia*, (Oct. 1983): 29–31. In Aug. 1984, Arafat gave an interview to the same magazine in which he appeared endorsing the notion of jihad. He also called the Palestinian struggle the "longest Arab-Islamic revolution of our time" and referred to the Palestinians as the "Muslim people of Palestine." See "Arafat Renews Call for Jihad," *Arabia*, (Aug. 1984): 6–7.

14. On the subject of the PLO-Iranian alliance and its potential destabilizing effects in the Gulf, see John Cooley, "Iran, the Palestinians and the Gulf," *Foreign Affairs* 57 (Summer 1979): 1017–34.

15. By the middle of 1980, Gulf Shi'a had rather mixed attitudes towards the Iranian revolution. On one hand, they admired Ayatollah Khomeini as the Imam and as an incorruptible leader who stands up to America. On the other hand, they were quite wary of the bloodshed in the wake of the revolution and the ongoing Iran-Iraq War. These conclusions are based on the author's observations during a visit to the Gulf in the summer of 1985. The reactions of Gulf Shi'a to the Iranian revolution are also discussed by James Bill, "Islam, Politics and Shiism in the Gulf," *Middle East Insight*, 3(3) (Jan.-Feb. 1984): 3–12; James Bill, "Resurgent Islam in the Persian Gulf," *Foreign Affairs* (Fall 1984): 108–27.

16. Quoted by Cooley, *Iran*, 1027.

17. On PLO expectations for the forming of an Arab-Iranian front against Israel, see the extensive interview of Hanni al-Hassan in *Monday Morning*, Beirut, 2–8 Apr. 1979. See also the interview of Abu Iyad in *Al-Ray*, Kuwait, 29 Mar. 1979.

18. See Arafat's interview in *Der Spiegel*, 19 Mar. 1979.

19. *Monday Morning*, 2–8 Apr. 1979.

20. *Der Spiegel,* 19 Mar. 1979.

21. For the text of the joint PLO-Iraqi declaration, see *Iraqi News Agency,* 31 Mar., 1979 in *FBIS.*

22. For Abu Iyad's interview, see Al-Ray, Kuwait, 29 Mar. 1979; For Hani al-Hassan's interview, see *Monday Morning,* Beirut, 2–8 Apr. 1979.

23. On the Shi'a of Iraq, these ties with Iranian Shi'ism and with Khomeini, and their opposition to Saddam Hussein, see Hanna Batatu, "Iraq's Underground Movements: Characteristics, Causes and Prospects," *Middle East Journal* 35(4) (Autumn 1981): 578–94.

24. *Tehran Domestic Service,* trans. in *FBIS* 15 Oct. 1979.

25. See Saddam Hussein's interview in *Al-Mustaqlal,* Paris, 13 Oct. 1979.

26. During a visit to Tehran in February–March 1980, the author had the opportunity to conduct extensive interviews with the hostage-takers inside the occupied American Embassy. For details on the embassy takeover, the planning, the groups involved, and the protagonists of the affair, see Christos P. Ioannides, *America's Iran: Injury and Catharsis* (Lanham: Univ. Press of America, 1984), 91–129.

27. Personal interview with Ahmed, an embassy militant, Tehran, Feb. 1980. See also the militants' 22d Communiqué denouncing the PLO mediation, *Tehran Domestic Service,* trans. in *FBIS* 8 Nov. 1979.

28. *Tehran Domestic Service,* trans. in *FBIS* 19 Nov. 1979.

29. On the tactical support for Khomeini and the embassy takeover by Marxist PLO groups, see *Middle East Reporter,* Beirut, 24 Nov. and 1 Dec. 1979.

30. Speech by Arafat at a Beirut rally, *Voice of Palestine,* trans. in *FBIS* 7 Dec. 1979.

31. The ties between the PLO and the Iranian Mujahedin and Feda'iyan guerrillas are examined in Christos P. Ioannides, "The PLO and the Radical Iranian Opposition: 1965–1979." Paper presented at the *20th Annual MESA Conference,* Boston, 22 Nov. 1986.

32. The argument on the primary role of the PLO in the Iranian revolution was advanced among others, by Michael Ledeen and William Lewis, *Debacle: The American Failure in Iran* (New York: Vintage Books, 1982), 110–12; Claire Sterling, *The Terror Network* (New York: Berkeley Books, 1982), 120–21. When the Iranian turmoil intensified in the fall of 1978, several stories which appeared in the three major American news magazines, described the important role which the PLO and especially the Marxist PFLP were presumably playing in this turmoil. See *Time,* 11 and 18 sept. 1978; *U.S. News and World Report,* 2 Oct. 1978; *Newsweek,* 20 Nov. 1978.

33. Personal interview with Bahonar, Tehran, Feb. 1980.

34. See the Mujahedin official organ, *Mojahed,* 25 Feb. 1980.

35. See *Middle East Reporter,* 18 Oct. 1981, 13.

36. For Khomeini's speech to the Islamic Delegation, see *Kayhan,* Tehran, 8 Mar. 1981.

37. On King Hussein's statement about the "new confrontation states," see *New York Times,* 12 Nov. 1987.

38. The secondary role of the Palestinian issue is reflected, among others, in the final declaration of the summit. See *New York Times,* 12 Nov. 1987.

39. The February 1985, Amman agreement did not refer specifically to the U.N. Security Council Resolution 242 which Arafat has been reluctant to endorse. Following the collapse of the agreement in February 1986, all Fatah offices in Jordan were closed down in July 1986. In August 1988, King Hussein renounced all Jordanian claims to the West Bank. Coming in the midst of the Palestinian uprising, the move seemed to favor the PLO, but its consequences are still unclear.

40. For Khomeini's speech denouncing the Fahd Plan and all those who supported it, see *Tehran Times,* 18 Nov. 1981.

41. In August 1981, Hani al-Hassan met secretly with Massoud Rajavi who had escaped in Paris along with Bani Sadr a month earlier. The PLO denied the meeting but Rajavi didn't. On this meeting and the deteriorating of PLO-Khomeini relations, see *Iran Times,* Washington, 11 and 25 Sept. 1981.

42. The ties of Khomeini and his associates with Lebanon's Shi'a, area examined in Ioannides, "The PLO and the Radical Iranian Opposition."

43. On Lebanon's Shi'a and the role of Musa al-Sadr in Lebanon's politics and the AMAL movement, see Augustus R. Norton, *AMAL and the Shi'a: Struggle for the Soul of Lebanon*

(Austin: Univ. of Texas Press, 1987); Fuad Ajami, *The Vanished Imam: Musa al-Sadr and the Shi'a of Lebanon,* (Ithaca: Cornell Univ. Press, 1986).

44. In a speech from the Jamaran mosque, Khomeini stated the following with regard to the Israeli invasion of Lebanon: "Our cause is that we should go to Lebanon via Iraq, not directly. All our speakers and Friday Imams should proclaim that we should go to Lebanon by defeating Iraq. Iraq should not be allowed to rest and rally its resources. All the speakers should be aware of this conspiracy. . . . We want to liberate Jerusalem but we cannot do it until we deliver the Iraqi nation from this [Ba'th] party. We consider Lebanon as part of ourselves. But before we liberate it, we must liberate Iraq." *Tehran Domestic Service,* trans. in *FBIS* 21 June 1982.

45. See the editorial, "PLO and the Politics of Despair," *Tehran Times,* 20 Feb. 1983.

46. The highjacking of TWA Flight 847 from Athens airport precipitated a crisis in US-Greek relations. Citing lax security at Athens airport, the Reagan administration announced a travel advisory to Greece. The author happened to be at Athens airport on the morning of 14 June 1985 and underwent the airport security check. Circumstances of the highjacking and the ensuing crisis in US-Greek relations are examined in Chris P. Ioannides, "Greece, Turkey the US and the Politics of Middle East Terrorism." Paper presented at the UCLA Conference on *Greece: On the Road to Democracy, 1974–1987,* Los Angeles, 2–5 Apr. 1987. With regard to the possibility that AMAL was involved in the highjacking, see *New York Times,* 20 Nov. 1987.

47. On Shi'i resentment of the Palestinian Feda'iyun, the contentment to see the PLO expelled by Israel, and the subsequent Shi'i opposition to the Israeli army, see Augustus Richard Norton, "Making Enemies in South Lebanon: Harakat Amal, the IDF and South Lebanon," *Middle East Insight* 3(3) (Jan.-Feb. 1984): 13–20.

48. On the composition of the Islamic Resistance Movement (IRM) and the Lebanese National Resistance Front (LNRF) and the dominant role of the Shi'i groups in the anti-Israeli resistance, see "Success of Resistance Movement and Impact," *Middle East Reporter,* Beirut, 23 Feb. 1985; "South Lebanon: Philosophy, Strategy and Finances of the Resistance Front," *Middle East Reporter,* 15 Sept. 1984; "Hizbollah Defines its Militant Policy," *Middle East Reporter,* 23 Feb. 1984; "Hizbollah and Islamic Amal Promote Islamic Revolution," *Middle East Reporter,* 3 Dec. 1983.

49. See the interview of Dr. Velayeti, the Iranian Foreign Minister, in *Tehran Times,* 1 Jan. 1984; Dr. Velayeti also denounced Yasser Arafat at the U.N. General Assembly. For Velayeti's speech at the General Assembly, see *New York Times,* 30 Sept. 1984.

50. On the anti-Arafat faction and the backing it received from Syria, Libya, and South Yemen, see "Hardliners: Bid to Rally Ranks against Middle East Initiatives," *Middle East Reporter,* Beirut, 16 Mar. 1985.

51. On the visit of the dissident PLO leaders in Iran and the extensive coverage of that visit by the Iranian media, see *Ettela'at,* 4 Aug. 1985; *Kayhan,* 11 Aug. 1985; *Tehran Times,* 15 Aug. 1985; *Kayhan,* 15 Sept. and 22 Sept. 1985.

52. See *Amman Domestic Service,* trans. in *FBIS* 29 Nov. 1984. For the PNC Political Statement supporting Iraq, see *Amman Domestic Service,* trans. in *FBIS* 29 Nov. 1984.

53. See "Resolutions of the Political Committee of the 18th Session of the PNC, Algiers, April 26, 1987," *Journal of Palestine Studies* 16(4) (Summer 1987): 198.

54. Arafat made this statement during the Islamic summit meeting held in Kuwait at the end of Jan. 1987. See *Al-Ittihad* (Abu Dhabi), 31 Jan. 1987.

55. On the "war of the camps," see Elaine Hagopian, ed., *AMAL and the Palestinians: Understanding the Battle of the Camps,* (Belmont, MA: Arab-American Univ. Graduates, Occasional Papers, No. 9, 1985).

56. See the editorial, "Israel Laughs at Recent Lebanon Clashes," *Tehran Times,* 19 June, 1986.

57. *Tehran Times,* 26 June 1986.

58. *Baghdad Times,* 4 Jul. 1986; *Arab News* (Riyadh), 4 Jul. 1986.

59. See the editorials: "Arafat Reveals Himself," *Jumhuriye Islami,* 8 Jul. 1986; "PLO Downfall for Arafat's Treacheries," *Tehran Times,* 9 Jul. 1986.

60. See "Resolutions of the 18th Session of the PNC," 198.

61. Arafat made this statement during his speech at the Islamic summit meeting held in Kuwait, 25–28 Jan. 1987. See *Voice of Palestine,* Baghdad, trans. in *FBIS* 29 Jan. 1987. See also Arafat's interview in *Der Spiegel,* 19 Mar. 1979.

62. The analysis of the Islamic resurgence in the occupied territories and Israel is partially based on the author's observations during a visit to the area in the summer of 1987. On the impact of the Iranian revolution and the growing influence of Islamic fundamentalism in the occupied territories as well as in Israel, see: "Extreme Muslims Spread in Israel," *Times* (London), 21 Jan. 1980; "Islamic Resurgence Spreading among Israeli Arabs," *Middle East Reporter,* 14 Mar. 1981; "Muslim Fundamentalists: Inter-Arab Friction in West Bank Laid to Muslim Brotherhood," *Middle East Reporter,* 20 Mar. 1982, 11–13; Thomas L. Friedman, "An Islamic Revival Is Quickly Gaining Ground in Unlikely Place: Israel," *New York Times,* 30 Apr. 1987; "Islamic Fundamentalism in the West Bank and Gaza," in "Outlook," *BBC,* 11 Nov. 1987; Elaine Ruth Fletcher, "The New Muslims," *Jerusalem Post* (international ed.) 21 Nov. 1987.

63. On the emergence and activities of the Islamic Jihad Organization, see Eli Rekhes, "Violence: the Next Stage?" *Jerusalem Post* (International ed.) 21 Nov. 1987.

64. See Friedman, "An Islamic Revival;" Fletcher, "The New Muslims."

65. Quoted from the article of Said al-Ghazali, "Islamic Movement vs. National Liberation: Friendly Cooperation or State of War?" *Al-Fajr Weekly,* (Jerusalem), 6 Sept. 1987, 8–9.

66. al-Ghazali, "Islamic Movement."

67. Abd al-Aziz Udeh made this statement on the radio program "Outlook," *BBC,* 11 Nov. 1987. On 11 April 1988, the Israelis expelled Udeh and al-Quka to Lebanon. Three days later, they were given a hero's welcome at the Iranian Embassy in Beirut.

68. See al-Ghazali, "Islamic Movement.

69. al-Ghazali, "Islamic Movement."

5 THE SOVIETS AND THE PLO
The Convenience of Politics
JOHN C. REPPERT

In the more than forty years since the end of World War II, no geographical area has generated more attention, frustration, fear, and anger among the world's powers than the Middle East. Within this turbulent region a curious alliance has evolved between the Union of Soviet Socialist Republics, the largest nation on earth, and the Palestinian Liberation Organization, a nation in search of a homeland. While separated by geography, history, and ideology, these two nations have found adequate practical advantage in their relationship to span threats of war and offers of peace. Recent events, following the twentieth anniversary of the founding of the PLO in 1985, have brought the partnership under severe scrutiny by both sides. A new leadership in the Kremlin has begun to ask hard questions about the utility of continued association with the independently minded Arabs of Palestine, while a PLO leadership still under siege has questioned the willingness and ability of the Soviet Union to further the Palestinian cause.

The high stakes in the current bargaining for peace, as well as the continuation of the intrafratricidal warfare among the Arabs, make even more urgent the understanding of the role of the superpowers in the region. This chapter will focus on the bilateral contacts and conflicts between the PLO and the USSR from the Arab-Israeli War of 1973 through the rise and fall of the latest versions of the Jordanian-Palestinian peace initiatives. [1] Within this context, the author will rely on documents of both parties, as well as two years recent experience in the diplomatic community in Moscow, to analyze the motivations and goals of the two actors. The binding ties of the Soviet pursuit of a leading role in an international conference on the Middle East and the PLO's search for recognition and a homeland will be traced through international events and regional issues.

BACKGROUND

When Mikhail Gorbachev, as the new leader of the Community party of the Soviet Union (CPSU), singled out Yasser Arafat for special attention at the meeting of the new Kremlin leader with visiting world leaders at the burial of Konstantin Chernenko in Moscow, March 1985,[2] he added but one more signal to the tortuous cryptography which has defined the relationship in the past few years. The mixed signals transmitted between Moscow and Beirut, Fez, Tunis, or wherever the PLO could be located at a given time, have suggested both strain and promise. What had appeared to be the relative indifference of the USSR to the decimation of the PLO fighting forces through the Israeli invasion into their former strongholds in Lebanon, as well as the considerable internal strife which racked the PLO from their struggle in Lebanon to the 1984 session of the Palestine National Council in Amman and the internal friction which has followed, may be one of the many areas of Soviet international commitment which Gorbachev will seek to reevaluate as he achieves a degree of security and confidence within the leadership of the CPSU.

Three major events in the past fifteen years have had the most decisive effect on the nature of the Soviet-Palestinian relationship. The first of these was the 1973 Arab-Israeli War with the simultaneous wavering, then defection, of Egypt from its position as the bulwark of Soviet influence in the Middle East. The second was the brief 1977 effort to renew the Geneva peace process in which the Soviet Union would play a major role in international negotiations and the PLO would take a direct role as a participant, representing the interests of the Palestinian people. This effort was followed instead by Sadat's surprise visit to Israel, the Camp David accords, and a continuation of the step-by-step process which has, thus far, kept both the Soviets and the PLO out of a direct role in the negotiating process. The final event, which continues to play a major role in the nature of understanding between the Soviets and the PLO, revolves around the Syrian and Israeli incursions into Lebanon, which had become the primary PLO stronghold in the Middle East. Each of these events and the subsets of actions connecting them will be briefly examined to evaluate the evolution of relations which the Soviets and the PLO are currently attempting to clarify and redefine.

Along with the understanding of the major events, it is necessary to set the context of the relationship in terms of the aspirations of the two partners. Although their relative importance has varied over time, it appears that PLO interests in their relations with Moscow have centered around several basic issues. The first issue is the desire of the PLO to move their struggle for "just rights and a homeland" from the regional arena to the international stage. To this end, it was clearly beneficial to draw in one of the superpowers as a spokesman for the Palestinian cause. A second goal is that of obtaining material support for the continuance of the PLO conflict with Israel. A direct relationship with a superpower offers the opportunity for significant material support and loosens the leash of control that the regional powers maintain in conjunction with their provision of financial support. A third goal is the enhancement of the legitimacy of the PLO as the representative of the Palestinian Arab people. This was clearly improved by recognition on the part of the Soviets of the PLO as the "sole legitimate spokesman of the Arab people of Palestine" in 1978.

The Soviets, too, entered the relationship with the PLO in pursuit of several goals, which are fundamental to understanding Soviet behavior. For the Soviets, the PLO was seen as a vehicle to obtain direct access to the political and economic decisionmaking centers of the Arab camp. To obtain and maintain this access the Soviets have publicly championed the convening of an international conference in which the Soviet Union plays a leading role and the PLO serves and is recognized as spokesman for the Arabs of Palestine. This posture fit well with both Soviet efforts to maintain a favorable image on "anti-imperialism" within the Third World and with their hope of establishing a permanent, legitimate presence in the oil-rich Middle East. The Soviets found the Palestinian issue an effective tool for focusing Arab hostility toward the Israelis and then toward the US as Israel's superpower supporter. This was presented in contrast to expressed Soviet interests in supporting Arab causes in the Middle East.

THE IMPACT OF THE 1973 WAR

The buildup of tensions in the Middle East in the early 1970s came at an inopportune time for the Soviets; they were in the midst of the pursuit of detente with the United States. In a prelude to the immediate causes of the war, the primary Soviet client in the region, Egypt, sought to redefine its relationship to the superpowers. In what seemed to many a dramatic reversal of the steady drift toward Soviet influence begun under Nasser, his successor, Sadat dramatically reduced the number of Soviet military personnel in Egypt during the summer of 1972. Indeed, the entire year had produced a see-saw relationship. As early as February, reports in the West reflected a strain in military cooperation with the Egyptians. Egypt's war minister was quoted as telling a group of senior officers, "if you feel like kicking your [Russian] advisors in the butt, please do it discreetly."[3] Yet, in the following two months of March and April, the reports flowing out of the Middle East looked like the relationship with Egypt had never been stronger. The Soviets were reported to have agreed to build a factory in Egypt for the production of MIG-21 aircraft,[4] although subsequent events precluded the confirmation of any such plan. By April Israeli sources identified MIG-23 aircraft in Egypt with Egyptian crews in charge of their operations.[5] Later that month Sadat was in Moscow for two days, and the joint communiqué on his departure cited an "agreement on further strengthening of military cooperation." The military nature of the visit was stressed by the presence of then Commander of Egyptian Air Force, Husni Mubarak.[6] Despite this seeming momentum which would enhance the Soviet role in the region, the trend was rudely reversed in July when Sadat returned to Moscow, reportedly demanding more military hardware. When the Soviets were less forthcoming in response to his request, Sadat sent thousands of Russians in both advisory and direct combat roles home from Egypt, greatly reducing their presence in this country.

While the PLO's initial access to the Russians had come courtesy of Nasser, who took Arafat along on a trip to Moscow in 1968 and introduced him to the Kremlin leadership, the PLO seems to have been willing to seize the initiative in their relations with the Soviets during this time of friction between the Kremlin and Cairo. Tangible results from Soviet-PLO contacts gradually emerged as a follow-up to Arafat's October 1971 trip to Moscow. By January of 1972, reports were received that the Soviets had agreed to train Fatah guerrillas in the Soviet Union and to provide hospitalization to the wounded from that organization.[7] As relations between Cairo and Moscow deteriorated, PLO ties with Moscow were strengthened. It is unlikely that it was by coincidence that on 18 July 1972, the deadline Sadat had set for the expulsion of 17,000 Soviet advisors, that Arafat was present in Moscow at the head of a PLO delegation emphasizing Soviet-PLO cooperation.[8] By September of 1972, Fatah leadership was reporting that the Kremlin had agreed for the first time to directly supply weapons to the group, as opposed to the earlier practice of providing arms through other Middle East intermediaries.[9] A return visit to Moscow by Yasser Arafat and George Habash during the period of strain with Egypt reportedly produced the new agreement. Thus, it appeared that the goal of obtaining Soviet material support was beginning to pay off for the PLO, despite continued Soviet reservations on PLO goals and methods.

Faced with the possibility of continued difficulty with Sadat and with the desire to maintain a prominent role in the region, the Soviets modified their policy to create an alternative to Egypt through a series of initiatives with the PLO, Syria, and Iraq. The Soviets, who had previously been vocally critical of Palestinian terror, were even willing to transform the image of the October 1972 killing of Israeli athletes at the Munich Olympics by Palestinians into a form of support for Arafat and his leadership of the PLO. The Soviets defended their support for Arafat and the PLO as a moderate alternative to the Black September movement, which had claimed responsibility for the slayings in Munich.[10] In line with this position, the East Germans, in apparent coordination with the Soviets, permitted the PLO to open an official office of representation in East Berlin in August of 1973.[11] This choice of a symbolic opening in East Germany in light of the events of the Munich massacre seemed even more dramatic.

The October 1973 war itself further affected the precarious balance in the Middle East and ended in advancing PLO relations with the Soviets. The Soviet decision to actively encourage the PLO to counter attempts of Sadat to improve relations with the US or other moderate Arab states, such as Saudi Arabia, brought the PLO relationship closer to center stage in Soviet-Middle East policy than it had ever been before.[12] The Soviet decision to materially support the Arab forces in the October conflict by increasing military deliveries to the region from $970 million in 1972 to an estimated $2.655 billion in 1973 again proved the repeated lesson of the Soviets' difficulty in translating presence into influence.[13] During the actual conduct of the 1973 conflict, Soviet actions were extensive enough to result in a decision to bring US forces in NATO to alert status. Yet both powers exercised adequate restraint to avoid a direct confrontation. The Arab oil weapon was employed to good effect in restraining traditional US allies from supporting American operations. However, while applauding the effectiveness of this weapon, the Soviets realized that they were as unable to control this political/economic lever as they were in controlling the extensive military hardware they had placed in the hands of the Arab armies.

The lessons of the 1973 conflict were important for both the Soviets and the PLO in defining their relationship. In addition to the recognition of the limitations on their ability to directly control the nature and extent of the conflict, the Soviets were also made aware that the gains they had previously achieved in Egypt had proven transitory. Egypt, in fact, appeared to have been drawn closer to the US, rather than to the Soviet Union, as a result of the recognized ability of the US to impose a cease-fire on the fighting. The increasingly expensive and sophisticated arms which they had provided their Arab client in the region, while escalating the Israeli cost of victory, failed to alter the fundamental balance of power.

The PLO, despite their increasing prominence as the conscience of the Arab peoples, had to recognize their very limited capabilities in a high intensity, regional military conflict and their equal limitations on affecting the course of the peace which followed the conflict. The Soviet desire to begin rebuilding their position of influence in the region and the PLO desire to regain a more influential role in the region brought the two closer together. Though the PLO, in its current state, was incapable of providing any support to the Soviet material goals of ports as bases for logistical operations, it could give the Soviets increased claim to its position as a friend of the Arab people and as a central player directly involved in any meaningful settlement of the on-going Middle East crisis. This capability on the part of the PLO was strengthened by the actions of the Arab nations at the Rabat Conference of October 1974, where the PLO was recognized as the "sole legitimate representative" of the Palestinian Arabs. [14]

The Soviets, for their part, did exhibit increased activity at the United Nations and in bilateral relations with other countries on behalf of the Palestinians. In their own press they declared their role in the UN to be that of the defender of the rights of the Palestinians. [15] This support at the United Nations was not always made easy by the actions of the PLO, who refused to acknowledge or abide by UN Resolutions 242 and 338 on the settlement of the Middle East conflict. To the dismay of the Israelis, 105 members of the UN overlooked this attitude by inviting Arafat to speak there in November 1974. In Arafat's memorable address, he noted that he had come with the "olive branch and the gun of a revolutionary" and that it was the duty of the international community to keep the olive branch from slipping from his hand. [16] The response of the members of the General Assembly was to vote in the week following the speech in favor of giving the PLO observer status in that body.

In this context, contacts between the PLO and the Kremlin were stepped up once the fighting in the Middle East had been halted. Arafat returned to Moscow in November of 1973. Although still not received as an official visitor in the full sense, this visit did produce the first official communiqué on the outcome of his talks with the Soviet leaders. [17] Shortly after these talks, Moscow began to speak in public about the "national rights" of the Palestinians and a homeland for them on the West Bank. [18] In February and March of 1974, Soviet Foreign Minister Gromyko visited the Middle East to assess the results of the war and the current Soviet position. He met Arafat on two occasions during this trip to the region and again on a return trip to Damascus in May of the same year. Radio Moscow characterized these meetings as a "brilliant confirmation of the steadfastness of the Soviet Union's stand of comprehensive support for the just struggle of the Palestinian Arab people for their legitimate national rights."[19]

These contacts led to Arafat's first invitation to visit the Soviet Union in an official capacity in July of 1974.[20] Although this visit led to the opening of an office in Moscow where the PLO would maintain a permanent representation, this recognition still did not achieve what the PLO had hoped for in obtaining status. The PLO did, however, make progress on the goal of moving their issues to the world stage. Following the direct contacts, the Soviets allied with Palestinian supporters of the Third World to bring about the previously discussed invitation to participate in the affairs of the UN.

The PLO acknowledged this support through their role as a spokesman for increasing Soviet involvement in the Middle East and the necessity for a direct Soviet role in any international negotiations to resolve the continuing Arab-Israeli warfare. The PLO increasingly carried the banner for Arab unity in opposition to the Israelis and spoke with greater frequency in support of espoused Soviet goals and programs in the region (specifically, in the 1973 official communiqué and subsequently in PLO statements of their willingness to pursue a political solution to the problems of the region with direct Soviet participation). The 1973 Conference of Arab States in Algiers, which followed immediately the official visit of Arafat to Moscow, stressed the unity theme by citing for the first time the PLO as the "sole representative" of the Palestinian people. By the 1974 conference in Rabat, the Arab states added the need to "secure the legitimate rights of the Palestinian Arabs, including the right to a national home."[21]

Despite the progress in their relationship with the PLO, it seems apparent that following the 1973 conflict the Soviets reduced the intensity of their focus on the specific issue of the Israeli-Arab conflict and began to consider the broader issues of the Persian Gulf nations. The basis of this shift was most likely a function of the impact of the oil weapon with its influence on NATO and a sense of frustration in achieving Soviet goals in the region through the Arab states directly involved in the conflict with Israel.

THE GENEVA PEACE PROCESS AND CAMP DAVID

The mid-1970s brought the Middle East situation back to the superpower agenda, not in the context of war, but of peace. The strain that the Middle

East fighting had placed on detente between Washington and Moscow had been clearly recognized by both and efforts were undertaken to maintain effective controls on the tensions of the region. In an official Soviet government statement of 9 January 1976, the Soviets called for a reconvening of the Geneva Conference with the PLO as the legitimate representative of the Palestinian people. The statement added that any settlement would have to insure the "legitimate rights of the Palestinian Arab people," including its "inalienable right to create its own state."[22] In pursuit of this goal, the Soviets were successful in including the PLO in UN Security Council deliberations of 12–13 January 1976 on methods for resolving the Middle East dispute. In this regard the Soviets found the PLO an able and willing spokesman on the necessity of convening the Geneva Conference in which the Soviets would assume an equal role with that of the US in permanently resolving the basic issues separating the powers in the Middle East. Thus, by Twenty-fifth CPSU Party Congress in 1976, Brezhnev had clearly aligned the interest of the Soviet Union with those of the Palestinians in terms of their "legitimate national rights," although the Soviet Union had not formally recognized the PLO as the sole spokesman for all Palestinian interests.

Three weeks after the Party Congress, Egypt again played an inadvertent role in strengthening Soviet-PLO relations by abrogating the 1971 Soviet-Egyptian Treaty of Friendship and Cooperation. The PLO was called upon by Moscow to cooperate in isolating Sadat from the rest of the Arab world for his actions. A spokesman for the PLO held a press conference in Moscow in April to support the Soviet position. For their own reasons, Syria, Jordan, and Iraq joined in supporting the Soviet line.[23] Prospects for the Geneva process were brightened once again that fall. On 1 October, one day after Kissinger at the UN had publicly expressed doubt about the future of the step-by-step process, Moscow submitted a formal proposal for a reopening of the Geneva Conference with PLO involvement "on an equal footing from the very outset."[24] In the midst of the US presidential election, no results were achieved, but the proposal was left on the table for the new US administration.

Arafat returned to Moscow in March of 1977 where he was received by Brezhnev and treated cordially. In the following months, Arafat consistently attempted to put pressure on the United States to resume the Geneva peace process with the convening of an international conference. In this effort the PLO naturally received the assurance of public support by the Soviets that the Palestinians would be properly recognized and represented in any comprehensive negotiations. This seeming unselfish concern about the fate of the PLO illustrates the utility of the alliance for the Soviets. The complex challenge the Soviet position created for the US was that any agreement to include the PLO as a full participant in the negotiations strengthened the necessity to directly involve the Soviets as the major power most capable of exercising a positive influence over the PLO.[25] Once again, Security Council 242 was cited by the US as the primary block to a PLO role in the negotiations.[26]

By October of 1977 it appeared that the coordinated policy of the Kremlin and the PLO was bearing fruit. A joint US-Soviet statement was made on the desirability of renewing negotiations in Geneva not later than December of 1977. In this statement the Palestinian issue was identified as "pivotal" and the US began to speak publicly and officially, if still ambiguously, about recognition of Palestinian rights in the negotiations.[27] President Carter at this point had accepted without public reservation the position of the Soviet Union as the cochairman for the conference. At this moment, when the joint goals of the Soviets and the PLO seemed closer to success, the Soviets made clear the priority of their interests. When the US began to drag its feet over admitting the PLO as long as continued to refuse to recognize Resolution 242, the Soviets suggested that the PLO could be brought in later in some undetermined second stage of the talks.[28] The hostility to even this prospective change in policy which quickly developed on the part of Israel and among pro-Israeli political lobbies in the United States was both vociferous and predictable. The momentum to renew the Geneva process quickly stalled in the hierarchies of the US administration.

The entire concept of a Geneva conference in its previously proposed form was drastically transformed by Sadat's dramatic visit to Jerusalem in November.[29] As had now become the pattern, Soviet frustrations with Egypt benefited the relations with the PLO.[30] Arafat quickly joined in condemning Sadat's initiative, and by 2 December 1977, the heads of state of Libya, Syria, Algeria, and South Yemen and an Iraqi deputy premier were meeting with Arafat in Tripoli to coordinate their opposition to Sadat's peace initiative.[31]

The Carter administration, however, frustrated in its previous efforts to reach a lasting solution to the Middle East crisis through Geneva, decided after some deliberation to seize on the Sadat initiative to continue an effort which would be a major part of the Carter presidential legacy. After lengthy negotiations and despite broad expressions of concern with the Arab camp, as well as from the Soviet Union, the leaders of Egypt and Israel joined President Carter in September of 1978 to pursue a settlement to the Middle

East conflict. The result, of course, were the Camp David accords in which
two of the primary antagonists in each of the previous wars, Israel and Egypt,
mutually agreed upon conditions of peace and disengagement.

Although the accord did not refer to the establishment of self-government
on the West Bank and Gaza and included unspecified calls for Israeli
withdrawal at a subsequent date, the reaction of the PLO was swift and
included a rare show of unity. On 18 September, one day after the accords
were announced, Arafat called an emergency session of the PLO Executive
Committee. The result was a universal PLO condemnation of Camp David
with the threat that "those who announce their support for the conspiracy of
Camp David will face the will of our people and its just retribution." [32]

Whatever differences they may have had over the specific form of
representation in a Geneva peace conference, both the Soviets and the PLO
were quick to condemn the Camp David accords on a series of charges. The
PLO, in its capacity as the conscience of the Arabs, charged Sadat with
betraying the fundamental elements of Arab unity. The Soviets, although
primarily upset about once again being bypassed in an attempt to resolve the
Middle East problems, couched their opposition in terms of concern for their
PLO allies. Brezhnev declared on 22 September, "[t]here is only one road" to
a real settlement, "the road of full liberation of all Arab lands occupied by
Israel in 1967, of full and unambiguous respect for the lawful rights of the
Arab people of Palestine, including the right to create its own independent
state." [33] They swiftly assured the world that the Camp David accords were
doomed at the outset, because they "did not permit a Palestinian State, or
recognize the PLO as the only legitimate representative of the Palestinians." [34] Both the PLO and the Soviet Union renewed their call for Arab unity
of all "progressive" states and for the ostracism of Egypt by all other powers
in the region. Both renewed calls for true international talks involving all of
the concerned parties, specifically the Soviet Union and the Palestine
Liberation Organization. The US step-by-step process became synonymous
in their speeches and writings with US efforts to divide the Arab states and to
dictate the terms of any peace to those individual countries.

PLO documents released by the Israeli government after reportedly being
captured in PLO headquarters in Lebanon describe Soviet-PLO coordination
of their policy following Camp David, revealing common goals but recognizing the continued existence of barriers. The documents report that in talks
between Arafat and Soviet Minister of Foreign Affairs Gromyko in Moscow
November 1979, both parties agreed on common measures to isolate the US,

Israel, and Egypt within the Middle East and to undertake measures to economically punish Egypt for its perceived "betrayal" of the Arab cause. Both agreed that achieving Arab unity would be a key function of the PLO and that the PLO should use its influence over states such as Saudi Arabia where Soviet influence was weakest. The Soviets continued their insistence on the right of Israel to peace and sovereignty as part of a comprehensive settlement, despite PLO objections. The PLO refused to recognize the provisions of Security Council Resolution 242, despite Soviet urging.[35] Even in periods of extensive practical cooperation, both sides recognized fundamental differences in their positions.

Elements of the political platform of the Fourth Fatah Conference of May 1980 also show the continuity of their agreed policy. In this extensive document it was noteworthy that the USSR was the only non-Arab ally cited by Fatah and this in a most favorable context. In the international domain the platform called the "strengthening of our strategic relations with socialist countries, foremost among them the USSR, to frustrate American and Zionist plots against the Palestinians."[36]

Despite the problems of Camp David, the agreement reached there did not break down entirely with a return of Egypt to a "unified" Arab camp. This caused both the Soviets and the PLO to reshape their alliances in the region. What emerged from this process was the "Pan-Arab Front for Steadfastness and Confrontation," consisting of Algeria, Libya, South Yemen, Syria, and the PLO. This was a far cry from the goal of a unified Arab world lining up behind the interests of the PLO and the Soviet Union on Middle East issues. In many ways it appeared that the massive Soviet aid to the Arab powers and the powerful political support of the "second superpower" in the United Nations had produced nothing of value for either the Soviet Union or its clients. The Soviet Union remained a recognized force for change only within one of the two warring camps in the Middle East. The US appeared to be gaining, rather than losing, influence in the region. Even though the Camp David accords were fraught with difficulties, it did remind both the Soviets and the other Arab states that the US alone had the power, prestige, and influence necessary to bring together the warring sides. Simultaneously, the PLO seemed to have lost some of its earlier relevance as a force (while militarily weak) capable of bringing together and focusing Arab interests in the region. Thus, not only were both sides still far from achieving their basic goals, but each now saw the other as increasingly less capable of effectively serving as the vehicle for the achievement of those basic interests.

CONFLICTS WITHIN LEBANON

The final event in this period that would fundamentally reshape the Soviet-PLO relationship came in the context of another war in the Middle East, yet this war and its consequences were unlike those which had preceded it. It was the struggle, or seemingly unending series of struggles, within Lebanon. Although PLO forces were present in several Arab countries, Lebanon had served as the most important PLO base of operations since the Palestinian organizations were driven out of Jordan as a result of the 1970 and 1971 fighting.

Following the 1973 war, the PLO had created what was effectively recognized as a "state within a state" inside Lebanon. Because of internal weaknesses based on the factional basis of its body politic, Lebanon found itself unable to effectively control the activities of those who used its territory for their own purposes. In an uneasy truce with the PLO, the official Lebanese government stood by as the PLO continued to conduct cross-border operations into Israel and as the Israelis in turn responded by attacking Palestinian targets within Lebanon. The critical divisions within Lebanon, which have played a vital role in its history, were once more brought into conflict in regard to the Palestinian question. While groups generally identified on the Moslem left of the Lebanese political scale supported the PLO, those referred to as "Christian rightists" were involved in direct conflict, frequently resulting in casualties on both sides.[37]

The nature of the conflict was seriously altered in 1976 when the Syrians entered Lebanon and began actions against the PLO. To the frustration of the PLO leaders, both their traditional supporters in the Arab world and the Soviets hesitated to come to the defense of the PLO, either politically or materially.[38] Although the initial Soviet public response did not reflect their frustration with Syria, perhaps in the anticipation of strengthening its influence in the region through the Syrian action, this quickly changed when they noted that on some occasions the Syrians had joined the Christian militias within the country in fights with the units of the PLO and their Lebanese allies. Brezhnev on behalf of the PLO came out in opposition to these acts, in part because of the Soviet interests in the PLO and probably even more so because it pitted two of the Soviet' diminishing number of allies in the region against each other. Conflicting reports of the time about Soviet decisions to curtail arms shipments to Syria as a sign of displeasure have yet to be finally resolved.

In the cause of ending intra-Arab fighting, the Soviets were formally joined later that year by Arab leaders meeting in Riyadh, who also took steps to end the hostilities. The Syrians were recognized as the Arab Peacekeeping Force. Actual conflicts between the two armed camps were greatly constrained, although the situation was more one of truce than peace. By 1980 and the Pan-Arab Front of Steadfastness and Confrontation in Tripoli, it appeared that the hostility between the two Soviet allies was more fully under control. Later that same year, Soviet relations with Syria improved considerably with the signing of a Treaty of Friendship and Cooperation between the two countries.

The 1970s had ended with both promise and threat for Soviet interests in the Middle East. The shah of Iran, who along with Israel had been one of the few staunch US allies in the region, had fallen from power and had been replaced with the Ayatollah Khomeini, whose hatred of the US was known. Khomeini's equal dislike of the communists, as seen in the later suppression of the Iranian Tudeh Party, would transform promise to threat. Iran and Iraq, a Soviet ally, were soon at war, further thwarting Soviet efforts to make a gain of a US loss, and the invasion of Muslim Afghanistan in December 1979 worsened Soviet relations with nations of the Middle East.

At this same time the PLO took steps apparently designed to broaden and perhaps alter its own base of support. The PLO became far more active politically in Western Europe with Arafat pursuing a publicly announced goal of "erasing the terrorist image and achieving legitimacy in the eyes of the world."[39] Arafat personally visited with Chancellor Kreisky of Austria in 1979 and travelled to Spain in 1980. Favorable comments on the PLO became common in Europe, and in April 1980 the European Parliament called on Israel to recognize the PLO as the representative of the Palestinian people in negotiations.[40] In their quest for legitimacy and recognition on the world stage, the PLO may have considered that direct action on their part paid far richer and faster benefits than those they had gained through Soviet actions on their behalf.

In his address to the communist party congress in Moscow in February 1981, Brezhnev stuck with the then familiar approach to the Arab-Israeli conflict. He insisted first that the Soviet Union must be allowed to take an active role in international negotiations on a lasting peace in the region and that the PLO must "naturally" be a party to the talks. He supported the "inalienable rights of the Arab peoples of Palestine up to and including a homeland."[41] The volatility of the area was again stressed by a leading Soviet foreign policy spokesman in noting that "the Middle East is the most dangerous area of conflict within the developing world. The Soviet Union suggests a collective search for a Middle East settlement . . . with the participation of all interested parties, including the PLO and Israel."[42] Stressing the accuracy of this assessment, the Israelis that same summer stepped up their pressure on the Palestinian organization with increased military strikes within Lebanon, to include bombing the PLO headquarters in Beirut.[43] Though dramatic in the regional context, neither superpower seemed inclined or able to attempt to control the increasing tensions.

Attention of the world was quickly refocused on the Middle East in October of 1981 with the assassination of Sadat in Egypt. Sadat had been a major stumbling block to both Soviet and PLO interests in the region and a hasty reevaluation of the situation was called for by his death. This process was further spurred by comments of former President Ford and Carter on their return to the US from Sadat's funeral that the US would have to deal with the PLO to achieve peace in the region.[44] Two weeks after the assassination, Arafat was in Moscow on an official visit. At this time the Soviets announced that the PLO office which had been operating in Moscow since 1976 would be accorded full diplomatic status.[45] At this same meeting in Moscow, both parties joined once again in the call for an international conference to settle the Arab-Israeli dispute, in which both would play leading roles.

The decision of Israel to launch its long anticipated[46] "Operation Peace for Galilee" invasion of Lebanon in 1982 quickly unravelled many of the factors essential to PLO operations and influence. The operation was remarkable in several aspects. The rapid neutralization of the Syrian forces, which had been generously supplied with Soviet aircraft and air defense weapons, again raised questions over the value and quality of Soviet military aid. While the PLO was also effectively defeated in a military sense by the Israelis in Lebanon, the Palestinians proved to be militarily far more capable than they had previously been considered, by friend or foe. Though quickly driven from their camps in southern Lebanon, they stubbornly held on to facilities within Beirut. It was nearly three months after the beginning of the invasion before the remnants of the main Palestinian forces were evacuated from Beirut and dispersed to a series of host nations. Even in the forced evacuation, stalwart supporters of the PLO publicly proclaimed a moral victory for the Palestinians based on the tenacity they had shown in their struggle. The three-month period is especially remarkable when contrasted with the far briefer time required of Israel to dispatch the combined forces of several major Arab nations in previous conflicts.

To many observers the goal of the Israelis made the stakes in this conflict higher for the PLO than any previous conflict. The apparent, if unannounced, goal appeared to be the "destruction of the organized Palestinian movement," to once and for all resolve the Palestinian problem for the people of Israel. To the consternation of the PLO, this crisis, as in 1973 where this survey began, caused an unfavorable contrast in superpower capabilities and willingness to use influence. Several PLO officials leveled harsh criticism against the Soviet Union on this issue.

Despite the very real threat to the PLO, their Soviet allies remained on the propaganda sideline and, ultimately, it was necessary to rely on the US to assist in the PLO evacuation from the besieged capital of Lebanon. Any Soviet efforts in this area would have been frustrated by the lack of diplomatic ties to Israel since these ties were broken in 1967. Yet, in some ways the success of the Israelis in moving substantial numbers of PLO leaders and military forces out of Lebanon only enhanced Arab support for a Palestinian homeland, if only to remove an armed and potentially disruptive minority from within their borders.[47]

Another attempt at a superpower solution to the Middle East problems was provided as an immediate follow-up to the successful PLO evacuation from Beirut, when on 1 September 1982, President Reagan proposed a peace plan which would subsequently bear his name. The element of most immediate concern to the PLO was the president's proposal that an autonomous Palestinian entity be created and linked to Jordan, rather than the straightforward establishment of a Palestinian state. To the surprise of the Soviets, the PLO did not immediately reject the plan. Regardless of the specific provisions, the Soviet Union was predictably hostile to any plan bringing credit to the US and excluding the Soviets from the peace process. Two points stressed by the Soviets in distinguishing their plan from that of President Reagan were: (1) the PLO as the *sole* legitimate representative of the Palestinians, (2) the Palestinians' right to their own independent state, prior to any subsequent confederation agreement.[48] The atmosphere which had made such considerations possible was, however, swiftly dissipated by the massacres at the Palestinian camps in Sabra and Shatila. The situation in the region once again shifted from negotiation to invective; accusations of betrayal flew among and within the forces of the region; and the superpowers returned to the sidelines and the propaganda struggle.

Those PLO forces which remained in Lebanon in the Syrian controlled territory soon turned any sense of military pride that the PLO may have had in the Lebanon operation into a political disaster. In June 1983 conflicts began within factions of the PLO in what was later to be called the "Al-Fatah Mutiny."[49] With Arafat far away from the situation in his new headquarters in Tunis, a segment of the PLO with support and encouragement from Syria started military operations against those units still loyal to Arafat. This created a clear dilemma for the Soviets, as they once more watched two of their reduced numbers of supporters in the Middle East at war with one another.

The predictable, initial Soviet allegation was that this was but another Western plot to destroy the alliance of Syria and the PLO.[50] The Soviet response reflected their growing frustration with occurrences within the region. Foreign Minister Gromyko met with a PLO official in Moscow in July and spelled out the Soviet position. "The Soviet side expressed its firm opinion about the impermissibility of strife and internecine dissension among the Palestinians faced with the Israeli aggressor, for they weaken the forces of the Palestinians and disunite the ranks of the Arabs. Discord within the PLO can and must be overcome by political means."[51] Subsequent Soviet reporting on the conflict through 1983 stressed the need for unity. Arafat continued to be listed in Moscow's reporting as the leader of the PLO, suggesting that Moscow either felt that his position was preferable to that of his Palestinian foes or that he represented the more likely victor in the struggle. In the Byzantine form of Soviet communications, it has been noted that Arafat's personal stock rose by the end of this period in Moscow. At the time of Brezhnev's death in November 1982 Arafat was listed last of all named participants; while fifteen months later at Andropov's funeral, his listing in the official press had moved ahead of all other leaders of national liberation groups.[52]

Unable to resolve the dispute between their Middle Eastern allies, the Soviets sought gain by pushing blame for the crisis on the US. As Soviet academician Yevgeniy M. Primakov, director of the Oriental Studies Institute and commentator on the Middle East stated early in 1984:

> Of course, one should not ignore the contradictions within the Palestinian movement and the disagreements, at times acute, between the PLO and the individual Arab countries. But do these contradictions and disagreements block the solution of the Palestinian problem, as alleged by the Western press? Isn't the solution being blocked by the policy of the USA which refuses to recognize the PLO's right to represent its people in the Middle East settlement, the right of the Palestinians to decided their own fate?[53]

Though the Syrian backed elements were able to prevail in the territory controlled by Syria, they were unable to achieve any fundamental restructuring of the PLO to bring it under effective Syrian domination. They did succeed in highlighting the basic divisions within the fragile coalition which comprised the Palestinian organization. This internal fighting has weakened the PLO in terms of its ability to achieve its own goals and in terms of its utility as a representative of Soviet interests in the Middle East. Earlier the PLO had recognized the relative advantage of direct pursuit of its own goals in dealing with the countries of Western Europe. Now the Soviets seemed to have concluded that it would benefit them to structure their policy to appeal to the traditional national interests of Syria and the other Arab States, rather than on relying on ephemeral Arab unity through the PLO.

CURRENT SOVIET-PLO RELATIONS

Though the complex relations in the Middle East defy neat compartmentalization into time frames, the current era may be defined as revolving about three events. These are the Moscow Peace Initiative of 29 July 1984, the tumultuous Palestinian National Congress of November 1984, and the 1985 joint Jordanian-Palestinian peace proposal. In terms of the present state and future prospects of Soviet-PLO relations, these events spell out the prospects and uncertainties of this political partnership.

The Moscow Peace Initiative followed the standard format of calling for an international conference on the Middle East in which the Soviet Union and the PLO would be full participants, the Israeli withdrawal from occupied lands, and the establishment of an independent Palestinian state. The proposal called for the mutual recognition of the rights of Israel and the PLO, which would serve as the sole legal representative of the Arab people of Palestine. While not unfamiliar, this program did launch the Soviets into a new round of active involvement in the region. In the following months, leaders of several Arab states with close relations to the Kremlin scheduled visits to Moscow, where the merits of the "new" Soviet plan were extolled. The Soviets claimed strong approval for the proposal on the part of Syria, Jordan, Lebanon, and the PLO and stressed the theme of unity with the Arabs by noting the similarities of the Soviet proposal and the recommendations of the Arab leaders at Fez.

In terms of the struggle within the PLO and the conflict between the Arafat grouping of the PLO and Syria, the Soviets seemed to try to cover all bets. The Soviets commented frequently on the harmful nature of internal conflict and suggested that this depleted the good the Soviet Union was attempting to accomplish through its initiatives. Gromyko met with Arafat in Berlin in October, and articles with favorable interviews with Arafat appeared periodically in the Soviet central press. In these Arafat adopted the Soviet position that efforts to "undermine the unity of the PLO" and separate that organization from Syria were externally inspired.[56] Western sources blamed Syrian intransigence with preventing substantial progress. Syrian President Hafiz al-Asad was credited with refusing to compromise, despite Arafat's desire to do so, and with blocking the scheduled Palestinian National Council meeting in Algiers.[57] At the same time, the Soviets sought to strengthen their relations with Asad of Syria. Asad visited Moscow in October of 1984, where he was well received and assured of continuing Soviet support for his needs. Ignoring the impact these acts might have on the internal actors in the Middle East, Soviet articles stressed the theme that this effort at achieving unity was a source of great dismay among the "forces of imperialism."[58]

Despite Soviet misgivings, the friction and frustration among her allies in the Middle East continued. While Soviet statements still insisted on the PLO as a prime party to any negotiations, they were less reassuring on other occasions. On the 26 October Day of International Solidarity with the Syrian People, the Soviet statements discussed only their common view with Syria on the "inalienable rights of the Palestinian Arab people" with no reference to the PLO or its various factions.[59] With his forces scattered and his power under immediate challenge and without the direct support of the Soviet Union, Yasser Arafat decided by November of 1984 to make a bold play for unity and/or power within the PLO. He determined to proceed with the previously scheduled meeting of the Palestinian National Council. The initial attempt at unity failed when the Syrian-backed members of the PLO resolved to boycott the Executive Committee meeting, which was to precede the Council session.[60] Accepting the disunity reflected in their absence, he continued to drive for power within the council. This public "referendum" was largely made necessary by the challenge for leadership which had dragged on for eighteen months and by the physical scattering of the leading elements of the PLO which had existed since the evacuation of Beirut.[61]

While this was clearly an internal matter, it was one which had a profound effect on the nature of the Soviet-PLO alliance. To sound out the Soviets on the upcoming assembly and to clarify the PLO approach, several prominent PLO leaders spent the week before the council meeting gathered in Moscow. According to Soviet reports, they emphasized their determination to "preserve the cohesion" of the organization, to continue to cooperate with other anti-imperialist Arab forces, and to "overcome difficulties" so that the PLO could continue an active role in the region.[62] The Soviets, though, were quick to point out that "a number of Palestinian organizations refused to take part in the session." While it is not apparent that the Soviets felt that one group or the other would oppose the relations with the Soviets, they were aware that a divided organization was ineffective in securing Soviet interests in the region, much less serving as a source of unity for the Arab nations.

The Seventeenth PNC assembly in Amman, Jordan surely ranks as one of the most dramatic gatherings of an organization which has not lacked for excitement in its past. Arafat was barely able to summon a quorum of the delegates required. In a calculated gamble, he submitted his resignation to the body after fifteen years of leadership, only to be recalled to his post by the delegates on the following day. As opposed to previous sessions, the unspoken threat to the PLO at this session was its "ally" Syria and not its declared foe, Israel. The Soviet Union, breaking with past practice, sent no official delegation to observe the session and the reporting from the session did not indicate that the relationship with the USSR was a subject of discussion.[63] At the Soviet Day of International Solidarity with the Palestinian People, immediately following the session, the Soviet government again stressed the need for cohesion in the Palestinian ranks and for close cooperation between the PLO and other Arab peoples.[64]

By the first week of 1985, a PLO delegation was back in Moscow to discuss the results of the PNC gathering. In public they reaffirmed the traditional goal of an international conference to solve the Middle East issues, but talks in private, as reflected in later statements, must have dealt with the use of Soviet influence to narrow the gap separating the PLO from Syria. While the Soviets have consistently denied playing such a role in the internal politics of the Arab nations, they have been publicly thanked by the PLO for their "efforts to normalize relations between the PLO and Syria."[65] In this atmosphere the twentieth anniversary of the founding of the PLO on 2 January passed without the fanfare Soviets normally provide for such occasions. The Soviets did restate their position that the PLO should be considered the only legitimate representative of the Palestinian people and noted that the PLO now had offices in more than one hundred states of the world. Even in light of the current crisis, the PLO must have reflected positively on their success in moving their issue out of the regional context and onto the world stage.

Perhaps reflecting the lack of unity within the organization and its changing goals, Yahya Habash, as the official PLO representative in Moscow, used the occasion of the anniversary to hold a press conference in Moscow attacking the intrigues of those who would seek to divide the Arab peoples through imposing "separate deals" as the path to peace in the Middle East.

He specifically voiced support for the Soviet peace initiative of the previous July and the need for an international conference. [66]

Only one month later on 11 February and in Amman, rather than Moscow, Yasser Arafat and King Hussein announced that they had reached a framework for a joint peace initiative. Although the details were far from clear, several elements were evident in the agreement. The reported agreement committed Jordan and the PLO to direct negotiations with Israel as a step preceding any broad internationl conference. Arafat on behalf of the PLO had agreed to a confederation between a Palestinian state on the West Bank and Jordan, rather than a fully independent nation. Furthermore, Jordan and the PLO agreed to accept all UN resolutions. While this did not specify Security Council Resolution 242, as the US had long insisted, it did not obviously exclude it. Thus, in a brief period of time the PLO, as represented by Arafat, had moved from the Soviet plan of July 1984 to something much closer to the Reagan plan of 1982, in accord with the interests of the moderate Arab powers, Egypt, Jordan, and Saudi Arabia. The selling of this plan to the US was entrusted to Saudi King Fahd and Egyptian President Mubarak, both of whom had scheduled trips to Washington for the following month. King Hussein continued the effort during his visit to Washington in June 1985.

While the Soviets may have been as uncertain of the contents and intent of the Jordanian-PLO plan as the US, their response gradually shifted from ignoring it to opposing the provisions of the agreement. In comments on King Fahd's visit to Washington, the Soviet press continued reports about the US refusal to enter into broad international negotiations and its refusal to recognize the PLO as the sole representative of the interests of the Palestinian Arabs. A single negative comment referred to attempts of the US president to revive the Camp David process. [67] An article by a Palestinian journalist in the Soviet press at the same time voiced solidarity with the July Moscow proposal and expressed disdain for those who would attempt to split the PLO by pursuing a "separate solution," like that advocated by Jordan and "other Arab states" without reference to Arafat's participation in the latest initiative. [68] Likewise, in joint US-Soviet discussions on the Middle East held in Vienna beginning 19 February, the Soviets pushed their proposal for an international conference while the US again expressed preference for direct negotiations of the regional powers, with neither reportedly referring directly to the new initiative. [69]

The Soviet attitude quickly became more negative and took on some interesting aspects. The first descriptions of the new initiative were to define it as a personal agreement worked out between King Hussein and Yasser

Arafat. The Soviets explicitly argued that the majority of Palestinian organizations opposed the agreement and that there was "no unanimity of views" even within Fatah, "whose leadership includes Yasser Arafat." The Soviet reporting noted that, while the agreement pleased Washington, Egypt, Morocco, and Saudi Arabia, it was resolutely opposed by Syria, Democratic Yemen, and others. The Soviet interpretation of the agreement was that it thwarted an international conference, forfeited the legitimate Palestinian rights to full participation in negotiations, and gave up their right to an independent homeland.[70] A meeting of representatives of "communist and workers parties of the Arab East" was hastily convened in Damascus, where the delegates decisively condemned the new initiative and encouraged others to begin work to frustrate the plan.[71] Subsequent Soviet reporting concentrated on views of Arabs, particularly within the PLO, critical of the accord. It is not without irony that the Soviet Union, which had argued throughout the long crisis within the PLO leadership of the importance for unity in the organization, was now placed in the position of supporting viable opposition within the PLO to the organization's acknowledged leader, who had been confirmed at the just concluded Palestinian National Council meeting.

Under the severe Soviet criticism and the opposition which existed within the PLO itself, Arafat also seemed to seek some failure insurance. Despite US appeals, he refused to advance to the open and explicit acceptance of Resolution 242 and seemed to reject statements made by Mubarak that a Palestinian delegation in talks with the US could consist of Palestinians not clearly identified with the PLO leadership.[72] He undertook no obvious efforts, though, to rebuild his damaged bridges to restore the PLO-Soviet partnership. The PLO gamble was considerably complicated by the hesitation of the US to enthusiastically endorse the plan. While it did exclude the Soviets and did match closely the president's own plan of 1982, the US had been made very cautious by its experiences in Lebanon and recognized the difficulty of carrying through even when agreements with Middle East principals were reached.

During the early summer of 1985, a familiar scene had returned to the Middle East. Representatives of the superpowers were shuttling to the capitals of the region to clarify positions and explore new options. Israel continued to refuse to negotiate directly with members of the PLO, while the US repeated the necessity of the PLO to explicitly accept Security Council Resolution 242. Arafat on behalf of the PLO leadership continued to advocate progress under the terms of the agreement he had created with King Hussein, while King Hussein urged greater use of "positive" American influence to resolve the disputes of the region. The Soviet Union stuck to its position that only a broadly based international conference would bring peace to the region and that "separate deals" could only increase hostility. The Soviets retained their claim as defenders of the interests of the Palestinian people but distanced themselves from the Arafat leadership of the PLO.

In a further ironic twist the AMAL Shi'i movement in Lebanon launched attacks on Palestinian camps around Beirut, in essence continuing the drive begun by Israel in 1982 — though for quite different reasons — to eliminate the PLO as an independent military force in Lebanon. The Soviets urged progressive organizations in Lebanon to refrain from entering the struggle and to seek an end to the bloodshed. [73] Soviet pressure on Syria resulted in the Damascus-backed Palestinian National Salvation Front going to Beirut to negotiate on behalf of the Arafat PLO elements fighting the Shi'a in the camps. The Soviet central press ran articles favoring an introduction of Syrian troops in the Lebanese capital. [74] Soviet frustration was well summed up in a June TASS release. "Another tragic page is being added to the tragic history of the Palestinian and Lebanese people." [75] The Soviet charges that the intra-Arab fighting was incited and directed by the CIA and Israel thinly masked its frustration in resolving disputes among its potential allies in the region.

The Soviet plan to discredit the Jordanian-Palestinian peace program continued throughout the summer and fall of 1985. Soviet representatives in the Middle East openly challenged the plan, while the Soviet central press moved as far as to call the plan "Camp David in new packaging." [76]

What had been a critical stage in the Middle East relations of Jordan, the PLO, the Soviets, and the West in the summer of 1985 moved closer to a crisis in the fall. The Soviet criticism of the Amman peace plan and their coolness toward Arafat resulted in a stream of Palestinian visitors to Moscow in August and September. Both supporters and opponents of Arafat and his plan presented their positions to officials in the Kremlin. [77] Nearly simultaneously, King Hussein of Jordan and President Mubarak of Egypt were paying visits to Washington, urging that the Americans lend more support to the Amman plan while the opportunity still existed. [78]

A PLO nemesis in their relations with both the Soviet and the West captured the headlines in late September and October. The incidents began when Palestinians seized, then murdered, three Israelis in Cyprus. Israel retaliated by an air raid on Arafat headquarters in Tunis. The following week Palestinians seized the Italian cruise ship, *Achille Lauro,* and proceeded to kill an elderly wheelchair-bound American. Had the Israelis written the script for a PLO public relations disaster, they could hardly have done better. The Italians had been among the most vocal and consistent supporters for due recognition of the PLO, but this murder inflamed public opinion among them and throughout the West. Furthermore the incident took place shortly after four Soviet officials had been seized in Beirut and one had already been murdered. Only the week before the *Achille Lauro* incident, Arafat's foes in the Palestinian National Salvation Front had publicly tried to lay the blame on Arafat for the Soviet's murder.[79] Not surprisingly under these circumstances the Soviets showed solidarity with the US in condemning terrorism and, implicitly, the PLO.

The most obvious result of these incidents was a stormy session involving King Hussein and Arafat in Amman for several days in October. Hussein seemed especially concerned about his association with an organization which either intended to conduct a campaign of international terrorism in the face of universal condemnation or was unable to control the activities of its subordinate units. With the Soviets watching from the sidelines, Arafat adopted a position of public belligerence and private accommodation. Threatened with being cut out of the Middle East process, Arafat reminded his critics of the obvious, "If they thought they could achieve peace without us, they wouldn't have hesitated."[80] More accommodatingly, recognizing the challenges to his position from all sides, Arafat concluded the meeting with a pledge "not to carry out any act that could hurt the February 11 agreement."[81] The following week he went even further in talks with Mubarak promising to punish any PLO members guilty of violating the ban on terrorism.[82]

While Arafat was working to restore international respectability, the Soviets were focusing on the upcoming Soviet-American summit. Though the Soviets pledged to defend Arab interests at the summit and criticized President Reagan for failing to include the Middle East in his regional issues speech at the United Nations, the crux of their agenda was clearly arms control. The 29 November Day of International Solidarity with the Palestinian People was passed over in relative silence in Moscow, with the exception of an elaborate defense of the Palestinians as a separate and distinct nationality, which was carried in *Aziya i Afrika Segodnya*.[83]

The massacres at the Rome and Vienna airports in December again challenged Arafat's power and credibility. With the PLO somewhat lamely calling for jurisdiction over the perpetrators of these acts, a member of the Fatah central committee openly acknowledged the crisis in Soviet-Palestinian relations.[84] Soviet irritation was adequate that Karen Brutents, deputy chief of the International Department of the CPSU Central Committee, could acknowledge in an interview in Kuwait that "We do not put the matter within the framework that Yasser Arafat is the PLO and that the PLO is Arafat. We cannot link all our relations with the Palestinian people's liberation movement to those with Arafat."[85]

A hastily arranged visit of Faruq Qaddumi, the leader of the PLO political department, to Moscow succeeded in reducing the tensions. In a final meeting with Foreign Minister Shevernadze, Qaddumi pledged PLO interest in internal unity and their continued interest in an international conference on the Middle East in which the USSR would play a prominent role. Whether truly convinced of the PLO's good intentions or not, the Soviets evidently concluded that they had no better alternative currently available. In a move reminiscent of the Black September group incident at the Munich Olympics, as Soviet-PLO relations were just developing, the Soviets and their allies began a campaign to separate Arafat from the Abu Nidal group, which had been blamed for the attacks at Rome and Vienna.[86]

Arafat's attempts to align himself with the moderate states in the Middle East suffered a serious blow on 19 February 1986, when King Hussein announced in a three and one-half hour television address to his people that he was abandoning the year-long effort to forge a joint peace strategy with Arafat. In this talk Hussein continued to insist that the PLO could be the only legitimate representative of the Palestinians but noted that the current leadership refused to advance peace by specifically recognizing UN resolutions necessary for progress. He called on the Palestinians to consider alternatives to Arafat's leadership.[87] Bilateral relations continued to deteriorate to the point where the PLO liaison office in Amman was officially closed in April.

This surprise move both expanded and restricted Arafat's room to maneuver. On the negative side, the move openly brought Jordan and Syria closer together, threatening to render Arafat as odd-man-out in the region. On the positive side, the termination of the plan removed a significant thorn in PLO-Soviet relations and also removed a major source of controversy within the PLO ranks. Additional PLO representatives were swiftly dispatched to Moscow, although results were unclear. If the Twenty-seventh Party Congress in Moscow were to serve as a guide, the PLO did not fare well. Unlike Brezhnev at the last congress in 1981, Gorbachev made no direct reference to the PLO or their rights. He did include a strong attack on terrorism, stating that "the Soviet Union rejects terrorism in principle and is prepared for effective cooperation with other states to root it out."[88] Two later speakers, the deputy secretary of the Syrian Ba'thist Party and the representative of the Palestinian Community party, spoke to the congress to call for unity and to attack the Hussein-Arafat agreement.[89]

Gorbachev did agree to meet with Arafat one more time in the spring of 1986 as both attended the East German Party Congress in Berlin in April. The public reporting of the meeting stressed the standard themes of unity and Arab solidarity in the struggle against imperialism but little else. If this represented a Soviet desire to concentrate on superpower relations and on the Soviets' own domestic concern, events in the Middle East continued to make this difficult. Through the summer of 1986 fighting continued to flare up in Lebanon among the Arab groupings. Specifically, the Shi'a with Syrian backing maintained political and military pressure on the PLO, determined to preclude a restoration of the relative autonomy that the PLO enjoyed in Lebanon prior to the Israeli invasion of 1982.[90]

The basis of Soviet-PLO cooperation, which survived for more than ten years, has been severely strained. Despite Gorbachev's warm welcome for Arafat at the burial of Chernenko in March of 1985, the Soviet leader has recognized that the original basis of Soviet-PLO cooperation has changed. The Soviets clearly find the PLO alliance less and less useful as an entry into direct Middle East negotiations, and the use of the PLO to enhance Arab unity in favor of Soviet interests has been vastly undermined, for even the Soviets have been forced to emphasize differences within the Arab world and even within the PLO leadership. Although of considerable importance in the past, the utility of the PLO to illustrate the consistent anti-imperialist position of the Soviets in search of peace in the Third World became less credible when it appeared that the PLO itself wished to work more closely with the "leading imperialist power" instead of the Soviet Union in its effort to obtain peace and a homeland.

In their own reassessment, following the twentieth anniversary of their founding, it was similarly obvious to the PLO leadership that the initial interests which had brought them into partnership with the Soviets were diminished. The PLO struggle for recognition of their claim for "just rights and a homeland" in the international arena had been largely acknowledged. The major nations of western Europe, as well as the United States, now primarily discussed the form such a homeland should take, rather than question its feasibility or desirability. The scattering of the PLO forces after Lebanon had at least temporarily reduced the PLO demands for material support. Even the legitimacy of the PLO to speak on behalf of the Palestinian Arabs, while still opposed by Israel and bottlenecked by the issue of UN

Resolution 242, was far less a question than it had been in 1973. The PLO has offices in more than one hundred nations, and even three former US presidents had agreed that the PLO was an essential element in obtaining a meaningful peace in the Middle East. With this recognition, the PLO seemed more inclined to rely on the influence of regional powers, than upon the USSR.

As the Soviets are diligent in reminding the West, the troubled Middle East is virtually upon the border of the Soviet Union and must, therefore, be of constant concern. Gorbachev in his mid-50s has taken over leadership in the Soviet Union with vast power and great ambitions. Arafat, his chronological peer, yet vastly his senior in years of leadership, has shown a skill and cunning in survival that is uncommon in the lethal struggle in which he has been involved for two decades. Despite the changes which have taken place, it would be premature to write the epitaph on the Soviet-PLO partnership. By all accounts, the relationship has always been one of convenience and not love, and history has shown that convenience is more flexible and far less demanding than love, and for these reasons it is often more enduring. Neither the Soviet Union nor the Palestinian Liberation Organization has accomplished its basic goals in the region, and both may well continue to maneuver for allies in the pursuit of these goals. The situation in the Middle East is hardly more settled or less tense than it was in the previous decades, and the future is no more certain.

NOTES

1. Several excellent works trace the early contacts between the Soviets and the PLO. See, for example, Galia Golan, *The Soviet Union and the Palestine Liberation Organization, An Uneasy Alliance* (New York: Praeger, 1980). For another account of the early period, see Mehmood Hussain, *The Palestinian Liberation Organization* (Dehli: Univ. Publishers, 1975).
2. "World Leaders Size Up Gorbachev," *USA Today,* 14 Mar. 1985, 5A.
3. "Cario Puts Chill on Russia," *Newsweek,* 28 Feb. 1972, 32–33.
4. "Egypt Will Build Its Own MIG 21's" (AP report), *The Kansas City Star,* 23 Mar. 1972, 21.
5. "Egyptians Fly MIG 23's" (AP report), *The Kansas City Star,* 17 Apr. 1972, 5.
6. "Moscow Gives Sadat Pledge of Military Aid," *The Kansas City Star,* 30 Apr. 1972, 11B.
7. William Beecher, NY Times Service, "Reds May Aid Arab Guerrillas," *The Kansas City Star,* 3 Jan. 1972, 6B.
8. Helena Cobban, *The Palestinian Liberation Organization* (Cambridge: Cambridge Univ. Press, 1984), 223.
9. Eric Pace, NY Times Service, "Russians Are Reported Supplying Arms to Al Fatah," *Stars and Stripes,* 19 Sept. 1972, 4.
10. Y. Kornilov, "Meeting with the Fedayeen," *New Times* 42 (1972): 24–25 as reported in Robert O. Freedman, *Soviet Policy toward the Middle East Since 1970* (New York: Praeger, 1975), 96.
11. Freedman, *Soviet Policy* 106.
12. Freedman, *Soviet Policy,* 106, 117–18.

13. Wofgang Berner, et al., eds. *The Soviet Union, 1974–75* (New York: Holmes and Meier Publishers, 1976), 246.

14. Ammon Sella, *Soviet Political and Military Conduct in the Middle East* (New York: St. Martin's Press, 1981), 131.

15. K. Borisov, "The 29th UN General Assembly Session," *International Affairs* (Moscow), Oct. 1972, 35.

16. Yehuda Lukacs, ed. *Documents on the Israeli-Palestinian Conflict, 1967–1983* (Cambridge: Cambridge Univ. Press, 1984), 181.

17. Augustus R. Norton, "Moscow and the Palestinians," in Michael Curtis, et al., eds. *The Palestinians: People, History, Politics* (New Brunswick, N.J.: Transaction Books, 1975), 240.

18. Freedman, *Soviet Policy,* 135.

19. "Palestinian Issue Increasingly Central to Soviet Middle East Strategy," *Soviet World Outlook* 1(2) (13 Feb. 1976): 4–5.

20. Freedman, *Soviet Policy,* 242–43.

21. Lukacs, *Documents,* 223.

22. "Palestinian Issue," 4–5.

23. "Moscow Scorns Sadat, but Not Egypt. Steps Up Support of Left Elsewhere in Middle East," *Soviet World Outlook* 1(5) (15 May 1976): 8.

24. "Modified Soviet Proposal on Near East," *Soviet World Outlook* 1(10) (15 Oct. 1976): 3.

25. Robert O. Freedman, *The Middle East Since Camp David* (Boulder, Westview Press, 1984), 10.

26. The efforts of the Carter administration to find an acceptable solution to this dilemma are described in Ismail Fahmy, *Negotiating for Peace in the Middle East* (Baltimore: The Johns Hopkins Univ. Press, 1983), 197–98.

27. Sella, *Soviet Conduct,* 165–66.

28. Mark V. Kauppi and R. Craig Nation, eds. *The Soviet Union and the Middle East in the 1980s* (Lexington, MA: Lexington Books, 1983), 191.

29. Despite the trouble that would follow, the second of five conditions for peace which Sadat presented to the Israeli Knesset during his visit was "achievement of the basic rights of the Palestinian people and their right to their own State." Fahmy, *Negotiating,* 286.

30. In this case, as in the past, Sadat argued that his efforts were truly aimed toward helping the Palestinians and, ultimately, Arab unity. This theme is well presented in Felipe Fernandez-Armesto, *Sadat and His Statecraft* (London: Kensal Press, 1982). Fahmy in his book argues that Sadat in private recognized that he was betraying the PLO, if not the Palestinian people, in his relations with Israel.

31. Cobban, *The Palestinian,* 93.

32. Cobban, *The Palestinian,* 100.

33. "Moscow Condemns Camp David Agreement," *Soviet World Outlook,* 3(10) (15 Oct. 1978): 4.

34. A. A. Gromyko and B. N. Ponamarev, eds. *Soviet Foreign Policy (Vol. II) 1945–1980* (Moscow: Progress Publishers, 1981), 608.

35. Raphael Israeli, ed. *PLO in Lebanon, Selected Documents* (New York: St. Martin's Press, 1983), 35–36, 48, and 51.

36. Israeli, *PLO in Lebanon,* 18. Another version of this same document appears in Lukacs, 193–97. Although longer and with a different English translation, this second account agrees with the first in regard to the material cited.

37. A graphic, if perhaps biased, report of the struggle within Lebanon is presented in this book by one of the founders of the Palestinian Resistance Movement, Abu Iyad [Salah Khalaf] *My Home, My Land* (New York: Times Books, 1981), 159–201. A somewhat more impartial assessment is presented in Cobban, *The Palestinian,* 58–80.

38. Iyad, *My Home,* 194.

39. Freedman, *The Middle East,* 206.

40. Freedman, *The Middle East,* 208.

41. L. I. Brezhnev, "Report of the Central Committee to the Communist Party of the Soviet Union" (Moscow: Novosti Press Agency, 1981), 20–21.

42. Henry Trofimenko, "The Third World and U.S.-Soviet Competition: A Soviet View," *Foreign Affairs* (Summer 1981): 1039.

43. Freedman, *The Middle East,* 32.

44. "Carter and Ford Say U.S. and PLO Will Have to Talk," *New York Times,* 12 Oct. 1981, 1.

45. Kauppi, *The Soviet Union,* 191.

46. Discussion of the anticipated invasion seemed to rest more on appropriate weather and occasion than on the basic issue of whether or not it would occur. Even in the US, academic discussions on the nature and consequences of an Israeli invasion were discussed some four months before it occurred. See, for example, John Yemma, "The Palestinians: Politics and Conflict," *Christian Science Monitor,* 19 Feb. 1982, 12–13.

47. Harold H. Saunders, "An Israeli-Palestinian Peace," *Foreign Affairs* (Fall 1982): 101.

48. Galia Golan, "The Soviet Union and the PLO Since the War in Lebanon," *The Middle East Journal* (Spring 1986): 291–92.

49. A lengthy and detailed account of this conflict is found in Adam M. Garfinkle, "Sources of the Al-Fatah Mutiny," *Orbis* (Fall 1983): 603–40.

50. "Moscow Tells Palestinian Liberation Organization to Shape Up," *Soviet World Outlook* 7 (15 Jul. 1983): 5–6.

51. "Moscow Tells," 5–6.

52. Golan, "The Soviet Union and the PLO," 293.

53. Yevgeniy M. Primakov, "USA: Policy of Destabilization in the Middle East," *International Affairs* (Moscow) 3 (March 1984).

54. R. Davydov, "The Middle East: The Potential of the Soviet Initiatives," *International Affairs* (Moscow) (Oct. 1984): 116–19. These claims are seriously disputed in Western analytical reporting. See, "Soviets Seek Initiative in Near East," *Soviet World Outlook* 9(11) (15 Nov. 1984): 5–6.

55. R. Vasilyev, "Strengthening Soviet-Arab Cooperation," *International Life* (Moscow), (Dec. 1984): 77–79.

56. L. Pavlov, "Egypt: Yasser Arafat Interview," *Izvestiya,* 26 Aug. 1984, 4.

57. Louis Wizniter, "Efforts to Reconcile Syria's Assad and PLO Chief Arafat Collapse," *The Christian Science Monitor,* 22 Oct. 1984, 16.

58. Valentin Chemodan, "Growing Development of Soviet-Syrian Relations," *Al-Ba'th* (Damascus), 17 Jan. 1985, 3. Trans. in *FBIS* USSR International Affairs, 24 Jan. 1985, H1–2.

59. K. Georgiyev, "Syria's Resolve," *Izvestiya,* 27 Oct. 1984, 5.

60. "PLO Unable to Hold Full Leadership Talks," *New York Times,* 19 Nov. 1984, A10.

61. A good preview of the quandaries faced by the PLO leadership are presented in John Kifner, "For Arafat, Effort to Convene Palestinian Assembly is a 'Matter of Survival,' " *New York Times,* 19 Nov. 1984, A10.

62. "Palestinian Leaders Visit USSR 19–23 Nov.," Moscow TASS, Trans. in *FBIS* USSR International Affairs, 26 Nov. 1984, H1.

63. John Kifner, "PLO Parley: Arafat Survived, but Now What?" *New York Times,* 30 Nov. 1984, A10.

64. "Council of Ministers Sends Message to PLO," Moscow TASS, 6 Dec. 1984. Trans. in *FBIS* USSR International Affairs, 11 Dec. 1984, H2.

65. Abdul Wahab al-Khashan, Kuwait KUNA, 11 Jan. 1985. Trans. in *FBIS* USSR International Affairs, 14 Jan. 1985, H1.

66. "Habash Holds Press Conference," Moscow TASS, 3 Jan. 1985. Trans. in *FBIS* USSR International Affairs, 7 Jan. 1985, H1.

67. Farid Seyful-Mulyukov, "World Today," Moscow television, 18 Feb. 1985. Trans. in *FBIS* USSR International Affairs, 19 Feb. 1985, CC 1–2. Also see L. Koryavin, "Washington Alternative," *Izvestiya,* 15 Feb. 1985, 5.

68. Rami Muhammad al Sha'ir, "Near East: Time for Constructive Solutions," *Sovetskaya Rossiya,* 15 Feb. 1985. Trans. in *FBIS* USSR International Affairs, 19 Feb. 1985, H2–3.

69. James M. Markham, "Soviet and U.S. Open Vienna Discussions on Middle East Problems," *New York Times,* 20 Feb. 1985.

70. "Opposition to Hussein-Arafat Agreement Noted," Moscow TASS, 19 Feb. 1985. Trans. in *FBIS* USSR International Affairs, 20 Feb. 1985, H1–2.

71. "Damascus Meeting Statement," Moscow TASS, 27 Feb. 1985. Trans. in *FBIS* USSR International Affairs, 28 Feb. 1985, H1–2.

72. Judith Miller, "Arafat Denounces U.S. Response to Jordan Accord as 'Shameful,' " *New York Times,* 3 Mar. 1985, 1.

73. "Counter to Lebanon's Interests," *Pravda,* 24 May 1985, 5. Trans. in *FBIS* USSR International Affairs, 29 May 1985, H1.

74. Ye. Korshunov, "Lebanon: Seeking a Solution to the Problem," *Izvestiya,* 20 May 1985, 1. Trans. in *FBIS* USSR International Affairs, 21 May 1985, H1.

75. "Middle Eastern Knot," Moscow TASS, 9 June 1985. Trans. in *FBIS* USSR International Affairs, 12 June 1985, H1.

76. V. Lashkul, "International Commentary: Camp David in New Packaging," *Izvestiya,* 21 Aug. 1985, 4. Trans. in *FBIS,* Middle East and North Africa, 22 Aug. 1985, H1.

77. "Moscow Said to Urge Palestinians to Reject Talks," *The New York Times,* 8 Sept. 1985, 6.

78. Gerald M. Boyd, "Reagan and Mubarek Differ on PLO," *The New York Times,* 24 Sept. 1985, A3.

79. Ihsan A. Hijazi, "Pro-Syrians Point to Arafat Allies in Soviet Killing," *The New York Times,* 6 Oct. 1985, 15.

80. John Kifner, "Warning by Arafat: Peace Will Not Exist Without the PLO," *The New York Times,* 30 Oct. 1985, 1 and A6.

81. John Kifner, "Arafat Pledge on Hijackings Is Reported," *The New York Times,* 31 Oct. 1985, A3.

82. "PLO chief disavows terrorism," Associated Press as reported in *The Times Herald Record,* 8 Nov. 1985, 44.

83. V. Mishin, "Solidarity with the People of Palestine," *Aziya i Afrika Segognya,* 11, Nov. 1985. Trans. in *JPRS,* USSR, 28 Feb. 1986.

84. Interview with Fatah central committee member Salah Khalaf in *AL–QABAS,* 31 December 1985. Trans. in *FBIS,* Middle East and North Africa, 3 Jan. 1986, A2–6.

85. Interview with Karen Brutents, Kuwait *AL-WATAN,* 4 Jan. 1986. Trans. in *FBIS,* Middle East and North Africa, 7 Jan. 1986, H8–21.

86. See for example, Peter Lang, "The Machinery of Assault," *Magyar Nemzet,* Budapest, 6 Jan. 1986. Trans. in *FBIS,* Middle East and North Africa, 7 Jan. 1986, H1.

87. "King Hussein Ends Joint Peace Bid," *The New York Times,* 20 Feb. 1986, 1 and A4. Also see Judith Miller, "Hussein Questions Who Should Speak for Palestinians." *The New York Times,* 23 Feb. 1986, 1 and 7.

88. Mikhail Gorbachev, "Political Report of the CPSU Central Committee," *Pravda,* 27 Feb. 1986, 1.

89. "Speech by Comrade Sulayman al-Najeb," *Pravda,* 4 Mar. 1986, 8, and "Abdullah al-Ahmar, "Speech before the XXVIIth Party Congress," *Pravda,* 5 Mar. 1986, 8.

90. For a more detailed account of the Shi'i-PLO conflict, see Augustus Richard Norton, "Estrangement and Fragmentation in Lebanon," *Current History,* Feb. 1986.

6 THE PEOPLE'S REPUBLIC OF CHINA AND THE PLO
From Honeymoon to Conjugal Routine
RAPHAEL ISRAELI

The recent opening of China to the West, one of the most dramatic transformations of Chinese domestic and external policies in the post-cultural revolution era, tends to blur the harsh, hard-line reality of the 1960s under which the People's Republic inaugurated her relations with the Palestinian national movement.[1] Therefore, in order to comprehend the nature of this extraordinarily close relationship, it is necessary to go back to those years and explain the developments which have occurred since in terms of the wider Chinese view of global national interest versus their ideological commitment and of the alternately rising and sagging fortunes of the PLO.

Chinese-Palestinian links were never preponderant in the calculus of power or in the national interest of either party. China had always had to worry about threats posed to her by the superpowers, about the border tensions with her immediate neighbors, and about her place in the world, not to speak of her immense domestic problems such as demographic pressures or the exigencies of economic development. The PLO, on its part, has been much more concerned about its bases of action against Israel; its sources of political and economic support; the building of its forces; and its relations with the Soviet Union, than about its link to China. Thus, neither part has been absolutely vital to the other, and each could easily dispose of its ties with the other without incurring substantial damage. For China has never had any direct interest in the PLO per se, nor did the PLO ever hedge its existence on China.

Nevertheless, seen in the context of China's obligation, until recently, to aid movements of national liberation; of the centrality of the Palestinian problem in Middle Eastern, inter-Arab, and Third World affairs; and of China's struggle with the other major powers for influence in the Afro-Asian arena, it is possible to see, all proportions guarded, why China would be interested in the PLO. Conversely, the Palestinian national movement—

138

which desperately sought acceptance and recognition in the world at the expense of Israel if possible, on a par with her if necessary — was eager to ally itself with potential sources of weapons and diplomatic support, either for their own sake or as leverage against other powers. It took comfort in the success of the Chinese revolution as a model for its own and had every intention to yield to China's charm and respond to its propositioning, if not as a permanent marriage, at least as an exciting, low-risk and promise-bearing love affair.

THE SINO-ARAB SETTING

Since its inception in 1949, the People's Republic of China has made clear its intent to restore to the country its pride, independence, and international stature — lost during the preceding century of Western domination — and has regarded itself as the vanguard of national liberation from the yoke of imperialism and as the pioneer of establishing a new world order in the Marxist-Leninist-Maoist vein. This messianic self-conception in fact dictated the double-edged foreign policy to be pursued in years to come: designed to further her perceived national interests such as security, international legitimacy, prestige, alliances against potential enemies, secure border, and the like; and to fulfill her ideological objectives, not the least of which was world revolution. These two sets of considerations may have at times contradicted each other, but the interplay between them — namely, ideological flexibility when the national stakes were too high or ideological resilience when the harm to her national interest did not seem irreparable — allowed her to chart her way the best she could.

And so we find China of the 1950s until the 1970s sometimes maintaining relations with governments not to her liking but regarded as vital to the nurturing of good neighborly or commercial links, to the balancing of foes, or to gaining entrance to the UN. At the same time, she cultivated groups such as communist parties or individuals who were in opposition to those same governments if that satisfied her ideological concerns. For that purpose, China developed institutional tools to deal simultaneously with the officials and the unofficial levels of her foreign activities. Thus besides governmental delegations sent abroad or received in Peking, she maintained a second channel of visits and contacts whereby trade unions, journalists, cultural organizations, and friendship associations could sustain the parallel avenue of informal relations. Visitors of both kinds were lavishly and thoughtfully guided on tours to the most impressive landmarks of Chinese communist achievements—such as selected agricultural communes, industrial plants, military units, and development projects—and to meetings with the Chinese leaders who orchestrated all those tours de force. China wanted to pose as a model of a developing nation, whose determination, self-reliance, and ideological commitment had allowed for amazing accomplishments.

At the height of the Maoist Era (1949–1975), the PRC's commitment to Third World movements of national liberation was couched in terms of undermining bourgeois regimes and the interests of imperialistic powers who supported them but was also formulated as part of the permanent state of revolution that would ultimately pit the proletarian parts of the world against their industrialized capitalist exploiters. The PLO and Israel were perceived as fitting, respectively, the two counterparts in that struggle.

Since the Bandung Conference of 1955, where Chou En-lai made his debut in the Arab arena, China has succeeded in establishing relations with a growing number of Arab countries, beginning with the "progressive" or "revolutionary" among them. In May 1956, of all Arab countries, Egypt pioneered diplomatic relations with Peking, to be followed by Syria and most of the rest, including the more conservative pro-Western among them such as Tunisia and Morocco. This was a spectacular success on the part of the PRC if one remembers that in August 1950 the Arab League had adopted a resolution not to recognize Communist China. This turnabout was effected as China fully exploited the break between the Arabs and the West: Egypt was struggling to evacuate the British from the Suez Canal Zone; the American embargo on arms sales in the Middle East had forced the Arabs to turn to the Communist Bloc; the ill-fated, American-initiated Baghdad Pact fell through; and the security situation along the Arab-Israeli borders was deteriorating. Thus, some Arabs overcame the fear of Communist countries that the West had instilled in them, especially as they themselves were moving toward centralist-authoritarian regimes characterized by state monopolies on foreign trade, a planned economy, five-year plans to develop heavy industries, and a unipartisan system, all dubbed as "Arab socialism" which could exist in alliance with Communist nations. The common front against world (especially American) imperialism and China's hostile pronouncements against Israel since the 1960s made this alliance all the more palatable to the Arabs.

During Bandung the Chinese found a way to cater to Arab policies by supporting, if mildly, their views on the Arab-Israeli conflict. Though the question of Palestine was not part of the Bandung plenary agenda, Chou En-lai supported a moderately pro-Palestinian resolution at the meeting of the political committee of the conference. After the conference, in what developed as a consistently pro-Arab policy which included support for the Arab views of Palestine, China naturally accumulated points to its credit vis-à-vis the Arabs. She unceasingly and vitriolically attacked Western imperialism and Israel during the Sinai War of 1956 and offered technical and economic help to her Arab friends. In 1958 she recognized the Qassim revolutionary government in Baghdad; she established relations with Algeria when it declared independence and in 1965 lent official recognition to the PLO, headed by al-Shuqairy, and allowed it to open its offices in Peking with quasi-diplomatic status and privileges.

As China expanded her relations with the Arab world, she marked her presence there by large missions which distributed propaganda materials, invited groups of Arab students to Peking University, sent Chinese Muslims on pilgrimage to Mecca, and offered economic, technical, and financial support. She was particularly generous with Algeria and the Yemen, perhaps due to their perceived strategic importance, and identified with the Gulf emirates against British imperialism. Despite the cultural suspicion towards China of pro-Western elements in the Arab world, who accused the PRC of plotting to conquer the world or condemned the Chinese penetration of Syria, radical Arabs were not deflected. On 15 November 1956, the Ba'th daily of Damascus proclaimed.:

> We love the Chinese, because they are revolutionaries and they never stabbed us in the back. They never plotted against us and never tried to hamper the construction of the Euphrates Dam. They never extended one hand of friendship while holding a dagger in the other . . . . The Chinese have said plainly that they support us against Israel and stand at our side on the Palestine issue. They have also declared that they regarded our frontiers with the enemy as China's first line of defense against World Imperialism and Zionism. Why, then shouldn't we cooperate with them?[2]

This statement, which would have certainly been endorsed by the fledgling PLO, did not tell the whole story, however. For the late 1950s and the early 1960s also marked the ideological split between China and the USSR and the consequent repercussions on China's foreign policy in general and her competition with the Soviet Union in the Third World in particular. Domestically, following the failure of the "Hundred Flowers," China set out to oppress the voices of criticism against the leadership. Externally, China, which had taken immense comfort from the technological success of the Soviets when the first Sputnik was launched in October 1957, decided that the Communist Bloc should desist from its policy of accommodation towards the West—namely, put an end to coexistence and increase the anti-imperialist struggle everywhere, including support of Afro-Asian Communist factions. China's zealotry in this regard generated hostility against Nasser's imprisoning Communists in both Egypt and Syria (after the creation of the United Arab Republic) and concern that he might do the same in Iraq if he could sweep the Qassim regime to his camp. Chinese newspapers of those days indeed warned that "it would be difficult to refrain from taking a firm stand against those who once fell victim to pressures but now are themselves exerting pressures on others"; accused the UAR of having "desisted from firmly opposing Imperialism"; and attacked Nasser's neutralist slogan of "neither East nor West" as meaning "neither friends nor foes," for "those who have no friends cannot deter foes; they even make thereby a step towards the enemy."[3]

Egypt, having attacked China's oppression of the Tibetan Revolt, prompted in turn a violent reaction on the part of China, who for the tenth anniversary of the PRC ceremonies invited the exiled leader of the Syrian Communist party, Khaled Bakdash, to deliver an anti-Nasser speech. The Sino-Arab relations, which had begun cordially and with great bombast, sunk to their lowest point in 1960. But China was quick to reassess the situation and realize that she would lose all the good will she had accumulated among the Arabs if she pursued her onslaught against the vastly popular regime of Nasser. Thus, Peking began to rehabilitate and restore her damaged image in the hopes of displacing the USSR and regaining favor among the Arabs. By 1961 economic and commercial relations between Cairo and Peking were revived, and in 1963 during the Afro-Asian Solidarity Conference held in Tanganyika in February, the two countries acted in full cooperation. Chou En-lai visited Cairo in late 1963 and again in April 1965, this time to sign an agreement on nuclear energy cooperation. During the rampages of the cultural revolution (1965–1975) hardly any improvement could be expected in China's relations with the Arab world, especially following the aborted Communist coup in the sister-Muslim country of Indonesia in 1965. However, the 1967 six-day war gave Peking a golden opportunity to condemn Israel who had "initiated the aggression," the US who "stood behind the aggression," and the USSR who "condoned the Imperialistic plot." In a series of messages to Arab heads of state, including Nasser and PLO head al-Shuqairy, China continued to hammer in the slogan of the tri-partite (Israeli-American-Soviet) conspiracy against the Arabs, stressing the Soviet "treason" towards the Arabs in that they did not rush to their help while Palestine and other Arab territories were taken over by Israel.

The defeated Arabs, hard-pressed in their economic, military, and political dependence on the USSR, did not need the Chinese renewed outburst of support. They could take comfort, however, in what seemed to be Peking's consistently anti-Zionist and anti-Israeli rhetoric.[4] For unlike the USSR, which had recognized Israel and maintained diplomatic relations with it until the 1967 war, China could be blemished by neither. China's "clean" record vis-a-vis Israel became particularly important in view of the spectacular rise of the PLO after 1967 and the warm relations established between it and the Peking authorities. For unlike the battered Arab states who depended on the USSR for survival, the PLO, which claimed to be the new vanguard of the Arab struggle against Israel could only draw encouragement from China's support and her hostility towards Israel.

CHINA AND THE PALESTINIAN PROBLEM

Upon the establishment of the State of Israel, when China was not yet involved in the Middle East, it tended to regard the Arab-Israeli conflict mainly as a concoction of the Western imperialists who made contradictory promises to both parties while instigating them to wage war on each other. Thus, Peking was rather neutral in the conflict and imparted equal blame to Israel and the Arabs for the failure of the 1947 Partition Plan and the outbreak of the war. The peoples of the Middle East were the victims, in China's eyes, while their governments cooperated with imperialism. In those early years, China saw the solution to the conflict in the repudiated Partition Plan and in direct negotiations without Imperialist intervention between the parties.[5]

In April 1955 China veered for the first time and supported a pro-Palestinian resolution adopted by the leftist Conference of Asian Countries in Delhi. In Bandung, Ahmad al-Shuqairy, then the Deputy Secretary General of the Arab League and later to become the first chairman of the PLO (1964), met with Chou En-lai and intimated to him the details—as viewed from his side—of the Palestinian problem. Nevertheless, Chou En-lai continued to view the Palestine issue as one of "refugees" which was to be resolved through a peaceful settlement. Furthermore, the Chinese interpreted the conference's support of "Palestinian rights" as an urging to seek the implementation of the UN resolutions through peaceful means.[6]

In early 1956, there was still evidence that the Chinese stood for a directly negotiated peaceful settlement of the Palestinian issue, which took into consideration the interests of both parties, according to UN principles.[7] China's position was all the more remarkable since she herself was still boycotted by the UN, the very body whose ground rules she was prepared to accept as a matter of policy.

Following the Suez War in October 1956, and the growing identification in Chinese eyes of Israel with Western imperialism, on one hand, and the real progress made in the relations between China and the Arab world during that year, that included the establishment of diplomatic relations with Egypt and Syria, on the other, the Palestinian issue climbed one notch up in Chinese foreign policy. The Chinese admittedly only spoke of "Palestinian human rights" and the need to find a solution to the "Palestinian refugee problem," but hardly anyone else outside the Arab World went beyond that. The early 1960s saw the gradual shifting of China to a more outspoken pro-Palestinian stand in view of China's general trend towards mending fences with the Arab world following the crisis of 1958. Thus, during Chou En-lai's visit to Cairo in late 1963, he for the first time, stood publicly in favor of the "legitimate rights of the Palestinians" and of "restoring their rights and returning to their homeland." When the PLO was established in 1964 and became centerstage in inter-Arab affairs, it seemed only natural that as part of China's campaign to entrench herself in the Arab world and win its favors in world affairs, she should keep abreast of the developments and update her views on Palestine accordingly. The shift was clear—from a human problem of refugees needing to be settled by peaceful means to a problem of national liberation to be resolved only by armed struggle in the best tradition of other Chinese-supported, anti-imperialist movements of national liberation elsewhere.

No wonder then, that when the Arab Summit of early 1964 decided to back the establishment of a Palestinian entity, China rushed to apply her stamp of approval to this resolution. al-Shuqairy, who undertook to build the new Palestinian entity, called upon, among others, the Chinese ambassador to Cairo, probably in order to evince the broad international base and legitimacy of his fledgling organization. Yasser Arafat, one of the leaders of the Fatah at the time, attended in March the pro-Palestinian demonstrations held in Peking, and a year later (March 1965) al-Shuqairy himself headed a PLO delegation to China (the PLO had been established in mid-1964). The delegation was met by Mao in person, and the end of the PLO official visit was marked both by the establishment of official PLO-Chinese links and the celebration of Palestine Day on May 15, which fell on the Seventeenth Anniversary of the establishment of the State of Israel.

The Sino-Soviet rivalry, which was inaugurated in 1960 with the break between the two Communist powers and climaxed during the 1960s and 1970s, gave impetus to China's policy towards the Middle East as well. For the PRC not only wished to maintain its special relationship with movements of national liberation, of which she viewed herself as the natural leader, but she also sought to oust the Soviet Union from positions of influence in the Middle East which provided leverage on Europe and Japan who depended on Middle East oil.

In the mid 1960s China's relations with the PLO acquired a new impetus: due to Peking's widening rift with Moscow, which was further enhanced by the ideological excesses of the cultural revolution, China attempted to discredit the Soviet Union in Palestinian eyes, on account of the Kremlin's recognition of Israel and its diplomatic relations with it. The PRC, which was laboring towards the convening of a second Bandung Conference without the Soviets, indeed claimed that the Soviet revisionists collaborated with the American imperialists in robbing the Palestinians of their rights, for their acceptance of Israel in fact meant condoning the dispossession of the Palestinians. The Chinese thus evinced hostility to Israel's existence which was in line with Palestinian thinking. Add to that China's perception of the Palestinians as troublemakers against American interests in the Middle East versus Israel's perceived subservience to the United States, and you have the explanation for the ardent romance between China and the PLO in the 1960s, compared with Peking's vitriolic stand against Israel.

These trends were all heightened during the cultural revolution (1966–75), as China put primacy on ideological rather than pragmatic considerations. True, during that period the PRC's foreign relations were damaged due to the domestic upheaval which swept China, but Peking's ideological fervor did not let up as regards movements of national liberation. After Mao's death, the course charted by Deng Xiaoping became clearly more pragmatic. While the ideological passion was quieted down in general, the PRC lent precedence to maintaining relations with governments rather than movements of national liberation. In the Middle East, she preferred to cultivate relations with Sadat who had evicted the Russians from his country in 1972 and promised to keep the Soviet Union out of the peace process since 1977, rather than siding with the rejectionist views of the PLO.

THE CHINESE-PLO ROMANCE

Having solidly anchored its support for the PLO in ideological terms, the PRC, despite, or perhaps because of, the highly ideological pitch of its policies during the cultural revolution, now turned to implementation of their policies. Indeed, from the mid 1960s on, the first contingents of PLO trainees began spending rigorous military training periods in Chinese camps, and the first shipments of Chinese light arms began finding their way into Palestinian hands. The fact that China could not provide massive military support did nothing to temper the vows of devotion that were exchanged between the two newlyweds. It appears, however, that while the Chinese were wholeheartedly entranced by their involvement with the PLO, the latter remained somewhat wary of alienating the USSR, whose support they hoped to gain. It stands to reason that the PLO hoped to gain more fervent courting from both Communist powers by keeping equi-distance between them and playing up their mutual jealousies.

The Chinese were so eager to pursue their courtship of the PLO that the Palestinian leadership's ideological and organizational aberrations were irrelevant to them. They supported the Fatah which had never embraced Marxism and its doctrine, and at the same time they disregarded the splinter-fragments of the PLO which professed Marxism (the PFLP and the DFLP); they even accepted the 1967 purging of Ahmad al-Shuqairy, with whom they had dealt since 1964, and embraced without restraint Yasser Arafat, the head of the Fatah, who took over the PLO supreme leadership. And they continued to regard the PLO as the legitimate representative of the Palestinian cause even prior to the adoption of that course by the Arab Summit of 1974.

The aftermath of the cultural revolution signalled both the aggravation of Sino-Soviet relations and the return of Chinese foreign policy to the world of reality. That meant that while the ideological import of the PLO (and other movements of national liberation) was toned down, China's role in laboriously weaving a new array of international relationships with world powers became evident. However, this latter objective, like Peking's rapprochement with the US, was meant as a means to strengthen China's position in relation to the Soviet Union, its archenemy, all over the world. The mounting importance of the Middle East in world affairs following the oil crisis of the 1970s lent still more impetus to Chinese attempts to isolate the USSR or at least to check Soviet influence in and the Soviet menace against the oil producing nations of the Middle East.

The PLO admirably adapted to this shift in Chinese policy inasmuch as it had become one of the mainstays of Soviet influence in the Middle East. True, the fact that the PLO had grown from an ideological ally into a political partner (even if unwittingly so) occasioned a toning-down of Chinese fervor in pursuing it. Yet, it seemed as if the selfless ideological courtship had borne fruit and provided some welcome by-products which could only nurture with convenience the already-existing relationship.

CHINA'S "RADICALISM OF IMPOTENCE"[8]

It seemed, however, that the Chinese were unable to outdo the Soviets whose strongholds in the Middle East, including their sponsorship of the PLO in the 1970s, emerged relatively unscathed by the adversities which befell the Arabs, not the least of which was the 1973 war and its aftermath. Thus, China took to rhetorical radicalism by siding with the rejectionist elements in the Arab world, such as Syria, Algeria, Libya, and the PLO and by upholding their rejection of Security Council Resolution 242. Chinese propaganda lumped the Soviet Union together with the United States as undermining the interests of the Palestinians by its "collusion" with Israel[9] and even accused the Soviets of facilitating Jewish immigration into Israel in order to settle the occupied Arab territories.[10] In a meeting of the Security Council in April 1974, the Chinese repeated their pro-Palestinian vows of fidelity: "The Chinese Government and the people have always deeply sympathized with the Palestinians and the Arab people and have always firmly supported them in their just struggles to oppose Zionism and Hegemonism."[11] True to its commitment, China consistently condemned Israel and its policies, Zionism and its designs. By divorcing itself from any association with Israel[12] and by rejecting UN resolutions regarding the Middle East (242, 338, and the renewal of the mandate of the UN Emergency Forces), China, unlike the superpowers and the moderate Arab countries, stood as the sole herald of the PLO and the Arab rejectionists. The Palestinians were not amiss in recognizing their debt. One of their leaders in effect declared in Beirut, following a meeting with the Chinese ambassador there: "China's attitude toward the Palestine Revolution has always been extremely serious and effective. In the near future we shall carry out a joint Sino-Palestinian activity in the political and military domains."[13] China's consistently radical support for the Palestinian cause went hand-in-hand with her mending fences with the Arabs as well. Indeed, near the end of the 1960s, Peking reestablished full diplomatic relations with all Arab capitals where (except for Cairo) the embassies had been depleted of their senior officials since the cultural revolution. At that point, China's view regarding the centrality of the Palestinian problem in the Middle Eastern complex began to converge with that of most Arab countries who voiced the same idea, at least on the rhetorical level. Thus, China's policy of patching up its relations with the Arab world was accompanied by a rather stringent emphasis on the revolutionary role that the Palestinians were perceived as playing in the Middle East—hence, China's opposition to foreign interference in any Middle Eastern settlement, be it superpower- or

UN-sponsored. She continued to hold the view that if the Palestinians pursued their uncompromising path of total rejection of Israel and of any peaceful settlement in the area, that would somehow ensure the perpetuation of their revolutionary zeal which could in the long run serve her purposes. However, the Chinese, who were themselves seeking legitimacy on the world scene, carefully avoided publicly condoning such instruments of foreign policy as hijackings and terrorism.

China's extremist policies with regard to the Palestinian problem, however, did not yield the hoped-for results of Palestinian and Arab tilting towards her in her rift with Moscow. Not that the Palestinians were happy about Soviet propensities toward a political settlement of the Middle Eastern impasse; but they knew only too well that they could not afford to distance themselves from the USSR, by far the stronger, more reliable, more influential, and wealthier of the two parties. Be it as it may, both maintained a similitude of good relationships, if only not to completely estrange one another. It was evident, however, that China's radicalism had exposed her impotence more than her now-extinguished ideological passion. Yasser Arafat visited Peking in 1970; he was offered some arms, but the rhetoric was restrained in comparison to previous occasions.

SETTLING INTO THE CONVENIENCE AND PROBLEMS OF MARITAL LIFE

The 1970s and 1980s signaled the routinization of Chinese relations with the PLO, alongside the ups and downs which characterize such relationships. President Sadat of Egypt who first ousted the Soviet advisers in July 1972 and then gradually shifted toward the American camp following the 1973 war, looked much more like a bulwark against Soviet penetration to the Middle East than the revolutionary PLO could be under the most favorable of circumstances. Thus, China's foreign relations were gradually characterized less by ideological fervor than by pragmatic considerations, allowing the Peking government to strengthen its relations with Cairo and temper its commitment to the PLO. From the early 1970s, the Chinese ceased celebrating "Palestine Day" and "Palestine Week," a practice that they had held since the happy encounter between the two in 1965. It was as if the courtship which had necessitated presents and bouquets had faded, and the anniversaries became uncelebrated events. True, the oath of loyalty and devotion pronounced in past years was still paid lip service, but side-affairs would henceforth become the norm for both parties. If the relationship was not dissolved, it was simply because the partners felt this would cause more damage than benefit or that nothing would be gained by dissolution. It would be likely, in fact, to cause them to lose face in the eyes of other Third World or revolutionary movements.

Once she had become a respectable member of the UN (1971), China more openly condemned hijackings and terrorism so as to gain currency among antiterrorist countries. This did not prevent Arafat from continuing to visit China and meet Chinese diplomats in Arab countries[14] nor Chinese statesmen from repeating their loyalty to the Palestinian struggle which was "part and parcel of the struggle of the Third World against Imperialism, Colonialism and Zionism."[15] According to unconfirmed reports, China apparently even hinted her support to Palestinian aspirations to establish an independent state.[16] In August and September 1974, a Fatah delegation headed by Hani al-Hassan visited Peking and submitted a message from Chairman Arafat to Premier Chou En-lai in person. This was the first PLO delegation to China in two years,[17] and the fact that it was accorded the highest honors and received by the foreign ministry and no longer only by party bodies was indicative of the continued commitment of China to the partnership and of her desire that it appear so to curious onlooking neighbors. To top the achievement, the Chinese apparently promised the delegation that they would support a General Assembly debate on Palestine.[18]

These moments were immortalized by an important Palestinian organ which wrote:

China has been one of 34 nations which petitioned the inclusion of a Palestinian clause in the U.N. Agenda. . . . For the Palestinians China is very dear. . . . For there is a strategic convergence between the goals of the Palestinian Revolution and the Chinese Revolution. Moreover, there is mutual sympathy between the parties. The Chinese believe that movements of national liberation have a say in the destruction and removal of Imperialism, therefore they support them . . . they view Israel as the reflection of Imperialism in the Middle East and therefore they object to the very racist existence of Israel and are in favor of a Palestinian democratic state to be established on the entire territory of Palestine. They assured us, the Palestinians, that they would never recognize Israel neither today nor tomorrow nor in a hundred years. . . . Pro-Zionist Senator Jackson's version is a pipe-dream. . . .[19]

It is more likely that the pipe-dream was Palestinian, but the fact that the PLO delegation had been led to believe what it published is in itself significant. For if nothing else, it shows the degree of expectation that the PLO leadership entertained with regard to China. Incidentally, either because they were alarmed by the seemingly warming relations between China and the Arabs or just as a matter of routine precaution, a Soviet mouthpiece lashed out, shortly thereafter, at the "double-faced policy of Peking," which promised much in terms of support to the Arab cause but in fact did little. It blasted Peking for its absence from the UN vote which condemned Israel for its occupation of Palestine and its oppressive policies against the Palestinians and for scuttling the Geneva Conference in which Moscow was trying hard to impose Palestinian participation. The Moscow organ also condemned Peking for having looked on indifferently as the Palestinians were being massacred in Jordan during Black September 1970. The Soviets exposed the Chinese slogan of "self-reliance" as a pretext for cutting supply lines to the Arabs who were in need of help from the socialist world as a prerequisite of their victory.[20] The fact that the PLO had declared its adherence to the principle of "self-reliance" was, of course, of no consequence to the Soviets.[21]

In early 1975, as tension mounted on the Israeli-Lebanese border along which the PLO had built its bases of attack against the northern Galilee, the PLO-Chinese marriage seemed to warm up. Arafat often met with the Chinese ambassador in Beirut, and every time the PLO took a beating from the Israeli artillery or air force, a comforting Chinese message would follow.[22] The spirit of "comradeship" between the parties was accentuated in Arafat's message of congratulations to "Comrades" Chou En-lai and Zhu De upon the termination of the Fourth People's Congress. Arafat, who also congratulated newly elected Li Xiannian to the Presidency of the National People's Council, specified that the friendship between the parties was an "active" one.[23] Indeed, those years saw the height of the PLO "guerrilla" offensive in the "Fatahland" area which it had carved for itself out of Lebanese territory. In those years, myths and symbols were coined by the PLO, which derived from the Chinese and other revolutionary vocabulary, such as "guerrilla warfare," "Arafat trail," "revolution growing from the barrel of the gun," and "self-reliance." Weapons, especially small arms and explosives, began flowing into PLO-dominated Beirut and then south Lebanon,[24] and frequent meetings took place between the PLO leadership and high Chinese officials.[25] The Chinese ambassador to Beirut was even reported to have visited the front in March 1975.[26] These meetings, which were coupled by a similar activity in Peking,[27] also proved beneficial. In political terms, the most significant outcome was the Chinese ambassador in Beirut's reassurance that his country recognized the PLO as the "sole legitimate representative of the Palestinians," a formula that had been adopted by the Rabat Arab Summit some six months earlier.

Twice rehabilitated Chinese leader Deng Xiaoping, who since the death of Mao and Chou En-lai had been dominating the political scene in China, joined the choir of Chinese support for the Palestinians immediately upon his confirmation to the deputy prime ministership in 1975; according to press reports he said in Peking:

> The just struggle of the Arabs and the Palestinians against Israeli Zionism, has been disrupting Superpower designs. The problem lies in Israel's aggression and expansion. . . . The Superpower's competition to resolve the problem only produces an increased level of Israel's aggression. But we are certain that the Arabs and the Palestinians will be able to retrieve their rights, and the People and Government of China will support, as always, the just struggle of the Arabs and Palestinians until they achieve full victory.[28]

Chairman Arafat received a message from Prime Minister Chou En-lai in May 1975 which stressed the support of the Chinese people and the Chinese Communist party to the Palestinian revolution and struggle against imperialism and Zionism with a view toward "restoring the national rights of the Palestinian people and liberating occupied Palestine." According to Arab sources, the Chinese message emphasized the need for a "total victory of the Palestinian cause."[29] Chinese ambassadors in Damascus and Beirut repeated the essence of the message to PLO leaders together with pledges to increase Chinese support to the Palestinian struggle.[30] In June 1975 a Sa'iqa delegation went to China,[31] and in July 1975 a Fatah delegation visited Peking (and North Korea and Vietnam) in a bid to increase and diversify the Communist Bloc support to the Palestinian cause. The Chinese deputy foreign minister reiterated in Peking his country's commitment to the Palestinian cause, warned from the reversion of the Middle East to the no war-no peace situation, and predictably accused the Soviets of inciting one Arab party against another instead of struggling for Arab rights. On the same occasion, Abu-Jihad, the head of the Palestinian delegation, reiterated that "armed struggle anywhere is the basic form of struggle" and that it would take armed struggle to overwhelm Israel's military power.[32] It seems that the visit, which scheduled high-level encounters and wide-ranging tours of the country, including military installations, also ended in military deals which assured the Palestinians of more weapons as their involvement in the Lebanese civil war heightened the stakes of their military survival.[33] The PLO-Peking agreement of October 1974 to "create a new level of relationship" between the parties was now being implemented,[34] and China's pledge to help bring about a Palestinian "victory" (not a "solution" to their problem)— now seemed realistic.[35]

Arafat had visited Moscow in April 1974, and got assurances of large military supplies from Soviet arsenals. But the PLO, feeling threatened by the ongoing Kissinger efforts to arrive at an Egyptian-Israeli interim agreement which they felt could turn into a separate settlement harmful to their cause, rushed to Peking to rally its political support. Moscow's steady backing for a Geneva peace conference was not exactly what the militant PLO was hoping for. Instead, the PLO was seeking to obtain Chinese support to oust Israel from the UN[36] because it was hoped that, having never recognized the Jewish state, Peking would feel fewer qualms about lending her support to such a proposition. Indeed, the visits of PLO heads, including some from splinter groups such as the Popular Front for the Liberation of Palestine,[37] were primarily intended to prepare a back-up support system in case the USSR deserted the PLO politically and/or militarily. China apparently warned the PLO in July 1975 of demarches that were being concocted behind the scenes in the Middle East which might adversely affect the Palestinians.[38]

However, China surprisingly announced in August 1975[39] that she was in favor of Kissinger's efforts to reach an agreement in the Sinai and attacked the USSR for trying to hamper those efforts and for betraying the Palestinian and Arab causes. Clearly China had reversed its policy of supporting armed struggle and of dismissing superpower interference in the Middle East. Peking, which was keen on improving its relations with Washington, had also apparently awakened to the prospect that the Kissinger-sponsored negotiations would leave the Soviets out of the process and defeat their designs in the Middle East. What was worse from the PLO viewpoint was Foreign Minister Qiao Guanhua's reported speech in a Hong Kong newspaper in which he had allegedly reconciled to the existence of Israel as a "*fait accompli*" and as a favorable fact which encouraged superpower confrontation. He was also reported to have opposed the repatriation of Palestinian refugees lest "a new problem of Israeli refugees might be created as a result."[40] Nevertheless, the PLO went ahead with a planned visit of one of its chiefs to Peking[41] and sent another high-level delegation to China in September headed by Abu Iyad.[42]

Intensive diplomatic activity was maintained between the PLO and Peking after the Egyptian-Israeli second disengagement was signed on 1 September 1975 and well into 1976. Qaddumi went to Peking in April 1976 in the footsteps of Vice President Mubarak of Egypt, apparently to balance out whatever "moderating damage" the Egyptian President may have caused.[43] Peking reassured the Palestinians that her rapprochement with Egypt was not at the expense of her close rapport with the Palestinians,[44] and even pledged that she would fight "shoulder to shoulder" with the Palestinians and the Arabs in their confrontation with Israel.[45] China's leaders not only reiterated their warm support to the Palestinian revolution but also declared that this was a matter of principle for them.[46] No wonder, then, that when Chou En-lai died in January 1976, Arafat inscribed in the condolence book of the Chinese embassy in Beirut: "A great loss, not only to China but also the Palestinian people and to humanity,"[47] Nayif Hawatmeh, the head of the Democratic Front for the Liberation of Palestine, expressed his condolences for the death of Mao in September of that year: "He was the great friend of the Palestinian people."[48] Mao's death occasioned great obituaries in the Arab and Palestinian press, hailing him as the man who had defended the Palestinian revolution "without reserve," who had granted weapons, diplomatic support, and training facilities to the Palestinians. He was reported to have told Arafat in one of their meetings that the West had created Israel as a challenge to Arabs in the western gate of Asia and Taiwan as one to China in the eastern gate thereof—hence the community of interests between China and the Arabs and the common lot that they shared against the West and Israel.[49]

Again in November 1976 a delegation of senior PLO officials visited Peking and was warmly received by the authorities there, to be followed by a Fatah delegation in December.[50] Those visits bore some practical fruits too: already in September 1976, and not for the first time, shipments of medical equipment and food were reported to have landed in Cairo, destined to the Palestinians in Lebanon.[51] But then, during 1977, a flow of reports followed of Chinese weapons reaching the Palestinians: light arms for the PLA and the Asifa, ammunition, and other military gear. The shipments did not include tanks, long-range artillery, and missiles, which the PLO coveted, but they were given free of charge as was China's wont when it came to movements of national liberation and particularly friendly states.[52] The Chinese foreign minister made no secret of his country's commitment to help the PLO morally and materially,[53] and some Arab sources even went as far as to fantasize about the possibility of "Chinese nuclear assistance" to the PLO.[54]

Sadat's peace initiative, which was followed by the Camp David peace accords, produced yet another point of strain in the otherwise stable relationship between the PLO and Peking. In October 1978, merely a month after Camp David, Arafat dispatched a delegation to ask for Chinese succor, while he himself flew to Moscow to secure the same. All they could extract from the Chinese, however, was a declaration that there could be no solution of the conflict that would not also settle the Palestinian national rights and bring about the withdrawal of Israel from the territories she had occupied.[55] Chinese officials promised China's unrelenting support to the Palestinians and pledged not to recognize Israel.[56] That the Palestinians were invited and welcomed by the Association for Friendship with Foreign Countries[57] and not by officials of the government, as in the heyday of the relationship, indicated perhaps a certain cooling of past passion. The annual visits of Fatah delegations to Peking had become routine since China began her military and political assistance to the PLO strongholds in Southern Lebanon in the early 1970s,[58] and this routine relationship, where custom and habit and matters of expediency took the place of ideological commitment, was encouraged by the growingly pragmatic new leadership which took over after Mao. The Chinese apparently promised to step up their military aid to support Palestinian self-determination and to abstain from any decision that would run counter to PLO positions. But exactly as the Palestinians had to "explain" that they could not give up their close friendship with the USSR and that they sought a unified socialist world in order to beat American imperialism, so the Chinese could easily get away with their insistence on a unified Arab position—hence their reluctance to interfere in inter-Arab controversies—and on the importance of their relationship with Egypt and the United States.[59] Qaddumi's comment that the US-China rapprochement would not hinder continued Chinese commitment to the PLO[60] must be seen in this context.

In early 1979, as the Sino-Vietnamese tension escalated into an open conflict, the PLO took a pro-Vietnamese position. Abu Iyad openly condemned "Chinese aggression against Vietnam" and said that no country which claimed the tag of "progressism" could indulge in hostilities against the Hanoi regime.[61] That was the last straw. In 1979, rumors began circulating in diplomatic circles about the impending break of relations between the PLO and China, especially due to the latter's support of Sadat's peace initiative and the projected visit of the popular Egyptian leader to Peking.[62] A planned visit by Arafat to Peking at the end of 1979[63] was put off; instead, the chairman of the Palestine National Council (PNC) rendered the visit with a view of "mediating between Peking and Hanoi the termination of their conflict." But in fact, he attempted without success to alter China's positive stand toward the Camp David accords.[64] China, however, who was warming up her relations with the US, did not seem much impressed by PLO pressures. Understandably, the PLO, which had been pampered by years of

Chinese rhetorical and material outright and unreserved support, now felt let down. One of their chiefs poignantly said: We expect America to stand up for Israel . . . we don't like ti but we understand it. After all, New York is full of Zionists. But China![65]

China's alignment with the American-Sadat position in the Middle East was further reinforced following Deng Xiaoping's visit to the US in early 1979 and Egyptian Deputy Prime Minister Hassan al-Tuhami's visit to Peking in preparation for Sadat's trip to China. On that occasion, Tuhami expressed support for the Chinese invasion of Vietnam.[66] So the convergence of the Chinese inching towards the Washington-Cairo Axis and the PLO's outright support for the Vietnamese brought the PLO-Peking relationship to its lowest ebb since its establishment in the 1960s. But there was no separation, just a family quarrel which followed the two parties' straying into adventurous affairs with others. It is quite possible, although it was never admitted, that the PLO took its revenge on China due to the latter's betrayal with the US and Sadat on the Camp David issue. However, it was evident, despite rumors and indications to the contrary, that neither party wished to break the relationship. Abu Saleh, a Fatah chief, remarked bitterly: "We were astonished by the Chinese leadership's current position supporting Camp David. . . . Our experience with the present leadership indicates that it is shrouding its policy on our case in obscurity and political obfuscation."[67] There was indeed ambiguity. The Chinese delegate to the UN did send his annual message to Secretary General Waldheim and to Chairman Arafat in November 1979 for Solidarity Day with the Palestinian people.[68] This was completely in tune with China's stated position to the Palestinian leaders,[69] and consistent with China's condemnation of Israeli reprisals against PLO bases in south Lebanon, even at the height of the PLO-China crisis.[70] On the other hand, the PLO's efforts to obstruct the visit to Cairo of high Chinese officials in November 1979 ended in failure.[71] And despite the meeting with Chairman Hua Guofeng in an attempt to plead for China's return to its outright support of Palestinian rejectionism,[72] Peking held firm.

The PLO, after a bout of jealousy, reconciled itself to mending the relationship. Abu Jihad, who had not been in Peking since 1978, announced his plans to visit in January 1980 and to meet with Chairman Hua and Vice Chairman Deng,[73] and current consultations continued between PLO officials and Chinese ambassadors in the Middle East thereafter.[74] Finally in August of 1980, Abu Jihad's mission to Peking was carried out, and in high-level consultations the two parties seem to have made up. This time, the Chinese not only reiterated their support to the PLO and Palestinian national rights, but they also negotiated the provision of some Chinese military hardware to the Palestinian revolution.[75] There were even reports that the PLO requested antiaircraft missiles from China after their attempt to obtain them from Moscow had failed.[76] The very application of the PLO for this sophisticated weaponry was indicative of the atmosphere in the mended relationship, regardless of whether or not the requested weapons were ultimately delivered. In a visit of a Jordanian delegation to Peking, Deng Xiaoping again expressed warm support for the Palestinian struggle against Israeli "expansion and aggression" and pledged China's help in order for the Palestinians to "retrieve their lost territories, including Jerusalem, and recover their rights, including their right to statehood."[77]

Once the PLO had reconciled to the idea that it had to live with a partner who had shed its devotion in favor of a new open relationship with occasional or permanent strayings, the Chinese-PLO relationship stabilized again. The alternative for the PLO was to be forlorn and replaced by the many more attractive partners China had discovered. Where would a desperate PLO turn? Trapped in a marriage of convenience, it felt it was better to play on China's new terms that to break the long alliance. On China's part, a decision had been made by the post-Mao leadership to desist from support to the movements of national liberation and to embrace a more pragmatic and economically beneficial international course. If the PLO somehow fell victim to this new orientation, so be it. And if China could juggle between swearing allegiance and loyalty on the one hand, and doing what it wanted on the other, it saw no great inconvenience in pursuing one policy and its reverse at the same time.

Toward the end of 1980, the PLO was happy to report that the Chinese were still condemning Israel's aggression and acts of terror in the occupied territories and encouraging the Palestinians to redeem their legitimate rights under the PLO, their only legitimate representative. The PLO also delighted in quoting the *People's Daily* which had condemned Israel as "fascist and racist" for her expelling of Mayors Fahd al-Qawasmeh and Muhammad Milhem from the West Bank.[78] In 1981, Arafat visited Peking again and met with Deng Xiaoping the strongman of the new regime and the architect of its new policies. The PLO delegation again raised the Camp David issue and asked for new military assistance. However, far from hoping to dissuade the Chinese from their support of the peace process, they were content to remark that China had "recognized some negative elements in the Camp David Accords" and accepted China's disenchanting position that it could not be expected to extend much material help to the Palestinians.[79] Arafat's visit, for all its limited achievements, was the culmination of calculated efforts by the PLO, especially the Fatah faction thereof, to revive their alliance with Peking[80] and to renew Chinese military aid in order to replace the large quantities of weapons and ammunition they lost during their confrontation with Israel in the summer of 1981.[81] At the height of that confrontation, when Israel bombed PLO stockpiles in Beirut in September, the PLO contacted China's chief of staff and urged him to supply them with long-range guns and other needed materials. The PLO noted that the Chinese responded immediately, and within days they dispatched their "present" to the battered Palestinians.[82] But now, during the Arafat visit, the Chinese agreed to talk about arms sales to the PLO. Upon taking over from Hua Guofeng in June 1981, Hu Yaobang, the new Chinese Party Chief had also reiterated his support to the Palestinians to retrieve their lost territories, and condemned Israel's retaliations in Lebanon as "criminal acts."[83] However, their differences on the peace process soon surfaced: while the PLO spokesman said that the "trivial issue" of Sadat's assassination (on 6 October) was not even mentioned in those talks, the Chinese declared that they were "deeply grieved over the murder" and judged his death as a "tremendous loss to the Arabs."[84]

The issue of arms supplies remained unsettled. Mahmud Labadi, the PLO spokesman, said that his delegation brought up the topic and especially requested air-defense systems to protect their military encampments which were positioned in Palestinian refugee camps throughout Lebanon, but that the Chinese were unable to provide them. Therefore, in the final lists of purchases that they left behind in Peking, anti-aircraft missiles were omitted.[85] Deng's final message to Arafat, which was quoted by the New China News Agency, was quite reflective of the new Chinese ambivalence: "Our aid is limited. You have to rely mainly on your own efforts and on the unity of the Arab Countries and people. . . . You are at the forefront of the struggle for national liberation. You are our Comrades-in-arms. All along, we have supported the Palestinian people in their fight for liberation. The struggle of the Palestinian people is protracted, but you are bound to win."[86] The PLO was quite candid in its recognition of the hiatus which separated it from China. For not only did Arafat expect a reversal of the peace process after Sadat's assassination in the hope that the "Egyptian Army and people would never forget Sadat's betrayal of the Palestinian cause,"[87] but a PLO spokesman also acknowledged "our existing differences on several issues in our region and other areas of the world (presumably the peace accords in the Middle East and the attitude to the USSR and movements of national liberation elsewhere). [88] Another source in Beirut confirmed that Arafat had received Chinese promises for arms procurement "except for two kinds of weapons" (presumably long-range guns and anti-aircraft missiles) and that a senior Chinese official had referred Chinese response to PLO arms requests to "the future," due to the fact that "China's ability falls short of her aspirations." [89]

In 1982, China still persisted in her support of Palestinian state and in her condemnation of Israel's "aggression," although it also mildly lashed out at acts of terror committed by the Palestinians as "unfitting for a serious movement of national liberation." The Chinese also emphasized their opposition to recognizing Israel or to establishing any relations with them in the foreseeable future. [90] During the Israeli anti-PLO incursion into Lebanon and its siege of PLO-occupied West Beirut in the Summer of 1982, the Chinese again voiced their support for the Palestinians, condemned Israel's "aggression and inhuman war," and pledged to "join others in checking the Israeli aggression." [91] The Chinese Red Cross sent a special airload of a twenty-ton medical shipment to the Palestinian Red Crescent, [92] and the Chinese government allocated the sum of one million dollars in assistance and began delivery of the military equipment that had been promised to Arafat in 1981. [93]

In October 1983, when Arafat was besieged in Tripoli by the pro-Syrian and Soviet-supported Abu Musa group, he appealed to the Chinese for emergency aid. The Chinese new agency reported that the aid was sent immediately, and it included light- and medium-range guns, mortars, hand grenades, ammunition, and other military gear. It was rumored in Peking that Arab governments who support Arafat pressured the Chinese government to send the emergency help lest the Abu Musa faction take over the PLO, which would then come under direct Syrian and Soviet influence, ending its independent struggle. [94] In November, a PLO delegation rushed to Peking to ask for more emergency help. The Chinese expressed their support for Arafat's leadership and called upon the PLO to unify its ranks in order to deal with Israel's policy of "expansion and aggression." Deputy Prime Minister Wan Li who hosted the delegation could comfort it with aid and words: "Your struggle is arduous and tortuous, but justice is on your side. Persistence means victory. The Chinese people and government will always support you." [95] In January 1984, another Arab leader in search of weapons visited Peking: Tareq Aziz, the Iraqi foreign minister. He was told of Chinese support to the Arafat faction of the PLO and of their pledge to continue to assist the beleaguered Palestinian chief politically and militarily in addition to the medical and logistic shipments they had dispatched to him. The Chinese had in fact sent some of the aid to the various Arab countries where Arafat's men had been scattered after the 1 September 1982 evacuation of Beirut, in the hope that they would thereby contribute to the stabilization of the PLO.[96] During President Li Xiannian's visit to Amman in March 1984, Arafat went to meet him and expressed his desire to receive Chinese military shipments directly to his troops in Jordan. Peking asked that a PLO military mission be sent to China to discuss this matter.[97] Arafat, who had won Syria's enmity and Moscow's chill, was attempting to patch up his relations with Amman and to hold on desperately to his Chinese trump-card as a substitution for and a threat and warning against the USSR. In May, in response to Li's invitation,[98] Arafat went to Peking in person to step up Chinese assistance. This time, amidst reports that China was providing the PLO with tanks, artillery parts, and large quantities of light weapons and ammunition free of charge, the PLO chief attended military maneuvers of an armor unit and was delighted to hear that the Chinese were as committed as ever to lending their support to his leadership and to the Palestinian struggle which they regarded as "comparable to their own."[99] Arafat's visit, which marked twenty years of his own personal involvement with Peking, came one week subsequent to President Reagan's own trip to China, during which Chinese leaders had tried in vain to convince him to negotiate with the PLO. Arafat was grateful: "China has stood behind us since our very beginnings, we shall never forget."[100] He had every reason for his gratitude; he was welcomed, for the fourth time in Peking, as a head of government with a nineteen-gun salute (twenty-one were reserved for Reagan as a head of state); he got much of the military hardware he had coveted, which made China, for the first time, a larger arms supplier to the PLO than Moscow;[101] he was warmly received by the highest echelons of the Chinese government, including Deng Xiaoping;[102] and he got all the diplomatic declarations he so badly needed: that "the just and total settlement of the Palestinian problem remained the key to a Middle Eastern settlement," that "the Chinese people will always firmly support the Palestinian people in their just struggle against the expansionist policy of Israel,"[103] and that China would "oppose Super-power involvement in the Middle East."[104] The Chinese also agreed to discuss the proposal for an international conference on the Middle East, with the participation of the permanent members of the UN Security Council; Premier Zhao Ziyang even promised Chinese support at the Security Council for the convening of such a conference.[105]

China followed up on the renewed warmth in PLO-Peking relations by congratulating Arafat upon the gathering of the controversial PNC in

Amman in November 1984, and by expediting the shipments of weapons that had been promised: light arms, missiles, light guns, ammunition, and Chinese technical personnel to train the PLO.[106] It seemed that both parties now seemed easier about their relationships: Arafat's PLO, which was battered after the Beirut and Tripoli debacles, had inched closer to Mubarak's Egypt and entered into a new alliance with Hussein's Jordan. China, like Egypt, had pronounced her support of those steps, which made her policies in the Middle East more consistent. Vis-a-vis Moscow, Arafat was bitter at her client's — Asad of Syria's — sponsorship of the Abu Musa dissident group a situation that Peking was only too glad to exploit to bring the PLO closer to her fold. No wonder, then that in May 1985, Arafat was again invited to Peking, this time at the head of a joint PLO-Jordanian delegation which symbolized his new symbiosis with the Hashemite kingdom.[107] This time, Arafat lobbied mainly for the international conference on the Middle East on which he had agreed with King Hussein as a result of their 11 February 1985 accords.[108] Again, the Chinese went out of their way to evince their warmth and friendship and promised not only to support the conference but also to talk other countries into lending their voices to it. The Chinese delegation to the talks, headed by Premier Zhao Ziyang, renewed its upholding of the Palestinian "inalienable national rights" and its support for the termination of "Israeli occupation in all occupied Arab lands."[109] Those assurances were repeated in a message by the Chinese president to Arafat when Israel bombed the PLO headquarters in Tunis in October 1985.[110]

China's championing of an international conference to resolve the Middle East impasse is in itself an important departure from her former rhetoric of "armed struggle." Indeed, since that idea won China's approval, it became for Peking a formula for assuming a respectable and moderate stature as part of her newly-adopted pragmatic policies. Even while remaining true to her rhetorical and political commitments to the PLO, she can now afford, is indeed bound as a permanent member of the Security Council and a prospective participant in the international peace conference, to regard the Middle East in a wider perspective. Thus, China continues to maintain close contacts with the PLO, through which she reaffirms her traditional support for it.[111] During his Middle Eastern tour in late 1985, the Chinese foreign minister missed no opportunity to reiterate his country's commitment to the "legitimate national rights of the Palestinians,"[112] but his statement was diluted by the moderate formula calling upon "all countries of the Middle East to live peacefully and to exercise their right to existence," an addition that can definitely be interpreted as acquiescing in Israel's right to exist. Not that the Chinese had not hinted before to such a position, but doing so during the visits of Chinese high officials in Arab countries was quite novel, especially when coupled with their urging the settlement of the conflict through "peaceful negotiations" under the umbrella of a UN-sponsored international peace conference in order to reach a "just and reasonable settlement."[113] At the same time, however, the Chinese officials took the pains to ritually deny all reports of Chinese-Israeli military and commercial deals, condemned Israel's "savage crimes" against the Palestinian people, and expressed their government's and people's support for the Arabs in general and the Palestinians in particular in their "just struggle."[114]

PROSPECTS

China's more moderate and even-handed treatment of the Middle East in recent years was reflected in Foreign Minister Wu Xueqian's tour of the region in December 1985, which included rejectionist Syria, moderate Egypt, and middle-of-the-road Iraq. Vice Prime Minister Yao Yilin had visited the Gulf states in November 1985 and made statements that amounted to an implicit recognition of Israel.[115] There have been seasonal flurries of reports since the early 1980s regarding China's hidden relationship with Israel, be it on the military level, where Israel was rumored to have sold advanced weaponry and technology to the PRC, or on the commercial and economic levels, where Israel was said to have shared with the Chinese new irrigation technology or aided Chinese agriculture in various domains. Israeli tourists, who were never allowed to visit the PRC on their Israeli passports, are now selectively permitted to do so, although this matter is still apparently given to the whims of local officials. With Israel being the "obverse" of the PLO and since the latter's relationship with the PRC has been to a great extent predicated on Peking's outright rejection of Israel, it is fair to assume that the unmistakable recent relaxation of Chinese attitudes towards the Jewish state is also a reflection of the loosened and more routinized relations that China maintains with the PLO. In other words, the China-PLO wedlock has lost much of the jealousy and exclusiveness which characterize passion and has settled in a world of convenient routine and calculated expediency. Either partner could stray from stated policy, but not so much as to break the relationship. China has a stake in nurturing her links with the PLO for many reasons, even if the ideological fervor has faded: (1) The Palestinians are the one issue around which the Arabs are rhetorically unified, even if each of them regards the PLO and its leadership in a different light; if China wants to maintain its stature in the Arab world, she cannot escape aligning herself along the lowest common denominator which unites the Arabs regarding the Palestinian issue. (2) China has a huge stake in cultivating her relations with the Third World and the forty-two-countries-strong Islamic conference, in both of which the PLO has a strong standing as a revolutionary movement of national liberation and as the governing body of a would-be Muslim state. (3) China needs to win the support of rich oil-producing Islamic countries, especially the Gulf states, both in order to lure them away from their economic contacts with Taiwan and to qualify for their petrodollar investment money.[116] Peking believes that good terms with the PLO will provide a conduit for that policy goal. (4) China has turned into an important arms exporter to the Arab and Islamic world; they have already provided gunboats, guns, spare parts, and ammunition to Egypt, Jordan, and possibly the two contending powers in the Iran-Iraq War. A good relationship with the PLO might also serve to further that goal either by directly supplying weapons to the Palestinians or by using the battle experience of the PLO and its good offices to promote sales to other Arab and Third World countries. One has to remember, however, that Israel and the PLO are not necessarily an either/or affair for China. The latter realizes full well that countries who maintain a good relationship with both (like the European community) have also some leverage on both and can perhaps even play as intermediary between them. In the long run, therefore, China risks nothing in terms of her relations with the PLO, is she were to recognize Israel and tie diplomatic relations with her. It is in the short haul that Chinese considerations are centered, the stakes being that if Peking were to decide to improve her relations with Israel, she might raise the anger of the PLO and the Arab, Islamic, and Third worlds. China has evidently weighed the choice between recognizing Israel and losing those allies in the short term or continuing to exploit her estrangement from Israel in order to gain among her friends. And she has evidently decided that, for the time being, she can discretely get from Israel all she needed and wanted, in all domains, without having to pay any political price. However, when China's open-door and other pragmatic policies become irreversible and her relations with the rest of the Third World grow normal and relaxed, she should have no compunction about gradually inching towards a total normalization with Israel. The PLO (and other Arabs) may burst into bitter broadsides, but they will have to reconcile to the idea that China and other countries around the world, just like western Europe and Egypt, can very well maintain diplomatic relations with the PLO without having to exclude the Israelis.

NOTES

1. For much of the crude information material, I am indebted to the Israeli Ministry for Foreign Affairs, Department of Research and Planning, which graciously made available to me some of its resources. I am also deeply grateful to my research apprentice, Allegra Pacheco, who undertook the task of material-hunting despite short notice and her overburdened schedule of study.

2. An oblique reference to the US and a sarcastic sting to the Arab conservatives who still supported the US.

3. *The Red Flag* (The People's Army Organ), 1 Apr. 1959.

4. China had picked up some anti-Zionist rhetoric during the Korean War, but then relented during the brief thaw in 1954–55 when she indicated her interest in relations with Israel. Following Bandung, however, her anti-Israeli hostility grew more apparent.

5. Shichor, 34–35.

6. Shichor, 54–55.

7. Shichor, 56–58.

8. The term is borrowed from J. Schumpeter, *Capitalism, Socialism and Democracy,* (NY: 1950), 328.

9. Summary Record of the 883d Meeting of the Special Political Committee of the UN, 14 Nov. 1973, 6–7. This theme was expressed in the speech delivered by Wang Wei-tsai, China's representative in the committee.

10. See J. Cooley, "China and the Palestinians," *Journal of Palestine Studies,* Beirut, 1(2) (Winter 1972): See also the *Peking Review,* 26 Oct. 1973.

11. Speech by the Chinese representative at the 767th Meeting of the Security Council, 16 Apr. 1974, 16. By "hegemonism," the Chinese meant, of course, Soviet extra-territorial adventures.

12. See foreign minister of China's speech at the 2137th Meeting of the General Assembly of the UN, 2 Oct. 1973, 26.

13. *Al-Nahar,* Beirut, 6 June 1975.

14. MENA (Middle East News Agency), Cairo reported such a meeting on 27 Apr. 1974 between Arafat and China's ambassador to Damascus. Another one took place between Arafat and the Chinese ambassador to Cairo on 18 June 1974 (Radio Palestine, Cairo).

15. Radio Palestine, Cairo, 2 June 1974.

16. Senator Henry Jackson, who visited Peking in July 1974, was reported as having made a statement to this effect. He added, however, that China was interested in the existence of Israel as a check against Soviet expansion. It was not until 1979, following the Israeli-Egyptian peace accords, that China came out publicly in support of a Palestinian state.

17. See Radio Palestine, Cairo, 2 Sept. 1974.

18. *Al-Akhbar,* Cairo, 6 Sept. 1974.

19. *Filastin al-Thawra,* 9 Oct. 1974, 20. This reflects, of course, Palestinian perception of Chinese stands, not necessarily what the Chinese said or thought.

20. *Literaturnaya Gazeta,* 18 Dec. 1974.

21. *Filastin al-Thawra,* 9 Oct. 1974, 20.

22. For example, *WAFA News Agency,* 27 Jan. 1975, reported such a message from Mao and his government. *Radio Palestine* (San'a) reported similar meetings on 21 Jan. between Faruq Qaddumi, the foreign secretary of the PLO, and the Chinese ambassador in Beirut and on 7 Jan. between Qaddumi-Abu Iyad and the Chinese ambassador in Cairo, (MENA, Cairo, 7 Jan. 1975).

23. Al-Sha'b, 10 Feb. 1975; Radio Palestine, Cairo, 4 Feb. 1975.

24. See R. Israeli, ed., *PLO in Lebanon: Selected Documents* (London: Weidenfeld and Nicolson, 1983), 142–3.

25. On 17 Feb. Arafat met the Chinese ambassador in Damascus (MENA, Cairo); on 3 Mar. Tawfiq Safadi, a senior PLO official, met with the Chinese ambassador in Beirut. (PLO Radio, Beirut).

26. Radio Beirut, 27 Mar. 1975.

27. Chinese deputy prime minister met the new head of the PLO mission in Peking, Hamed Abd-el-Aziz 'Abadi in May 1975, and this encounter was reported to have underlined the friendship between the parties (Radio Damascus, May 12, 1975). 'Abadi was later reported to

have submitted his credentials to the Chinese foreign minister (Radio London in Arabic, 12 Apr. 1975), an honor reserved to ambassadors of foreign governments.

28. *Ma'ariv,* Tel-Aviv, 15 May 1975.

29. *Al-Quds,* Jerusalem, 19 May 1975. This message was seconded by a declaration of the Chinese minister of foreign trade during a reception for a visiting Egyptian trade delegation (*Al-Fajr,* Jerusalem, 30 May 1975).

30. For example, the Arafat-Chinese ambassador in Damascus meeting (Al-Sha'b, Jordan, 22 May 1975). Hanial-Hassan-Chinese ambassador Meeting in Beirut (*Al-Sha'b,* 6 June 1975; *Al-Nahar,* Beirut, 6 June 1975); Radio PLO from the Yemen, 7 June 1975.

31. *Al-Sharq,* Lebanon, 13 June 1975, 1.

32. *Reuter,* Peking, quoted by *Al-Quds,* 20 July 1975. See also Radio PLO, Cairo, 20 Jul. 1975.

33. *Al-Sha'b,* Jordan, 23 Jul. 1975; Radio PLO, Cairo, 21, 24 July 1975; MENA, Cairo, 23 Jul. 1975; *Al-Liwa',* Beirut, 23 Jul. 1975; AP Tokyo, 22 Jul. 1975; *Al-Nahar,* Lebanon, 20 Jul. 1975; *Al-Safir,* Lebanon, 27 Jul. 1975.

34. AP, Beirut, 18 Jul. 1975.

35. *Filastin al-Thawra,* 7 Jul. 1975.

36. *Al-Sayyad,* Lebanon, 13 Jul. 1975, p. 29.

37. *Al-Sha'b,* 13 Aug. 1975.

38. *Reuter,* Hong Kong, 20 Jul. 1975.

39. *Reuter,* Hong Kong, 26 Aug. 1975.

40. *Yediot Aharonot,* Tel-Aviv, 29 Aug. 1975.

41. *Radio PLO,* San'a, 29 Aug. 1975; *Al-Sha'b, Al-Quds, Radio Baghdad,* 9 Sept. 1975.

42. *Al-Sha'b,* 16 Sept. 1975.

43. *Radio Cairo,* 28 Apr. 1976; Al-Quds, 29 Apr. 1976.

44. *Radio Peking,* Arabic, 28 Apr. 1976.

45. *Reuter,* Hong Kong, 29 Apr. 1976.

46. Japan Television, 30 Apr. 1976, quoting the *Chinese News Agency;* PLO Radio in Lebanon, 15 May 1976.

47. *Reuter,* Hong Kong, 30 Apr. 1976.

48. *Reuter,* Beirut, 10 Sept. 1976; *Al-Fajr,* Jerusalem, 10 Sept. 1976.

49. *Al-Sha'b,* Jordan, 10 Sept. 1976.

50. *Reuter,* Hong Kong, 3 Dec. 1976; *Radio PLO,* Beirut, 28 Dec. 1976.

51. *Al-Sha'b,* 1 Sept. 1976.

52. *Akher Sa'a,* Cario, 13 Mar. 1977, 10.

53. *Radio PLO,* Cairo, 25 May 1977.

54. During Abu-Jihad's visit to Peking and his meeting with Li Xiannian this matter was brought up according to *Al-Mustaqbal,* Beirut/Paris, 9 July 1977.

55. *Reuter,* Peking, 30 Oct. 1978.

56. *Reuter,* Peking, 2 Nov. 1978.

57. *Reuter,* Peking, 2 Nov. 1978.

58. AP, Tokyo, 1 Nov. 1978.

59. *Filastin al-Muhtalla,* Lebanon, 20 Nov. 1978, 22.

60. *Filastin al-Muhtalla,* 20 Nov. 1978, 22.

61. *Al-Sha'b,* 20 Feb. 1979. The PFLP's organ *Al-Hadaf* (quoted by *Al-Nahar,* 25 Feb. 1979) joined in the litany of condemnations; The Popular Front for the Liberation of Palestine — General Command (PFLP—GC) also followed suit (*Al-Nahar,* 1 Mar. 1979). See also the *New York Times* of 22 Feb. 1979; and *Al-Quds,* 27 Feb. 1979. Qaddumi tried to mollify the PLO stand by taking a more "neutral" approach which called for the settlement of the conflict by "peaceful means" (*Al-Fajr,* 26 Feb. 1979), but the Chinese did not heed it.

62. *Al-Hawadith,* London, 3 Mar. 1979.

63. *Al-Hamishmar,* Tel-Aviv, 11 Nov. 1979.

64. *Al-Fajr,* 12 Nov. 1979.

65. *Events,* 23 Mar. 1979, 23.

66. *Events,* 23.

67. *Events,* 23.

68. *Radio PLO,* Lebanon, 29 Nov. 1970.

69. *Radio PLO,* Lebanon, 11 Nov. 1979; *Reuter,* Hong Kong, 18 Nov. 1979; *Radio Monte Carlo* (in Arabic) 31 Oct. 1979; *Reuter,* Peking, 22 Aug. 1979.

70. *Al-Mustaqbal,* Lebanon/Paris, 1 Jan. 1979; MENA, Cairo, 19 Apr. 1979; *Radio PLO,* Lebanon, 29 Apr. 1979; *Reuter,* Beirut, 19 Apr. 1979; *Kuwaiti News Agency,* 2 May 1979.

71. *Al-Bayrak,* Lebanon, 9 Nov. 1979.

72. *Al-Ba'th,* Syria, 12 Dec. 1979; Radio Tunis, 24 Dec. 1979.

73. *Al-Hawadith* (Lebanon/London) 6 Jan. 1980.

74. *Radio PLO,* Lebanon, 4 Apr. 1980; 9 Aug. 1980; *Xinhua,* Peking, 11 May 1980.

75. Radio PLO, Lebanon, 26 Aug. 1980.

76. *Al-Anba',* Kuweit, 2 Sept. 1980.

77. UPL, Peking, 18 Aug. 1980.

78. *Radio PLO,* Beirut, 26 Dec. 1980.

79. *Al-Safir,* Lebanon, 10 Oct. 1981; Reuter, Peking, 6 Oct. 1981.

80. *Al-Bayrak,* Lebanon, 2 June 1981.

81. *Radio Monte Carlo,* 3 Sept. 1981.

82. *Al-Yaqdha,* Kuweit, 27 Sept. 1981.

83. *Reuter,* Peking, 6 Oct. 1981.

84. *Reuter,* Peking, 8 Oct. 1981; Agence France Press, 7 Oct. 1981.

85. *Reuter,* Peking, 8 Oct. 1981.

86. *Reuter,* Peking, 10 Oct. 1981.

87. *Reuter,* Peking 8 Oct. 1981.

88. *Radio PLO,* Beirut, 10 Oct. 1981.

89. *Monday Morning,* Beirut, 18 Oct. 1981.

90. *Ma'ariv,* Tel-Aviv, 15 Jan. 1982.

91. A.P. Peking, 9 Jul. 1982.

92. *Radio Monte Carlo,* 22 Aug. 1982.

93. *Agence France Press,* 2 Nov. 1983.

94. A.P. 23 Oct. 1983.

95. A.P. Peking, 5 Nov. 1983.

96. *Al-Usbu' al-Arabi,* 4 Jan. 1984.

97. *Al-Yamama,* Saudi Arabia, 22 Mar. 1984.

98. *Radio Monte Carlo,* 10 Mar. 1984.

99. *Al-Qabas,* Kuweit, 21 May 1984.

100. *Reuter,* 4 May 1984.

101. A.P., 5 May 1984.

102. A.P. Peking, 5 May 1984; *Reuter,* Tokyo, May 14, 1984; *Reuter,* Peking, 9 May 1984.

103. *People's Daily,* 5 May 1984.

104. *Radio Monte Carlo,* 6 May 1984.

105. *Radio Amman,* 7 May 1984; Reuter, 6 May 1984.

106. *Al-Yaqdha,* Kuweit, 8 Aug. 1984.

107. *Agence France Press,* 10 May 1985.

108. *Reuter,* Peking, 10 May 1985.

109. *Filastin al-Thawra,* 18 May 1985; *Reuter,* 10 May 1985.

110. *Saudi News Agency,* 18 Oct. 1985.

111. For example, a Messenger from Arafat visited Peking in Oct. 1985. (*Bayader al-Siyyasi,* Jerusalem, 26 Oct. 1985); Abu Jihad met with the Chinese foreign minister in Amman in December 1985; (*Agence France Press,* 15 Dec. 1985); a message from the Chinese leadership to Arafat in Nov. 1985 (Radio PLO, San'a, 11 Nov. 1985); Arafat's meeting with the Chinese ambassador in Tunis who transmitted his president's greetings for the new year.

112. *Al-Watan-Al-Arabi;* Lebanon, 27 Dec. 1985.

113. *Sawt-al-Sha'b,* Amman, 16 Dec. 1985; Al-Ra'y, Jordan, 21 Nov. 1985.

114. *Sawt-al-Sha'b,* Amman, 16 Dec. 1985.

115. *Sawt-al-Sha'b,* Amman, 16 Dec. 1985.

116. Reuter from Peking reported on 5 Dec. 1985 that the Muslim-populated province of Ningxia has solicited Muslim investment now that development projects have been decentralized in China.

7 THE PLO IN LATIN AMERICA
ROBERT THOMAS BARATTA

Since 1974 there has been a sizeable increase in Arab, particularly Palestinian, activity within Latin America. Over the last decade, Palestinian Arabs, under the aegis of the Palestine Liberation Organization (PLO), have exerted varying degrees of political influence within Latin America. Some see PLO affiliation with regional governments as a result of political blackmail through a "terror network" while others offer a simple explanation based upon the supposed influence of "petrodollars." Close examination of Arab activity in Latin America reveal that neither explanation is accurate. Rather, evidence supports an orchestrated effort by distinct groups under the umbrella of the Palestinian nation-state-without-territorial-boundaries through both diplomatic effort and subversive military activity.

While the actual agenda of this effort remains muddled in political rhetoric, manifestations of its successes are undeniable and easily seen in Latin American capitals and in Washington DC and are felt in international and regional fora, such as the United Nations, the Organization of American States and the Inter-American Development Bank. Tactics vary and seem to be tailored to specific national needs or weaknesses. Overall strategy remains fixed and consistent but not without a touch of historical irony. It appears that Latin American nations, the very republics that were instrumental in creating the State of Israel and partially responsible for the diaspora of the Palestinians in 1947, are now politically and economically manipulated and massaged by the Arabs in a reverse direction.[1] In the discussion that follows, evidence of such manipulation is presented as well as examples of Arabs acting as a unified, purposeful body to that end.

Yasser Arafat removed any doubt of PLO intentions in the Western Hemisphere. At a celebration commemorating the second anniversary of the Nicaraguan Sandinista victory over Anastasio Somoza Debayle and without apology to Leon Trotsky, Arafat expressed traditional solidarity with movements of national liberation and unequivocally stated that "the way to Jerusalem is through Managua."[2] There is little doubt that Arafat's objective is Jerusalem. But, how does one get to Jerusalem through Managua? At the time, Arafat's comments were meant as reaffirmation rather than revelation. Yet, some years hence, observers are shocked by both the nature and extent of Palestinian political, economic, and military penetrations into Latin America.[3]

What follows is a discussion of Palestinian penetrations into Latin America and the direct relationships, if any, between governments of the region and the PLO. Primary analysis examines Latin American motivations for formal and informal links to the PLO. Later, specific national studies are followed by general speculation on future relations.

LATIN AMERICAN MOTIVATIONS

Palestinian penetrations into Latin America are rational developments as one considers the logic of Latin American motivations for beneficial symbiotic relationships with the Arab world. Latin America is a geographic region in the Western Hemisphere made up of various cultures, societies, and political systems. As such, it is grossly inappropriate to view Latin America as a monolithic entity as is any similar view of the Middle East. Each nation in Latin America is separate and has its own national agenda. Each has its distinct strengths and weaknesses. Yet most nations in the region share some bothersome commonalities such as underdevelopment and proximity to the United States. Generally, Latin American nations expend great amounts of economic resources and political energies to overcome these problems. Specifically, these problems serve as impetuses to Latin American nations establishing relationships with the Arab world—hence Palestinian Arabs— as a means to achieve greater national goals. The success of PLO presence and activity in Latin America does not necessarily signify a convergence of PLO and Latin American interests, rather an outgrowth of the convergence of greater Latin American interests with the Arab world.

The following list enumerates several motivations and explanations for the favorable relationships from the Latin American perspectives. These motivations, not necessarily mutually exclusive, include:

1. Cultural affinity
2. Large Latin American ethnic Arab Christian and Muslim minorities
3. Desire for preferential treatment on Arab-oil supplies/OPEC
4. Arab developmental aid to Latin American nations

5. A political and economic counterbalance within the Third World to United States regional hegemony
6. Solidarity with Third World movements of national liberation
7. Political insurance against transnational political violence
8. Institutional concern for Palestinians by the Vatican
9. Residual manifestations of anti-Semitism

CULTURAL AFFINITY

The luso-hispanic traditions of Latin America are culturally closer to those of the Arab world than to Western societies. The Iberian peninsula, home of the Spanish and Portuguese *conquistadores* and explorers, was ruled by Moslem Caliphs for almost eight centuries (711–1492 AD). The Moslems left clear marks on the Iberian cultural and political traditions. The Spanish and Portuguese then transplanted these traditions to the New World.[4] Several aspects of Latin American society and politics still reflect the Moslem influence. These can be seen in the language, architecture, political institutions and ideology, and so forth. Some of these common traditions, albeit separated by generations of socialization and development, today help facilitate relations between Latin America and the Arab world.

LATIN AMERICAN ETHNIC ARAB AND MUSLIM MINORITIES

Several Latin American nations have significant ethnic Arab and Muslim minorities within their populations. At present, their number approaches 2.5 million.[5] The significance of these minorities remains dependent on their size and influence in the host-nation domestic politics. The distinct nature of the Arab and Muslim minorities is somewhat complex and classification equally elusive. When addressing these minorities, the terms Arab and Muslim are not interchangeable although a strong political affinity may exist between the two groups. Arab minorities, both Muslim and Christian, have emigrated from various parts of the Middle East and Africa, principally from Syria, Lebanon, and Palestine. Muslim immigrants came to Latin America from various regions of the world. For example, the former Dutch colony of Suriname has the largest proportionate minority of Muslims in Latin America (about 16 percent) yet these Muslims did not emigrate from the Middle East. Rather, they came from former Dutch colonies half a world away, notably Java.

The history of direct Arab immigration to Latin America is hazy. Records of early immigration are virtually nonexistent. Some available historical records point to modern Arab immigration in the middle and late nineteenth century to the southern cone, the earliest waves to Paraguay and Brazil. Naturally, Arab immigrants went where they were most welcome. Paraguay offered economic incentives to immigrants in the late nineteenth century to overcome the disastrous effects of the loss of 60 percent of its population in the War of Triple Alliance (1865–1870). Brazil, a nation noted for racial and religious tolerance, offered a safe haven and opportunity for all immigrants. Notably, Brazil's Arab population grew to some eighty thousand by 1900.[6] Later, in the early twentieth century, Paraguay and Brazil were joined by Argentina, Chile, and Colombia as centers of large Arab immigration. In general, throughout Latin America, liberal anticlericalism removed most religious prejudice by the early twentieth century. Hence, Arabs could find a new home among the more progressive regimes in the region. Arab minorities are now distributed throughout the entire Americas including Mexico, Cuba, Venezuela, Honduras, Uruguay, El Salvador, Peru, Panama, Bolivia, Nicaragua, and Ecuador.

Why did the Arabs come to Latin America? Early Arab immigration came from the Christian communities of Syria and Lebanon. These Arabs were pushed from their homelands more than drawn toward Latin America. Some religious intolerance and political oppression coupled with unfavorable economic conditions within the Turkish Ottoman Empire contributed to the exodus of Christian Arabs from the region. Later, many Arab men fled to Latin America to evade the Turkish military conscription supporting World War I. Arab immigration intensified during later periods of strife in the Middle East. Notably, the Partition of Palestine in 1947 brought many Palestinian Arabs to Latin America and subsequent Arab-Israeli confrontations caused more migrations.

Regardless of the size of the ethnic Arab or Muslim community in a given nation, the political effectiveness is relatively small. Principally, ethnic Arabs in Latin America are not united. In may regards, they reflect the various cleavages of their homelands and transfer the concomitant divisiveness to their new communities in adopted lands. With few exceptions, ethnic Arab immigrants purposively assimilated into their adopted national societies. Many went so far as changing their ethnic names to hispanic surnames or phonetic equivalents.[7] Yet, many within these ethnic Arab communities in Latin America maintain traditional familial and property ties with the Middle East.[8] Nevertheless, their first loyalty has been to their adopted homeland.

The Latin American Arab and Muslim immigrant traditionally remained apolitical and consciously appreciative of the social and economic benefits and opportunity granted by the adopted nation. In short, they opt for a low political profile, except in the instances where they can participate within the dynamics of their adopted political system. Evidence of this is readily seen among the immigrant communities in Chile, Colombia, Argentina and Brazil where several ethnic Arabs hold national office or serve in the national bureaucracies.

Ethnic Arab support within Latin America for Palestinian issues principally has been evident through economic and political channels. For instance, some Palestinian support groups have been formed at local levels in Brazil, Colombia, Paraguay, and Nicaragua and funds have been forwarded to the PLO and Lebanon.[9] Lately, a new political identity and ethnic awareness is growing within these communities, especially among the middle class and the youth[10] and is manifested in support of Palestinian issues. This is partly a result of increased international participation by Middle East Arabs, in general, and is influenced by the recent immigration into Latin America by Palestinian refugees. This new awareness is militant in its approach to Palestinian issues, as witnessed by the appearance of radical organizations in nations like Brazil which are seeking to replace traditional informal familial support of relatives and friends with formal transnational solidarity on Arab issues. And as Latin American ethnic Arabs and Muslims become more politically active, it is likely that they will exert more pressure on regimes in favor of Arab and Islamic interests. This alone does not explain Latin American support for Palestinian issues. Yet, it is an important component of the complex exegesis.

FAVORABLE TREATMENT FROM ARAB OIL SUPPLIERS

All of Latin America is considered part of the developing world. Modernization and development in Latin America, like other areas of the world, are dependent on energy resources. Although large oil reserves continue to be proven in Latin America, current production is inadequate to meet the needs of national development agenda. As a result, critical gaps exist between oil production and consumption. Alternate energy sources such as hydro-electricity, coal, nuclear energy, and motor grade alcohol have not yet been developed at levels adequate to substitute for petroleum.

Several regional nations are net exporters of oil. Mexico, Venezuela, and Ecuador all export varying amounts and grades of oil. Yet, the combined output of these three nations is inadequate to meet regional fossil energy needs. Hence, alternate sources of oil resources are required. Since Arab nations control half of the world's oil reserves and export over one-fourth the world's oil, they are convenient suppliers for Latin American energy short-falls. Although Latin America's energy relationship with the Arab world has decreased significantly with falling oil prices over the past decade, it serves as a foundation for interregional cooperation today.

Smaller nations in Latin America remain relatively unaffected by Arab oil as they satisfy the bulk of their oil needs through domestic production and/or imported oil from Latin American sources in Mexico, Venezuela, and Ecuador. Also, Cuba and Nicaragua are beneficiaries of Soviet oil supplies in addition to regional and Arab sources. Other larger Latin American nations with developing industrial capacities have substantially greater energy demands, for which Arab nations fill the critical gap between domestic production and consumption. Brazil imports oil from virtually every available oil source. Argentina imports large quantities of oil from Iraq, Iran, and Saudi Arabia. Chile receives shipments from Iran and Saudi Arabia. Algeria services nearly all of Paraguay's fossil energy needs, albeit minor in comparison to the rest of Latin America. Uruguay imports oil from Kuwait, Iraq, and Saudi Arabia. In addition, Venezuela and Ecuador, both members of OPEC, maintain close relationships with all Arab oil producers.

Guaranteed access to Arab oil supplies and more importantly, favorable pricing of the oil, are conditional not only upon the buyer's ability to pay for the resource in cash or suitable trade, but also on favorable diplomatic relations. While the former conditions will be discussed at another time under the rubric of developmental aid and trade, the latter bears mention here. Since 1973 there has been little doubt about the value of oil as both a political and an economic tool by the Arab nations. Arab nations have used their oil resources through OPEC to gain diplomatic leverage in support of Arab issues, particularly the Palestinian homeland issue. Such a linkage was alluded to as early as 1973 when Lebanese foreign minster Fuad Naffah toured seven Latin American nations on behalf of the Arab League stating "no underdeveloped country that backs the just cause of the Arab world will suffer from an energy shortage."[11] Those Latin American nations dependent on Arab oil supply are most susceptible to this leverage. Coincidentally or not, Latin American positions relevant to Palestinian issues shifted considerably since 1973 in favor of the Arabs.

ARAB TRADE AND DEVELOPMENTAL AID

Arab trade and developmental aid are linked to Arab oil supply. Despite Latin America's great need for Arab oil, its ability to pay for it has been deteriorating over the years. This leads us to the following irony. Prior to 1970 Latin America was struggling to develop economically and break its bonds of dependency on the industrialized world, particularly on the United States. As previously stated, development programs are fueled by oil. The two OPEC oil shocks of 1973 and 1979 disrupted Latin American development plans by placing increased fiscal burdens on national governments. Some nations, like Argentina, Mexico, Peru, and Brazil, incurred huge debts that now threaten their political and economic stability. These debts are financed through the industrialized world's banks, hence strengthening Latin American economic dependence upon the industrialized world.

Latin America has sought alternate means of finance to fund both oil needs and development of alternate energy sources. The Arab nations have provided that alternate means. Especially since 1973, these two regions have been seeking closer economic cooperation. Although this economic cooperation is fading under the pressure of lower oil revenues, the Arab nations not only possessed the oil resources but also large money reserves for developmental aid and loans. On a cumulative basis, the Arab oil producers have cofinanced sixteen development projects at a total of $68 million through the Special Fund of OPEC and the Inter-American Development Bank (IDB).[12] Additionally, individual Latin American nations have negotiated favorable loans from Arab sources, such as the Saudi Fund for Economic and Social Development. Since 1977 Arab capital investment has been placed in several joint-venture banking operations in which Brazil, Argentina, and Peru have been major beneficiaries. The IDB itself is informally linked to Arab financial institutions like the Saudi Fund for Development, the Islamic Development Bank, the Abu Dhabi Fund for Arab Economic Development, and the Kuwaiti Fund for Arab Economic Development.[13] All this is in addition to private Arab investment.

Latin America, for its part, provides valuable resources to the Arab world. It is rich in the resources that the Arab world lacks. Latin America exports raw materials for construction, minerals, food products, technical "know-how," and armaments. Whereas Latin America still imports more from the Arab world than it exports to them, trade linkages are growing. Inexorably tied to these trade linkages are political interests. The quid pro quo for Arab developmental aid is Latin American political support for Arab interests. This will become readily apparent within individual national surveys later in this study.

A POLITICAL ECONOMIC COUNTERBALANCE WITHIN THE THIRD WORLD TO UNITED STATES REGIONAL HEGEMONY

Latin America has always been concerned about United States hegemony in the region. General Latin American nationalism assesses this hegemony as counterproductive to political and economic development. Hence, most nations in the region have sought convenient counterbalances to United States political and economic hegemony. Peruvian President Alan Garcia, a proponent on this issue, recently proposed the formation of a new regional solidarity organization with exclusive membership, slighting the United States, as a united front to address the perceived unequal North-South relationship with the United States. Other counterbalances have also been explored. The most obvious counterbalance candidate has been the principal American antagonist, the Soviet Union. Yet, this too has resulted in superpower hegemony and, at times, high political cost and risk.

The advent of the Nonaligned Movement or Group of 77 provided Latin America with a viable alternative. The Arab nations, through the Nonaligned Movement, projected economic and political influence into Latin America. A symbiotic relationship between the regions has developed over the past fifteen years within international fora and in coordinated efforts to bring about the New International Economic Order. Arab nations categorically have supported Latin American economic and political interests and have nurtured an interregional interdependence. Some broad interests areas include the Law of the Sea, international debt, trade, and nonintervention. For their efforts, Arab nations are able to tear Latin American nations away from classical dependence on the United States and the concomitant unqualified support for American foreign policy, especially in support of Israel. The result of new interdependence is favorable consideration by Latin American nations on Arab issues, notably the Palestinian homeland. Support for this issue and for Palestinian groups become symbolic of Latin American prerogative and independence of action. For instance, in the United Nations, Latin American nations vote consistently against the United States and Israel on Palestinian issues. This type of support is more convenient in that it is removed from the East-West confrontation and incurs little cost or risk. Obviously, not all nations are overly concerned about American hegemony nor do all nations support Palestinians as a counterbalance to American hegemony. Once again, this motivation is only one part of a larger explanation.

SOLIDARITY WITH THIRD WORLD MOVEMENTS
OF NATIONAL LIBERATION

One man's radicalism is another man's pragmatism. Not all nations view
relations with Arab nations strictly within the context of economics. Sometimes support for Palestinian groups can be viewed on ideological merit.
Within the Nonaligned Movement and the Third World there is considerable
support for movements of national liberation among national elites in Latin
America. At times, rhetorical support for these movements within international organizations is supplemented with significant material support in the
name of revolutionary solidarity. Solidarity is an important notion. The
official PLO information bulletin, *Palestine,* states in each of its issues that:
solidarity is an important weapon for helping the peoples of the world
overcome oppression and injustice. The world forces of liberation, of which
we are proud to be a part, are the emerging forces, and it is to us that the
future belongs. The forces of oppression have had their day, and shall be
consigned to the dustbin of history. Palestinian groups number prominently
among these liberation movements. Two regional regimes, Cuba and
Nicaragua, openly provide material support to Palestinian groups in the
forms of weapons, training, material sustenance, and diplomatic legitimacy.
Other progressive regimes in the region, such as Mexico and Peru, tolerate
the presence of these groups within their national borders, offer political
support and sanctuary, and provide diplomatic legitimacy in the form of an
interest section, trade office, or embassy.

POLITICAL INSURANCE AGAINST
INTERNATIONAL TERRORISM

In the individual country studies that follow, it will become clear that Latin
American nations which support Palestinian issues or lend support to
Palestinian organizations coincidentally tend to be spared the ravages of
international terrorism. Latin America in the past ranked among the lowest
in regions of the world victimized by international terrorism. Although
several Latin American nations currently are plagued by indigenous insurgencies that use terrorism as an integral part of their violent political
repertoire, few of these insurgent groups have solid links to the PLO.

Extraregional support for indigenous groups in Latin America, particularly from the PLO, is also minimized. What support there is, is largely in
the form of rhetorical expressions of solidarity. This is seen clearly in the

cases of Chile, Brazil, and Argentina. Yet, nations that support Israeli positions or are antagonistic to Palestinian organizations tend to find substantial extraregional support within their domestic insurgencies. This was the case in Somoza's Nicaragua where the PLO provided matériel and personnel to the Sandinistas and in Guatemala today where PLO rhetoric rails against a regime partly supported by Israeli arms. [14]

INSTITUTIONAL CONCERN FOR PALESTINIANS BY THE VATICAN

Over 90 percent of Latin America is nominally Roman Catholic and a slightly higher percentage Christian. Some estimate that one quarter of all Palestinians are Christian and about 35 percent of the PLO itself is Christian. Furthermore, Catholics allegedly appear in leadership positions in all eight factions of the PLO. [15] Although the institutional church has been weakened over the last century, it maintains political clout in some nations and moral clout in virtually all of Latin America. Papal concern for peace and social justice permeates the institutional church and the more radical elements of liberation theology of the popular church. While personal papal concern for the welfare of Palestinian refugees and over recent tragic events in Lebanon raise Palestinian issues about politics to the heights of morality, liberation theology weaves the morality of peace and social justice into the previous discussion on national liberation. The effects of papal concern are difficult to measure, but the solidarity between radicalized Christian groups and Palestinian groups is clearly evident in various Latin American capitals. Both papal and institutional concern lend the Palestinian cause a legitimacy on which national government actions may find justification.

RESIDUAL MANIFESTATION OF ANTI-SEMITISM

Strains of classical anti-Semitism still infect parts of Latin America. General disdain for Jews is rooted in the Iberian heritage. The Atlantic Ocean was no obstacle to the long arm of the infamous Inquisition. Spanish and Portuguese attempts to purify both religion and politics permeated colonial policy. As a result, Jews and converts alike were prohibited entry into the New World. Those who disregarded the royal decree tempted fate and came under the scrutiny of the New World Inquisition headquartered in Lima, Peru. Since the Portuguese were more relaxed in their enforcement of ecclesiastic ordinances, many Jews made their way to the Portuguese colonies. During

the Portuguese Babylonian Captivity (1580–1640), when Spain controlled
Portugal, many Jews and converts immigrated into Spanish America across
colonial boundaries. By the time of independence, Jews assimilated into the
criollo (Spanish descent born in South America) and *mozambo* (Portuguese
descent born in South America) population of Chile, Argentina, and Brazil.
Later Jewish migration from Europe and Russia, beginning in 1848, brought
significant numbers of Jews to Latin America. These immigrants set up
enclaves (ghettos) apart from the Spanish communities and preserved their
cultural identity. Because they maintained their sectarian identity in the New
World, the Jews were easy targets for suspicion and discrimination. At the
turn of the century, the Russian revolution and its radical ideologies shook
the sensibilities of the Latin American elites. The politically unsophisti-
cated, a clear majority in Latin America at the time, grouped all that was
Russian with Bolsheviks. As a result, many Russian Jews suffered. For
instance, in Argentina, the Tragic Week of 1919 (*La Semana Tragica*)
resulted in over eight hundred dead and four thousand injured.

Latin American politics during the 1930s were confused, at best. The
devastation of the Great Depression prompted regional social upheaval.
Reactionary regimes that stepped in to restore law and order functioned with
growing fascism in Europe as a backdrop. Additionally, refugees from all
over Europe migrated to the Americas. The Spanish civil war pushed many
Republicans into Cuba, Argentina, and Chile. At the same time Jewish
refugees were fleeing the Nazi encroachments into Europe and Stalin's
ruthless pogroms in Russia. Immigrations into Latin America placed additional burdens on economies already destroyed by the worldwide depression
and political corruption. Moreover, the xenophobia of the early twentieth
century reemerged in the late 1930s. As a result, most Latin American
nations closed their borders to immigrants. Bolivia, the primary point of
disembarkation of over ten thousand German Jews en route to other nations,
stopped issuing visas in May 1940.[16] Brazil, attempting to counter Nazi
infiltrations into domestic politics, started an enormous Brazilianization
project in 1938 aimed at ending any and all foreign influence and cultures
within its borders. The several ethnic enclaves within Brazil, including a
substantial Jewish community, were made to assimilate or emigrate. The
Nazi influence in Argentina during World War II kept Jewish activity there at
a low profile.

After the war, Latin America was instrumental in the creation of the State
of Israel and the subsequent diaspora of the Palestinians. All Latin American
nations established normal diplomatic relations with Israel; whereas until

1959 only six Latin American states hosted resident Arab missions. That number increased to thirteen in 1972 and today, sixteen Arab nations maintain missions in at least one Latin American state. Only Nicaragua, Cuba, and Guyana have no diplomatic relations with Israel. Nicaragua and Cuba are openly antagonistic toward Jews and Israelis.[17]

Generally, anti-Semitism is not a major factor in the international relations of Latin American and the Middle East, but anti-Semitism does occasionally appear. Rather, in addition to the resurgent neo-Nazism, the radical left has linked Jews with Israel and Zionism and in turn with imperialism and racism. These leftist groups are quick to point out Israeli material support for repressive regimes in Central America and chronicle Israeli arms sales to other Latin American governments. Regional national liberation movements find this Israeli support inconvenient and readily join Palestinian groups in denunciation of Israeli intervention and adventurism. Hence Latin American governments find themselves caught by this and Arab economic pressures. While this rarely results in anti-Semitism, it does pressure government policy away from Israeli support. Once again, not all Latin American governments or societies are affected. Not all Latin American nations have Jewish communities. Moreover, anti-Semitism is neither pervasive nor ubiquitous. Anti-Semitism, as a causal variable, is but another component of a larger explanation.

PALESTINIAN LIBERATION ORGANIZATION STRATEGY

Latin America is clearly peripheral to PLO interests. There is unlikely to be a cause within Latin America that would prompt the PLO to jeopardize its own political agenda let alone its survival. Despite PLO activism in Latin America, the main Palestinian agenda remains fixed: unconditional restoration of the Palestinian homeland. The ultimate aim of the PLO has been articulated within the Palestinian National Covenant and refined through the years. Simply stated, "Palestine is the homeland of the Arab Palestinian people; it is an individual part of the Arab homeland, and the Palestinian people are an integral part of the Arab nation."[18] The PLO has decreed that "armed struggle is the only way to liberate Palestine . . . the Palestinian Liberation Organization, representative of the Palestinian revolutionary forces is responsible for the Palestinian Arab people's movement in its struggle—to retrieve its homeland, liberate and return to it and exercise the right of self-determination in it. . . ."[19] The PLO is totally committed to the liberation of Palestine by any means, but primarily through armed struggle which implies a worldwide confrontation with its enemy, Zionism. To win the struggle, the PLO has pursued a fluid political program over the past two decades including the axes of "the linking of the Palestinian struggle with the overall Arab struggle via a front of all the national and progressive forces hostile to imperialism, Zionism and neo-colonialism; and solidarity with the world struggle against imperialism, Zionism and reaction, and for national liberation."[20] Linkages between the PLO and world revolutionary movements are a self-defined imperative. In Latin America this imperative is a double-edged sword. PLO cooperation with revolutionary movements in the region often conflicts with the legitimate Arab economic and diplomatic overtures previously discussed. As these overtures produce Latin American support for Palestinian issues and undermine regional support for Israel, they are complemented by domestic ethnic Arab minority activity supporting the overall Arab struggle.

Overt and determined support for Latin American revolutionary movements by the PLO tends to reverse or destroy favorable relations established through legitimate diplomatic means while politically embarrassing loyal domestic ethnic minorities. At the same time, regimes hostile to the Palestinian cause are open game. Nicaragua was a former PLO target because Somoza was a strong supporter of Israel and unsympathetic to the PLO. El Salvador, as a recipient of both matériel and training from Israel, has been another target of the PLO. In turn, El Salvador continues to support Israel in international fora and has moved its embassy in Israel to Jerusalem. Guatemala, another recipient of Israeli aid, is neither pro-Israeli nor anti-Palestinian in its foreign policy yet is victimized by insurgents in solidarity with the PLO. Areas of conflict between PLO support for revolutionary groups and Arab diplomacy are in virtually all nations in South America and Mexico. In this regard, Chile, Argentina, Brazil, Peru, and Colombia standout. At the same time, the importance of political support for the Palestinian Liberation Organization and its cause is underscored in the "Palestinian National Council Political Resolutions" at Algiers on 22 February 1983, when the organization indicated the necessity of "strengthening relations with friendly countries in Latin America and working to widen the sphere of friendship there."[21]

Recent events affecting the PLO, notably its forced departure from Beirut, have limited active PLO involvement with Latin American revolutionary movements. Yasser Arafat recently cautioned that PLO support "has not been weakened, but its accuracy has been reduced because of our involvement in the reconstruction operation."[22] When pressed to determine if the

PLO will renew its activities in support of national liberation movements once the institutions are revived, Arafat declined comment. Whether this is significant as a change in the PLO strategy advocating solidarity for national liberation movements or is a refinement in favor of effective Arab diplomacy remains to be seen. Meantime, PLO penetrations into Latin America persist.

In summary, PLO regional strategy in Latin America has followed two general paths. The organization has been involved in both subversive military activity and legitimate diplomatic missions. The greatest success has been obtained when PLO methods and individual Latin American organization goals converged into mutual supportive action. This is best viewed at the hub of Latin American PLO activity, in Cuba and Nicaragua.

CUBA

The beachhead in the Western Hemisphere for the PLO is Cuba. Although Cuba was the only nation in the Americas to vote against the partition of Palestine in 1974, it joined other world nations in extending diplomatic recognition to the State of Israel. With Cuba as the champion of regional "liberation organizations," coupled with its involvement as a Soviet surrogate around the world and with Fidel Castro's personal ambitions manifested in aspirations for leadership of the Nonaligned Movement, the Cuban international agenda and PLO strategy in the region were placed on a convergent path in the early 1970s. Castro's leadership of the national liberation movements was initiated at the first conference of the Organization of Solidarity of the Peoples of Asia, Africa, and Latin America held at Havana in 1966. By the close of 1967, Palestinians were being trained in Cuba at special guerrilla training camps directed by KGB Colonel Vadim Kotchergine.[23] Already in 1968, Cuban military personnel aided PLO activities in North Africa and Iraq. In early 1969, Cuban and PLO officers participated in joint training programs in the Soviet Union. Cubans from this training group were reported in some PLO guerrilla operations in the Sinai later in 1969. This type of loose cooperation continued through 1972 until Castro and PLO leaders formalized their relationship at Algiers.

In 1973 at the Algiers Nonaligned conference, Fidel Castro announced that Cuba no longer recognized Israel, and in 1974 Cuba allowed the PLO to open its first office in Latin America. This cemented Cuban-Palestinian relations and provided the PLO with a bridge into the Western Hemisphere. At the same time, the *mariage de convenance* affected between proponents of national liberation in the Middle East and Latin America not only strengthened Castro's leadership position within the Third World but also helped to solve numerous command and control problems for Moscow-coordinated mischief in the region.

Interestingly enough, interregional solidarity was not limited to rhetorical political support. An ersatz cultural exchange program between national liberation movements of Latin America and the Middle East, through Soviet sponsorship, provided scholarships to Patrice Lumumba University in Moscow with guaranteed employment after graduation. Training camps in Lebanon, Iraq, and Syria provided further technical skills and some on-the-job training for successful graduates. From there, the graduate guerrillas returned home to practice their new skills. Although the previous discussion may appear facetious, it is important to note that many soldiers of national liberation follow this pattern of education and training in the execution of political violence. And Cuba, for its part, provides support and guidance for both Latin Americans and Palestinians in military subversion activities. [24]

On the diplomatic side, Cuba is an outspoken supporter of Palestinian claims. Castro and his ministers consistently speak out in favor of the PLO and the restoration of the Palestinian homeland. Havana has hosted numerous meetings of several groups supporting the Palestinian cause. Significantly, Cuban activity in support of the PLO increased in 1979 — in conjunction with Sandinista National Liberation Front (FSLN) pressures on the Somoza regime — and continued into 1983, coupled with solidarity efforts for the Farabundo Marti National Liberation Front (FMLN) in El Salvador. In June 1982 Cuba permitted the PLO to upgrade its representation in Cuba to the ambassadorial level. Although disruption of PLO activity in Lebanon during 1983 may have crippled the PLO's capability to provide substantial support for Cuba and for Latin American movements of national liberation, it continued to support them with political rhetoric. Cuban rhetorical support for the PLO remained constant during its struggle in Lebanon although no reported Cuban matériel or troops were sent to protect the PLO.

Cuba has been the center of PLO activity in Latin America. Its relationship with the PLO seems to have grown out of mutual convenience rather than from deeply rooted ideological bonds or moral indebtedness. Castro and the PLO seem to cooperate as a gesture of solidarity complementing their own political agenda: Castro's quest for a key role in international leadership and a Palestinian homeland, respectively. With common enemies, they remain closely allied for the present. Sandinista Nicaragua, on the other hand, provides us with a different case.

NICARAGUA

Nicaraguan-Palestinian relations predate the FSLN (Sandinista National Liberation Front) victory over Somoza. It is reported that as early as 1969 Sandinista official Benito Escobar met in Mexico City with PLO representatives to discuss placing fifty-two Sandinista guerrillas in Tyre, Lebanon and in Fatah camps in Algeria for training.[25] The PLO intensified its support for FSLN rebels and was instrumental in the eventual overthrow of Somoza in 1979. By its own admission, the PLO provided not only military training but also matériel and troops.[26] In the decade between 1969 and 1979, several PLO-trained FSLN guerrillas remained in the Middle East and participated in terrorist attacks. Notably, FSLN adherent Patricio Arguello Ryan joined PFLP terrorist Leila Khaled in the failed hijack attempt on an Israeli El Al airliner from Tel Aviv en route to New York via London on 6 September 1970. (Arguello was shot dead and Khaled was captured.) FSLN press spokesman Jorge Mandi gave a testimonial to FSLN-PLO cooperation in an interview with the Kuwaiti newspaper *al Watan* on 7 June 1979. "In the early Seventies Nicaraguan and Palestinian blood was spilled together in Amman and in other placed during the Black September battles."[27] Yasser Arafat corroborated this to his Nicaraguan audience in June 1980: "The links between us are not new, your comrades did not come to our country just to train, but also to fight.[28] Sandinista Interior Minister Tomas Borge Martinez was trained by Fatah as were many other FSLN officials. Coincidentally, Borge spent a portion of the early 1970s as Castro's special emissary to the Middle East.

The PLO stepped up its aid to the FSLN as the FSLN appeared more confident of victory. In July 1979 a planeload of weapons was sent to the FSLN as military negotiations took place between PLO representative Abu Jihad and the FSLN representations in Beirut. A mutual assistance pact was adopted, and later—after Somoza's fall—full diplomatic representation was afforded the PLO in Managua. On 11 August 1979, just three weeks after the FSLN defeated Somoza, the Baghdad *Voice of Palestine* triumphantly proclaimed that a "PLO office will replace the Zionist enemy embassy in Managua."[29] In the meantime, the PLO dispatched personnel to Managua to assist in the FSLN consolidation of power. The PLO also facilitated over ten million US dollars in loans to Managua from Arab benefactors. In addition, they continue to participate in several facets of the Sandinista government but remain largely in the security forces. Clear evidence of this came from Arafat in 1982 when he admitted that PLO pilots were serving in Nicaragua,

El Salvador, and Angola.[30] In April 1985 the Danish Press reported a
Nicaraguan national airline Fokker F-27 Friendship aircraft crash in Green-
land. The dead pilot, Ahmed Khalid Abdallah Thamer, and surviving
copilot, Ibrahim Mansour, were both PLO members allegedly employed by
the Sandinista government.[31] Current estimates place around fifty to seventy
PLO diplomatic and military personnel in Nicaragua. It is the largest PLO
delegation in any Latin American nation.

Sandinista Nicaragua remains a staunch supporter of the Palestinian
cause. There is some indication from official Sandinista sources that this
support is a solemn obligation of the FSLN in partial repayment to the PLO
for its critical support of the Sandinista struggle.[32] Nicaragua today joins
Cuba as a bastion of PLO support in the Americas. The official Nicaraguan
government maintains a staunchly pro-Palestinian position. Ambassador
Javier Chamorro Mora articulated this position.

> Nicaragua has vehemently maintained, in the international arena, the need and the
> duty to find a just, lasting and peaceful solution to the problems of the Middle East.
> A key issue in this situation is the Palestinian question, to which there can be no
> solution without recognition of the respect for the right to existence of the
> Palestinian people and the need to restore to them their inalienable national rights,
> including the right to recover their own territory and to establish there own
> state."[33]

EL SALVADOR

The PLO is active in other areas of Central America. Particularly, PLO
relations with El Salvador demonstrate a conflict between the use of diplomatic leverage and military subversion. Prior to 1979 El Salvador could be
classified as a moderate supporter of the Palestinian cause. The Salvadoran
ambassador to the United Nations often added his nation's vote to the Arab
nations' on Palestinian issues in the United Nations General Assembly. But
PLO support for the Nicaraguan FSLN and its eventual victory over Somoza
seemingly encouraged PLO activism with other Latin American national
liberation movements. In August 1979, one month after the FSLN victory,
representatives of the Salvadoran LP-28 guerrilla movement—organizationally tied to the Popular Revolutionary Army (ERP)—petitioned PLO
officials in Beirut for aid. Later in 1980, while Arafat was in Managua
commemorating the first anniversary of FSLN victory, the PLO openly
admitted its "material and human assistance" to Salvadoran guerrillas
including "weapons, military training and Palestinian cadre . . ."[34] Conse-

quently, official diplomatic relations between El Salvador and Arab nations deteriorated. Further, PLO support for Salvadoran guerrillas politically compromised over two thousand Salvadorans of Palestinian descent and rendered them politically suspect. At present, El Salvador maintains no formal diplomatic relations with Arab nations and joins Costa Rica as the only Latin American nations with embassies in Jerusalem. El Salvador has accepted Israeli military arms and aid, at least since 1980. Needless to say, El Salvador has modified it support in international fora to more accurately reflect the political reality of its current diplomatic relations. For its part, the PLO maintains a steady vitriolic attack on the Salvadoran government, although PLO shipments of arms and other aid have been stopped through the concerted interdiction of the United States and the Salvadoran government. PLO capabilities to assist the Salvadoran guerrillas have deteriorated, as mentioned earlier, by the PLO dislocation from Beirut.

Institutional links between the PLO and Salvadoran guerrilla groups are facilitated through Nicaragua and Cuba. Additional contacts were made directly with the PLO in Beirut. The most important linkage has been Shafik Handal, a Salvadoran of Palestinian descent, who is Chief of the Salvadoran Communist party.[35] Both he and the late Salvador Cayetano Carpio met with Yasser Arafat, Abu Jihad, and George Habash's Popular Front in Lebanon to exploit pledges of revolutionary solidarity. "We and the Palestinian revolution are in the same trench fighting the same enemy . . . American imperialism . . . and Zionism."[36]

In the past, Salvadoran guerrilla groups have included Israeli targets in their attacks. When the Popular Liberation Force (FPL) kidnapped the South African Ambassador to El Salvador, as terms to the ransom, they demanded El Salvador sever relations with Israel and establish relations with the PLO. Following this, the Israeli embassy in San Salvador was bombed. Guerrilla forces have also claimed they destroyed Israeli military equipment at Ilopango airport in San Salvador.

PLO activity in El Salvador seems motivated solely out of solidarity for movements of national liberation and to its own vendetta against Israel. Perhaps the PLO was encouraged by its successful support of the FSLN in Nicaragua in prematurely pledging support for the Salvadoran FMLN. This time, the support resulted in severe diplomatic consequences. Open and continued support for the FMLN by the PLO threatens PLO relations with a large part of Latin America. It raises the visibility of the PLO as a radical element bent on military subversion and shows its willingness to meddle in Latin American domestic politics. This is anathema, not only to regimes on the political right but also to moderates, and undercuts the legitimate diplomatic efforts of other Arab nations. Since the PLO was forced out of Beirut in 1983, its support for the FMLN has waned. This may have given the PLO cause and circumstance to reassess its ill-advised adventure into El Salvador.

MEXICO

Mexico has been tolerant of national liberation movements since its own revolution in the early twentieth century. Some consider Mexico City the Paris of Latin America; as in Paris, revolutionary emigres from other Latin American capitals readily find refuge within the city and society. The single ruling party, the Institutional Revolutionary Party (PRI) permits this tolerance within certain limits; the limits are domestic politics and foreign participation in the Mexican political process. Violation of these limits places the emigres privileged status in jeopardy.

The PLO is one group among many revolutionary movements in Mexico City. PLO-Mexican relations reached their peak during the administration of Luis Echeverria Alvarez (1970–1976). Echeverria's leftist personal politics and anti-Zionist position placed the Mexican government closer than ever to the Palestinian cause and the PLO. In 1976 Echeverria allowed the PLO to open an information office in Mexico City. Later, his successor, President Jose Lopez Portillo, continued cautious support for the PLO in conjunction with Mexican support for other national liberation movements, particularly in Nicaragua and El Salvador.

Since 1982, however, Mexico has backed away from its close relationship with the PLO. President Miguel de la Madrid Hurtado does not hold the same views as his predecessors and has moderated Mexico's international position over the past three years. Nevertheless, the PLO continues its penetration into Mexican domestic politics. The PLO has active linkages with opposition parties such as the PST (Socialist Workers Party), the PSUM (Unified Socialist Party of Mexico), and the PRT (Revolutionary Workers Party), and with various student and community groups. The PRI, moving to curb PLO activity within Mexico, appears to be reassessing its present relationship.

HONDURAS

PLO activity in Honduras is unofficial and largely covert. The government of Honduras affords the PLO no special status, nor does it allow it free access within its borders. The PLO operates among the ethnic Arab community, centered in San Pedro Sula, from which it receives occasional financial support.

GUATEMALA

Guatemala is a popular target of the PLO. PLO rhetorical attacks are critical of Guatemalan domestic politics, but its major effort is aimed at Guatemalan-Israeli military cooperation.[37] Unconfirmed reports placed some PLO cadre in Guatemala, supporting indigenous guerrilla groups. This is possible yet unlikely, since the PLO has not established formal institutional links with Guatemalan guerrilla groups as it has in El Salvador and Nicaragua.

PANAMA

Panamanian international politics have appeared to be left-of-center ever since the Panamanian revolution under General Omar Torrijos. This was most evident in the Panamanian support for the FSLN.[38] (The broad coalition formed to defeat the dictatorship of Anastasio Somoza in Nicaragua brought together many forces from the entire political spectrum. Leaders in Panama, Costa Rica, and Venezuela, all had a personal dislike for Somoza.) Panamanian government cooperation with the FSLN facilitated greater interaction with support groups such as the PLO and the FMLN. Panama continued its relationship with the PLO beyond the FSLN victory in Nicaragua, and in September 1979 allowed the PLO to set up an unofficial office in Panama. Panama, under General Manuel Antonio Noriega, continues to support Palestinian issues and to benefit from Arab trade and investment throughout the isthmus.[39]

Arab support for General Noriega became especially important as the current political crisis erupted in June 1987, resulting in a marked deterioration of US-Panamanian bilateral relations. Later, after twin drug-related indictments in Florida courts against General Noriega and his subsequent de facto *coup d'état* in February 1988, the United States imposed broad economic sanctions. Initial actions caused severe liquidity problems for the Noriega regime as US dollars, legal tender in Panama, disappeared and banks closed. The Noriega regime, fighting for its survival in spite of the US sanctions, turned toward alternate sources of support and dollars to meet the government payrolls. Ousted Panamanian President Arturo Delvalle and his ambassador in Washington, Juan Sosa, claim that Libya provided the Noriega regime a $20 million loan during this critical time. Although neither

Libya nor the Noriega regime has confirmed this revelation, General Noriega presented to the secretary of the Libyan People's Bureau in Panama, Dr. Abu' Ajila al-Durayi, in late August a medal in honor of Colonel Mu'ammar al-Qadhdhafi for "leading international revolution against domination and colonialism the world over."[40] Other diplomatic efforts with the Arab world have begun to bear fruit. On 13 September 1988, the Noriega regime and the Republic of Sudan announced the establishment of diplomatic relations.[41]

VENEZUELA

Venezuela is a member of OPEC and a close friend of the Arab world. Yet, Venezuela continues to give the PLO the cold shoulder. In the past, Venezuela has been critical of national liberation movements since it was victimized itself by Castro-inspired revolutionaries in the early 1960s. Venezuelan support for Palestinian issues in the United Nations has been independent of its relations with the PLO but clearly linked to its affiliation with the Arab world through its OPEC membership. Given present circumstances, the PLO is likely to gain neither political recognition from Venezuelan nor unofficial offices in Caracas.

COLOMBIA

Colombia has been supportive of Palestinian issues in international fora but has rejected PLO political overtures categorically. Colombia's domestic problems with indigenous guerrillas place the PLO and the Colombian government at an impasse. The PFLP has expressed Marxist solidarity with Colombia's M-19 guerrillas. Moreover, the PLO has trained M-19 cadre in Lebanon. Colombia maintains friendly relations with Israel and participated in the United Nations Emergency Force (UNEF) in the Sinai. Colombia's leadership within the Contadora peace process in Central America and former President Betancur's rapprochement with three out of four Colombian guerrilla groups undercut legitimate revolutionary activity against the government. Alleged radical Arab complicity in Colombia's cocaine connection—principally through Libya and the PLO—adds to the unlikelihood of a change in current Colombian attitude toward the PLO.

ECUADOR

Ecuador attempts to maintain a neutral position in relation to Middle East politics. As a member of OPEC, it has close relations with oil-producing

Arab states; yet it hosts only one embassy from the Arab world, that of Egypt. Paradoxically, while Ecuador wants and receives Arab financial assistance for national development purposes, some of its military hardware needs are supplied by Israel. Ever since former President Carter's initiation of restraint in US conventional arms transfers to the Third World in the late 1970s cut US arms exports to Ecuador, Israel has willingly filled the gap.[42] With an active border dispute and growing domestic political violence, arms are essential to Ecuadoran national security. Additionally, some reports place Israeli security advisors in Ecuador.

Ecuador's status in OPEC, coupled with internal pressures from its domestic ethnic Arab minority, place Ecuador's delicate association with Israel in jeopardy. Late in 1981 Ecuador moved to counterbalance Arab pressures by permitting the PLO to open an office in Quito which served as an information office. It was subsequently blocked by the Ecuadoran National Security Council. There the PLO status is a direct result of Arab diplomatic pressures and Ecuadoran political convenience. Since Ecuador has no significant movements of national liberation threatening its national government, the PLO is not at risk following its solidarity strategy.[43] Yet from Ecuador the PLO can support any of its own activities in the Andes.

PERU

Peru today is a government under siege. While the size of its international debt burdens any economic recovery, Maoist-style guerrillas from the *Sendero Luminoso* (Shining Path) have terrorized large segments of its society since the early 1980s. Peru, after intense lobbying, was chosen as the headquarters for the petrodollars of ARLABANK (Arab-Latin America Bank) in 1977.[44] Subsequently, in 1979, Peru allowed the PLO to open an information office in Lima. The PLO representative, Issam Bseisso, established institutional linkages with both Peruvian student groups and radical political parties. Bseisso was recently replaced by Husain 'Abd al-Khalik.

Peruvian support for Palestinian issues has been consistently positive. For its part, PLO solidarity for Peru's notorious *Sendero Luminoso* has been guarded. The *Sendero Luminoso* is a nihilistic group noted for its indiscriminate attacks. Even the Soviet Union, which maintains both diplomatic and military presence in Peru, has not been immune from its wrath. If the PLO would support the *Sendero Luminoso* it could jeopardize its important relationship with Moscow. Furthermore, it is unlikely that the innately distrustful *Sendero Luminoso* would accept any foreign help. Since the PLO remains in Lima on a less than diplomatic basis, its survival there is at the pleasure of the Peruvian government. As long as the PLO avoids involvement in Peruvian politics, its favorable status is virtually assured.

PARAGUAY

Paraguay has always been sensitive to Palestinian matters and consistently supports the Arab world on Palestinian issues. As the site of early Syrian and Lebanese immigrations, Paraguay has developed close relationships with both Syria and Lebanon. At the same time, the autocratic government of General Stroessner is very intolerant of both foreign influence and political chaos. No guerrilla movement has been able to grow under General Stroessner's tight control of the country. The PLO has no official status in Paraguay. It is unlikely that General Stroessner openly would tolerate their presence within Paraguay, although some PLO members have been reported in Asuncion. The PLO is uncharacteristically silent about General Stroessner's regime while it attacks other repressive regimes, such as Chile.

Paraguay's strong support of Palestinian rights is an outgrowth of the affinity between its ethnic and Arab minority and virtual dependence on Algerian oil. Its support is independent of both Arab diplomacy and PLO activity. Paraguay will continue to support Palestinian rights and reject association with the PLO.

CHILE

General Pinochet of Chile has been ambivalent in his support of Arab issues. Chile, like many other Latin American nations, competes for Arab economic ties. It maintains official diplomatic representation with seven Arab states with special emphasis on ties to Saudi Arabia. Additionally, Chile has even begun to export cluster bombs from its nascent armaments industry to Iran. Despite Chile's position on Arab issues and its favorable relations with Arab states, the PLO has targeted the Pinochet regime and since 1979 cooperates closely with the MIR (Movement of the Revolutionary Left). Members of the MIR have been reported in training camps in Lebanon since 1981, and some Palestinians allegedly participated in MIR activities in Chile.[45] Yet, General Pinochet seems unwilling to risk his favorable Arab relations through confrontation with or criticism of the PLO.

BOLIVIA

PLO relations with Bolivia were cool under Bolivian military rule. However, because the PLO has been outspoken in its support for the civilian MNR (National Revolutionary Movement), relations with the present civilian government have warmed considerably. Although the PLO rhetorically supports the opposition Bolivian National Liberation Army (ELN), it has moderated its activities in Bolivia. Initiatives by the Bolivian government, begun in December 1982, to establish full diplomatic relations with the PLO have not yet been realized.[46] Late in 1985 the PLO pressed the Bolivian government through the PLO representative, Jorge Salamah, to establish formal ties with the promise of "undertaking some negotiations with the Arab world to aid Bolivia in its current crisis."[47] Domestic concern about a reassertive military in politics probably warranted that the civilian government keep a safe distance from formal ties with the PLO. Yet, the Paz Estenssoro administration announced on 2 April 1987 formalization of relations with the PLO and afforded its delegation all diplomatic rights and privileges. Barring any unforeseen changes in the near future, Bolivian need for oil and financial aid keeps its international agenda closely oriented toward the Arab world.

URUGUAY

Information on PLO relations with Uruguay is sketchy. The former military regime of Uruguay was another target for PLO criticism. Linked through the JCR (Revolutionary Coordination Junta) some remnants of Uruguay's *Tupamaro* guerrillas in exile maintain relations with the PLO. Uruguay's new reformist civilian government has eliminated much of the impetus for domestic protest, thereby removing political support for radical groups. As long as there is even a hint of PLO complicity with the *Tupamaro* movement, relations with Uruguay are improbable. The Uruguayan government, especially the military, is extremely concerned about domestic political chaos, particularly that caused by terrorist and guerrilla activity. Uruguay's dependence on Arab oil from Saudi Arabia, Kuwait, and Iraq will continue to favorably influence its position on Arab issues and help to moderate its image of the PLO.

ARGENTINA

PLO-Argentine relations have improved since the civilian government of Alfonsin replaced military rule. Argentine-Arab relations have been good.

Presently, Argentina maintains formal diplomatic relations with nine Arab states and has established strong trade relationships with Arab states beyond oil. In the international arena of the United Nations, Argentina has never voted against Palestinian rights.[48] Yet, Argentina is another case where Arab diplomatic efforts conflict with PLO strategic solidarity.

Since 1972 the PLO has supported the Peronist *Montonero* terrorists. After the Argentine military all but eliminated the entire movement during the 1974 to 1977 "dirty war," the *Montoneros* formed a tactical alliance, in exile, with Yasser Arafat and the PLO in August 1977. PLO-trained *Montoneros* infiltrated back into Argentina from 1979 to 1981, and renewed a campaign of assassination.[49] (These same terrorists were responsible for the assassination of former Nicaraguan dictator Anastasio Somoza Debayle in neighboring Paraguay).

Despite PLO complicity with Argentine terrorism, an Argentine congressional advisor leaked in early 1985 that "President Alfonsin has assured Arab diplomats that the PLO will have representation in the country before the end of the year."[50] That never materialized.

BRAZIL

In regard to the PLO and formal relations with Arab nations, Brazil is in a precarious position. While Arab diplomacy and Brazilian dependence on Arab oil push Brazil close to the Arab camp on Middle East issues, the PLO solidarity strategy worries the Brazilian government. As the largest and most powerful nation in the region, Brazil's traditional foreign policy has been international neutrality. Toward this end, it maintains formal diplomatic relations with virtually all Arab nations, as well as with Israel. Brazil's ambitious national development plans are dependent upon energy resources and capital investment, particularly from Arab oil and petrodollars. Although Brazilian exports of nonmilitary goods to the Arab world have averaged 1.3 billion US dollars per year since 1982, these revenues do not come close to managing the huge deficits created by Brazil's oil needs since 1973. These exports were expected to drop in 1986 as a result of weakened Middle East revenues from Brazilian oil imports. Brazilian exports to the Middle East cover a diverse range of manufactured goods. Most significant among these exports are Brazilian arms sales to nearly every nation in the Middle East, including Saudi Arabia (to include a $3 billion deal for one thousand tanks), Jordan, Iraq, and Libya.[51]

Coincidentally, Brazil hosts the numerically largest ethnic Arab population in Latin America. Unlike ethnic Arab minorities in other regional nations, Brazilian ethnic Arabs are politically active. The Brazilian newspaper, *O Globo,* reported that 300 members (out of a total of 479 representatives and 69 Senators) of congress belong to, or are sympathetic to the Parliamentary League of Friendship and Cooperation with Arab Nations. Additionally, 53 parliamentarians are ethnic Arabs.[52] The Parliamentary League was founded in November 1981 "as a result of a campaign for the recognition of the PLO and in support of the establishment of a Palestinian state" and it lobbies the Brazilian government to adopt pro-Arab positions.[53]

PLO activity in Brazil can be traced to 1971 with a tactical alliance between the PFLP and the Brazilian VPR (Popular Revolutionary Vanguard) facilitated by PLO agent Rubhi Hallum. No hard evidence exists to suggest PLO operations within Brazil beyond recruitment and fundraising, but the PLO has trained members of the VPR in Libya. Additionally, Brazilian-made arms exported to Libya have made their way to the PLO. The PLO has operated a bureau office in Brazil since 1975, as part of the local staff of the Arab League, and continues to pressure for full diplomatic recognition. The Brazilian government continues to consider the request.

CONCLUSION

Whether Latin America discovered the Arabs or the Arabs discovered Latin America is immaterial to this study. Since the first oil shock in 1973, Latin America and the Arab World, two regions of the Third World, have developed closer relationships that have resulted in mutual support on pertinent issues. In addition to improved trade relations, Latin America and the Arab world have aligned themselves on the same side of international political positions such as the Law of the Sea, international debt, and most notably, the Palestinian homeland. One of the principal beneficiaries of this close relationship between regions has been the PLO.

PLO presence and activity in Latin America reflect one aspect of PLO strategy to restore the Palestinian homeland through solidarity of national liberation movements. By definition, this implies an ideological linkage between the PLO and select groups in Latin America. This linkage tends to transcend national boundaries. The PLO is welcomed by Latin American regimes ruled by forces of national liberation in Cuba and Nicaragua and are only tolerated by democratic governments out of deference to Arab diplomacy. Similarly, authoritarian regimes in Paraguay and Chile cautiously turn a blind eye toward PLO activities there.

Seemingly, PLO efforts are most successful among the political left. Only movements of national liberation representing the political left in Latin America are considered candidates for PLO solidarity. For example, the PLO is unwilling to sacrifice its privileged status in Nicaragua to support the contras yet jeopardizes Arab diplomatic inroads in pro-Palestinian regimes, as Brazil and Chile, by supporting domestic Marxist-Leninist guerrilla movements.

This situation is painfully clear to Latin American governments and creates the following political dilemma: Arab diplomatic efforts and the politics of petrodollars have made Latin American governments sensitive to Palestinian issues. At the same time, however, the PLO has carried its solidarity strategy to Latin America through movements of national liberation. Logically, these movements exist outside of and work against the legitimate governments courted by Arab diplomacy. Yet the PLO is institutionally protected by Arab states. Hence an attack on the PLO not only buys increased trouble from the PLO but also ill will from Arab states. Consequently, the problem of PLO support for domestic insurgent groups is usually handled by governments in a quiet manner or completely ignored. But what remains is this: what will the PLO position on international solidarity for national liberation be once the Palestinian homeland is restored? More specifically, has the PLO established ideological linkages with movements of national liberation throughout the region that will translate into moral commitment and active support after Palestinian victory?

If so, then it is in the interest of regional governments with active guerrilla movements to keep the PLO factionalized and oriented toward its own goals, at least until domestic insurgent organizations are eradicated. A radical Arab state, with institutional links to guerrilla movements, which actively supports Latin American terrorism would be disastrous to regional stability. The PLO cannot expect legitimate recognition by responsible governments in Latin America unless it modifies its current strategy to alleviate any possible anxiety over its intentions and the ramifications for domestic political stability.

In the near term, no change is expected in PLO status within Latin America. Cheaper oil prices have reduced Arab diplomatic and economic influence in the region. Coincidentally, over the past two years PLO activity in Latin America has attenuated and has been restricted to diplomatic lobbying for political recognition. Perhaps the recent disruption of PLO activity caused by its dislocation from Beirut, gave it time and circumstance to reevaluate the efficacy of its solidarity strategy in favor of one aligned with Arab diplomacy, one tailor-made for Latin America.

NOTES

1. The United Nations General Assembly vote in 1947 on the partition of Palestine is recorded as Latin America republics voting 13 in favor, 1 against, and 6 abstentions. George Tomah, ed. *United Nations Resolutions on Palestine and the Arab-Israeli Conflict, 1943–1974* (Beirut: Institute for Palestine Studies, 1974), 4–14. See also Edward Glick, *Latin America and the Palestine Problem* (New York: Theodor Herzl Foundation, 1958).

2. Jillian Becker, *The PLO: The Rise and Fall of the Palestine Liberation Organization* (New York: St. Martin's Press, 1984), 166–67.

3. Some of this preoccupation is expressed in an article by Manfred Schonfeld, "PLO Presence in Latin America Seen as Attraction to Terrorism," *La Prensa* (Buenos Aires), 5 Jul. 1979, 11, as reported in *(FBIS)*, JPRS No. 73980/0001, 9 Aug. 1979. Schonfeld warns of the "transfer of the problems of the Middle East to Latin America through the network of transnational terrorism." See also "The PLO in Central America," *The White House Digest* (Wash. DC: White House Office of Media Relations and Planning, 20 Jul. 1983). Some other, perhaps partisan, sources include Eileen Scully, "The PLO's Growing Latin American Base," (Wash. DC: The Heritage Foundation, 2 Aug. 1983); "Radical Arabs Take Aim at Latin America," *Newsweek*, 1 Sept. 1980, 27; David J. Kopilow, *Castro, Israel, and the PLO* (Wash. DC: The Cuban-American National Foundation, 1984); and *The Washington Post*, 25 Jan. 1985, A1.

4. Fehmy Saddy, ed., *Arab-Latin American Relations: Energy, Trade and Investment* (New Brunswick, NJ: Transaction Books, Inc., 1983), 7–8.

5. Some population estimates of ethnic Arab minorities in Latin America run as high as 7.5 million. See Ignacio Kilch, "Arabs in Latin America," in *The Middle East* (Apr. 1986): 57.

6. For discussions about the Arab immigration to Brazil see Jamil Safady, *Panorama da Imigracao Arabe* (Sao Paulo: Editora Comercial Safady, c. 1973–1977) and to Paraguay, Humberto Dominguez Dibb, *Presencia y Vigencia: Arabes en el Paraguay* (Asuncion, 1977).

7. Kilch, "Arabs in Latin America," 58.

8. Juan Abugattas, "The Perception of the Palestinian Question in Latin America," *Palestine Studies* 9(3): 11.

9. Four prominent organizations in Latin America designed to mobilize Arab ethnic communities include: (1) the *World Lebanese Cultural Union* (WLCU), established in 1960 at a congress in Beirut under the leadership of Phalangist Pierre Gemayel to serve Lebanon, especially in terms of investments from emigrant communities; (2) the *World Maronite League*, established in 1979 at a congress in Mexico City with a regional headquarters in Sao Paulo, Brazil, under the guidance of the Phalange-dominated Lebanese Front against Palestinian Presence in Lebanon; (3) the *Federation of Arab Institutions* (FEARAB) establish in 1974 at Syrian instigation and supported by the Arab League aimed against Maronite hegemony in Lebanon; and (4) the *Federation of Palestinian Institutions* founded in 1984 as an all-Palestinian body of Yasser Arafat supporters in Latin America; from Ignacio Klich, "Arabs in Latin America," 59.

10. Edy Kaufman, Yoram Shapira, and Joll Barromi, *Israel-Latin American Relations* (New Brunswick, NJ: Transaction Books, Inc. 1979), 42–48.

11. "The Arab Contribution to Regional Stabilization," *Spotlight on the Americas* (Wash. DC: Center for International Security, Apr. 1984), 1.

12. Inter-American Development Bank, *Annual Report: 1985* (Wash. DC: IDB, 1986), 33.

13. Armando Prugue, "Financial Co-operation between the Arab World and Latin America: The Role of the Inter-American Development Bank," in Fehmy Saddy, ed. *Arab-Latin American Relations: Energy, Trade and Investment*, 79–80. The IDB 1985 *Annual Report* lists the OPEC Fund and the Islamic Development Bank as the only Arab participants in 1985.

14. See US Department of State, *The Sandinistas and Middle Eastern Radicals* (Wash. DC: US Government printing office, Aug. 1985), an unclassified report on Sandinista ties to Middle

Eastern radicals. See also Marlo Lewis, Jr., "Nicaragua: Mid East Connection," in *Midstream,* 32 (Jan. 1986): 3–7, and David J. Kapilow, *Castro, Israel, and the PLO* (Wash. DC: The Cuban-American National Foundation, 1984).

15. Robin Wright, "Strange Bedfellows: The Pope and the PLO," in *The Washington Post,* 24 Jan. 1982, 4:1+. The author notes that Pope John Paul II has been critical of Israel for "the exclusion of many Palestinians from their homeland. . . ." As a caveat, catholic membership in the PLO draws largely from Greek Orthodox Catholics. See also George Emile Irani, *The Papacy and the Middle East* (Notre Dame, IN: Notre Dame Univ. Press, 1986), 6. Irani claims that "two fundamental interests guide papal involvement in the Middle East: (1) protection of the welfare of Catholics and (2) the fostering of coexistence and dialogue between the followers of the three monotheistic faiths—Judaism, Christianity, and Islam." Irani also draws conclusions through analysis to specific papal perspectives in the Israeli-Palestinian dispute, Jerusalem, and the Lebanese war.

16. Judith Larkin Elkin, *Jews of the Latin American Republics* (Chapel Hill, NC: Univ. of North Carolina Press, 1980), 148.

17. Nicaraguan FSLN (Sandinista National Liberation Front) mistreatment of domestic Jews is recounted by Soshana Bryen in "The Sandinistas and the Jews," *The Wall Street Journal,* 24, Aug. 1983, 24. Joseph Berger, in "View of Jews of Nicaragua: Much Debate," *The New York Times,* 20 Apr. 1986, 11, gives a contrasting view of alleged Nicaraguan anti-Semitism under the present regime. Cuba hosted an international symposium on the Zionist influence in Latin America at Havana in November 1983 and published an edited volume "Simposis International Sobre la injerencia Sionista en America Latina" containing the conference presentations.

18. The Palestinian National Covenant, Article 1, from decisions of the National Congress of the Palestinian Liberation Organization held in Cairo, 1–17 Jul. 1968. From J. W. Amos III, *Palestinian Resistance: Organization of a Nationalist Movement* (New York: Pergamon Press, 1980), 296.

19. The Palestinian National Covenant, Articles 9 and 26, pp. 297, 299.

20. Y. Harkabi, *The Palestinian Covenant and Its Meaning* (London: Valentine, Mitchell, 1981) "The Political Program of the Palestine Liberation Organization," (Jan. 1973), 132+. The thematic solidarity with the forces of national liberation is further developed in succeeding years. "The Political Programmer of the Palestinian National Council," 8 June 1974, Cairo, proclaimed that "the PLO will struggle to strengthen its solidarity with the socialist countries and the world forces of liberation and progress to foil all Zionist, reactionary and imperialist schemes." From Yehuda Lukacs, *Documents on the Israeli-Palestinian Conflict, 1967–1983,* (Cambridge: Cambridge Univ. Press, 1984), 157. Later, on 22 Mar. 1977, the Palestinian National Council, in its Political declaration at Cairo, reaffirmed "the significance of cooperation and solidarity with socialist, non-aligned, Islamic and African countries, and with all the national liberation movements in the world." Lukacs, *Documents,* 182. The "Political Programme" of the Fourth General Conference of the Palestinian Liberation Movement (Fatah) at Damascus on 31 May 1980 declared that "our Movement is part of the international liberation movement in the common struggle against imperialism, Zionism, racism and their agents, and we establish our alliances with all international parties in conformity with our principles. . . ." Lukas, *Documents,* 196.

21. *FBIS* report (Middle East-Africa) on 23 Feb. 1983, A17 from Algiers Domestic Service, "PNC Political Statement," 22 Feb. 1983.

22. *Foreign Broadcast Information Service (FBIS)* report on 2 May 1985 (Middle East-Africa) from Aden, *Voice of Palestine,* "Yasir Arafat Discusses Palestinian Revolution" A2.

23. Kapilow, *Castro, Israel, and the PLO,* 32.

24. See Raphael Israeli, *PLO in Lebanon: Selected Documents* (New York: St. Martin's Press, 1983), 147–68. Israeli's book displays several PLO documents captured by Israel at the PLO Headquarters in Sidon, South Lebanon during the Peace for Galilee Campaign (June-Sept. 1982) that show Cuban-PLO cooperation in training and guerrilla activity.

25. Bryen, "The Sandinistas and the Jews," 24.

26. As reported in *al-Watan* (Kuwaiti Newspaper), 20 Jul. 1979, in "Arafat Says PLO Aids Foreign Guerrilla Units," *Wall Street Journal,* 14 Jan. 1982 and by Eileen Scully, "The PLO's Growing Latin American Base," 3–5.

27. Marlo Lewis, Jr., "Nicaragua: The Mid East Connection," *Midstream* 32 (Jan. 1986): 4.

28. Bryen, "The Sandinistas and the Jews," 24.

29. *Voice of Palestine* (Baghdad), 11 Aug. 1979 as reported in *FBIS* (Near East-North Africa) JPRS No. 74070/0026, 23 Aug. 1979.

30. "Arafat Says PLO Aids Foreign Guerrilla Units," *Wall Street Journal*, 14 Jan. 1982, 4.

31. *FBIS* report "Nicaraguan Plane Crashes En Route to U.S." on 23 Apr. 1985 (Western Europe), P1.

32. At a solidarity rally in Managua (13 Sept. 1981) memorializing Patricio Arguello Ryan, who died in 1970 assisting the PLO, the central themes honored "the role of the PLO's stand against Zionism in inspiring Nicaraguans to uproot Somoza, and its role as a world liberation movement." *Palestine* (PLO Information Bulletin) 7(16): 34.

33. *Palestinian Perspectives* (June/Jul. 1984): 14.

34. *Voice of Lebanon,* 22 June 1980 "PLO Providing Assistance to El Salvadoran Guerrillas," as reported by *FBIS* (Middle East-Africa) 25 June 1980, A3.

35. "Arafat Says PLO Aids Foreign Guerrilla Units," 4.

36. "Pro-PLO Newspaper Indicates Links to Guerrillas in El Salvador," *New York Times*, 29 Jan. 1981, A2, as reported by *Al Liwa* (Beirut).

37. Cheryl A. Rubenberg, "Israel and Guatemala: Arms, Advice and Counterinsurgency," *Middle East Report* (May-June 1986): 16–47. Israeli military cooperation with Guatemala began in 1971 and became increasingly important to the Government of Guatemala after the United States cut off military assistance to that regime in 1977. Rubenberg notes that this military cooperation includes materiel support and Israeli counterinsurgency advisors. See also Bishara Bahbah and Linda Butler, *Israel and Latin America: The Military Connection,* (New York: St. Martin's Press, 1986), 161–62.

38. See Shirley Christian, *Revolution in the Family,* (New York: Vantage Books, 1986), 63 + .

39. In June 1986, General Noriega was criticized in *The New York Times* for his alleged ties to regional drug trafficking and other illicit activities. Messages of support for General Noriega in the face of these accusations came from Fidel Castro, Daniel Ortega, Mu'ammar al-Qadhafi, Yasser Arafat, and Ayatollah Khomeini; from the US Department of State, telegram (unclassified) (PA 081639, Panama City) 8 Jul. 1986.

40. *FBIS* report from Tripoli *JANA,* 28 Aug. 1988, (Latin America), 29 Aug. 1988, 32.

41. *FBIS* report from Panama City *ACAN,* 14 Sept. 1988, (Latin America), 15 Sept. 1988, 20.

42. See Bishara Bahbah and Linda Butler. *Israel and Latin America.* They devote a chapter detailing Israeli-Ecuadoran diplomatic relations and arms transfers.

43. The terrorist movement, *Alfaro Vive, Carajo* (AVC) has been active in Ecuador since late 1983 but has not significantly expanded its size nor its activities enough to threaten the current national regime.

44. Tim Coone, "A Drop of Oil," *The Middle East,* (Dec. 1981), 32.

45. *Palestine* (PLO Information Bulletin) 7(5) (15 Mar. 1981): 34–35.

46. *FBIS* report (Middle East & Africa), 15 Dec. 1982, A1, of *Voice of PLO* (Bahgdad), "Bolivia Grants PLO Office Diplomatic Status," 14 Dec. 1982.

47. La Paz *Cadena Pan Americana* broadcast , 30 Dec. 1985, as reported by *FBIS* (Latin America), 2 Jan. 1986, C5.

48. *The Middle East* (Dec. 1981): 32. This record remained untarnished thorugh 1985.

49. *FBIS* reported (Middle East & Africa) from Tel Aviv *Ma 'ariv,* 14–15 Jul. 1980, N5–6 that "dozens of Argentine guerrillas are training in PLO camps near Damascus and Beirut."

50. "Politicians Advocating Recognition of PLO," *Ambito Financiero,* 20 Mar. 1985, as reported in *FBIS* (Latin America) 25 Mar. 1985, B3.

51. "Brazil and the Middle East: A Booming Arms Industry," *The Middle East* (June 1986): 34, 39. See also "Saudi Arabia Buys 1,000 Tanks," *O Globo* 21 Dec. 1985, as reported in *FBIS* (Latin America) 24 Dec. 1985, D1. *O Globo,* 7 Jan. 1987, 22 also reported an Iraqi purchase of 40 FILA Antiaircraft targeting systems from AVIBRAS (Brazilian Aerospace Industry) totalling $400 million. On 14 Jan. 1987 it reported shipment of SS-type (ground-to-ground) rockets to Saudi Arabia and Jordan.

52. "Brazil and the Middle East: Friends in High Places," *The Middle East* (June 1986): 40.

53. "Brazil and the Middle East," 40.

8 AUDITING THE PLO
ADAM ZAGORIN

How much money does the PLO have? How are its funds used? What do financial deployments reveal about the organization's politics and prospects? Such questions are not easy to answer, in part because the PLO maintains a low profile on financial matters. The organization believes, correctly, that focusing attention on its large and growing asset base can only make those assets less secure. The following analysis has, therefore, been drawn largely from research involving widely scattered public documents and other published material. Some members of the PLO were interviewed, but none of the figures or estimates have come from intelligence sources.

What emerges is a portrait of the PLO as a financially powerful organization with large assets at its disposal, at least in comparison with a number of Third World nations. Hardly an ephemeral body, the PLO uses its money to support key bureaucratic, diplomatic, and military functions. Importantly, however, such resources are not unlimited. And with the PLO's new imperative to fund the Palestinian uprising on the West Bank and Gaza and to fill the fiscal vacuum left by King Hussein's formal disengagement from the occupied territories, financial decisions are now more important than ever. Thus, the PLO's increasing use of limited assets to further key policy goals should, over time, exert influence in the direction of fiscal conservatism and, eventually, financial and even political reform.

FINANCES OF THE PLO

The main financial body of the PLO is the Palestine National Fund (PNF), about which the organization has officially released considerable but hardly complete information over the years. The cash reserve of the Fund is probably at least $1.5 billion, although some estimates run as high as $14 billion. Using the lower figure, such assets imply annual income of at least $125 to $150 million, representing an average rate of return of between 8 and 10 percent, earned through a variety of investment instruments.[1] Additional current receipts include some $87 million annually from Saudi Arabia, which continues to roll in despite declining oil revenues. Other oil-rich Gulf states have not met their aid commitments to the PLO in recent years, although they probably still contribute something. Then there is another 10 million to 15 million dollars furnished through the 5 to 7 percent "liberation tax" paid by some Palestinians, notably in the Gulf. Fund money is maintained largely but not exclusively in accounts of the Amman-based Arab Bank (listed assets: more than $10 billion).

A recent example of the PLO's growing focus on money came at the June 1988 Arab summit in Algiers, when the organization was turned down in its bid for some $300 million to $400 million in extra annual funding to help pay for the uprising on the West Bank and Gaza Strip. At the time, it was clear that this financial rebuke irritated the PLO, so much so that Arafat's close aide and spokesman, Bassam Abu Sharif, specifically cited the need for extra money in his denunciation of Arab leaders for their "dereliction of duty towards the Palestinian uprising."[2] Among other things, the money was to have been used to compensate strikers and protestors in the occupied territories for lost wages and other economic costs associated with their uprising. But Arab leaders balked at the prospect of handing such large sums and having to decide whether King Hussein of Jordan or PLO Chairman Arafat would manage its disbursement. The king's subsequent decision to stop paying the salaries of 24,000 civil servants in the West Bank and Gaza has so far produced no new financial initiative from the PLO. Israel, in any case, would almost certainly try to prevent any further PLO penetration of their occupied territories.

Set against its uncertain sources of income these receipts are a considerable array of expenditures which, according to the PLO, have ushered in an era of deficit spending. The Palestine Liberation Army (PLA), for example, requires an estimated $87 million per year to pay for a wide variety of military operations, including relatively inexpensive attacks on Israel—numbering 836 in 1985, according to the organization's figures—and far more costly initiatives such as attempted military rebuilding in southern Lebanon. Even if it is not fighting, the PLA employs a permanent force of roughly fourteen thousand. Another estimated $10 million goes to the operation of ninety or more diplomatic missions around the world; $52 million is allocated to a fund for disabled Palestinian fighters; $18 million for Palestinian universities and scholarships; $20 million for the Palestinian Red Crescent (with functions roughly akin to the Red Cross) and some $46 million for a variety of other activities. Therefore, the total Fund budget is about $233 million. And the annual deficit (covered by reserves) is about $100 million, according to the PLO.

Although figures on PLO expenditures are approximate, they do indicate the organization's priorities, at least in fiscal terms. Thus, roughly equal sums are devoted to social welfare functions and to the military. With the ongoing PLO buildup in Lebanon, military allotments may well be on the increase. Even so, the organization's attention to "butter" as well as "guns" is testimony to a keen social awareness and an appreciation that welfare payments constitute necessary and effective patronage.

Such are the rudimentary available facts concerning the Fund. In addition to the Fund, there are smaller assets belonging to dissident factions of the PLO—largely in opposition to Arafat and based in Damascus—as well as substantial sums under the control of Fatah, Arafat's own guerrilla organization. It is impossible to estimate the amounts under dissident control, except that they are relatively small, ebbing and flowing with the success of business operations on which they are based and with the generosity of hardline Arab governments which also provide backing. Only enough money is needed for bare-bones military/terrorist operations and a paltry administrative staff.

At the same time, recent press reports indicate that a self-sustaining corporate structure and income base were important to the Abu Nidal faction.[3] Operating through a now-closed Warsaw office, a firm called "SAS" was established by Abu Nidal and his close associates in 1979. The company functioned as the nexus of a network of other Abu Nidal firms operating in Europe. These commercial units had as their main business the export of goods, including arms, to Arab countries. Using a branch of a West European bank to funnel payments, arms shipments valued as high as $500,000 were made, bringing in large amounts of hard currency. SAS may still be in operation, but was apparently forced to close its Warsaw headquarters under US pressure prior to Vice President George Bush's fall 1987 visit to Poland.

As for Fatah, its considerable assets make it by far the wealthiest of the eight Palestinian guerrilla groups, perhaps even wealthier than the fund itself. A key characteristic of Fatah assets—unlike those of the PNF—is that their size is highly secret and their use is under the direct control of Arafat.

Responsible estimates of the size the Fatah fund run as high as 7 billion to 8 billion dollars,[4] although a lower figure may be more realistic. Managed by a small group of loyal employees, the Fatah account also receives contributions from Arab governments, some of which donate to Fatah (as opposed to the Fund) as a sign of goodwill or as a form of protection money to fend off PLO-sponsored trouble at home.

Control of Fatah's billions of dollars is important not only in sustaining Arafat's mainstream PLO, but also in relationships with rival Palestinians and external enemies. Maintenance of a standing army consumes at least $87 million annually. Apart from extensive weaponry, each soldier receives a monthly wage of just over $200, with officers (depending on rank) earning between $360 and roughly $1,150. Chiefs of missions abroad get almost $400 per month plus free housing and a generous cost of living allowance. Then there is the PLO social welfare network: $52 million in annual welfare payments for family support, housing, education, and so forth, with special attention to those who have lost wage-earners in battle or suffered at the hands of Israeli occupiers. SAMED ("Steadfastness"), a production unit which provides jobs for Palestinians in Lebanon and elsewhere, produces a wide variety of goods. According to a recently published report by Sami Fayez Mussalem, a close aide of Arafat's, SAMED is the "economic arm of the Palestinian revolution and the core of its public sector," with subsidiaries in thirty countries and on four continents.[5] Although much of SAMED's infrastructure was thought to have been destroyed in the Israeli invasion of Lebanon, Mussalem confirms that business is flourishing in industry, agriculture, construction, film production, publishing, and finance and commerce, among other areas.

For the industrial sector alone, Mussalem cities ready-to-wear, textiles, wool, furniture, hi-tech products, food, hygienic goods, construction equipment, and plastics as figuring in an output mix on display in twenty-six permanent exhibitions located in fourteen Arab and African countries, as well as Eastern Europe, with the US, Canada, and Latin America apparently being considered as areas for expansion. In agriculture, the movement has tens of thousands of acres under cultivation in Africa and the Middle East. Then there are the administrative employees, numbering at least five thousand, including accountants, secretaries, drivers, bureaucrats, and others, whose wages are divided into at least eight pay grades. At the top, Arafat and other senior officials determine high policy — for which they are paid about $900 per month plus a cost of living allowance.

POLITICAL CONSEQUENCES

The point about this work force, civilian and military, is not that its members are corrupt or misusing PLO money for personal gain. Nor are such cadres and soldiers particularly wealthy nor are many living undeservedly glamorous lives: one PLO midlevel accountant in a European capital, wearily pushing aside a stack of bills, said his salary hasn't gone up in years and then complains about worsening traffic that is making his commute to the office more arduous than ever. The bottom line on the PLO's far-flung bureaucracy and military is that it represents a huge patronage network. It is also very much a permanent, entrenched force, neither impressively capable nor imaginative in leadership. Self-perpetuation is inherently one of its most important major goals, irrespective of progress toward Middle East peace.

To understand what money means in political and practical terms to the PLO, it is useful to examine what the organization has had to say on the subject in recent years. In 1984 the Palestine National Council—or "parliament in exile"—met in Amman, in part to sort out a mess created by the PLO's then-tangled financial machinery. As a result of a still unhealed split the year before—the worst split in PLO history—a bloc of at least twenty-five officials in the fund's finance department had joined anti-Arafat dissidents in Damascus. Since many of the organization's financial records were maintained in the Syrian capital, payments to mainstream elements were being blocked. Shafik al-Hut, a mainstream PLO representative in Beirut, complained publicly that he no longer had enough money to meet the needs of thousands of war-stricken Palestinians in Lebanon. Hundreds, perhaps thousands of Palestinian students on PLO-scholarships in Eastern and Western Europe had been temporarily cut off, and many of the movement's offices around the world experienced interruptions in the flow of funds needed to function. In short, the PLO was on the verge of losing financial touch with vital operating arms and constituent groups.

Confronting this situation were thirty or more fund directors, whose deliberations produced a financial statement that was also a commentary on some of the key political issues facing the PLO. For anyone expecting the document to contain highblown revolutionary rhetoric, the surprise is that it reads more like the annual report of a large, if not particularly successful corporation.

In an introduction devoted to budget, regretful mention is made of a $31 million deficit. Fund directors then cite the fact that the year's Saudi contributions, "did not enter the account of National Fund income since the chairman of the Executive Committee [Arafat] deposited them directly into the account of the army's financial administration."[6] (Arafat's apparent hijacking of Fund money to an account under his direct control—no one suggests it was for his private use—is but one illustration of his consolidation of an independent financial powerbase.) In criticisms later echoed by PLO dissidents, Fund directors also comment that: "this measure is considered a violation of Fund and P.L.O. regulations." They say they have stopped "monthly payments to the financial administration [pending] a settlement" of the dispute.[7]

The fact that the board criticized Arafat is hardly surprising. It is known that some board members, with their pragmatic outlook, are occasionally at odds with what they see as the movement's ineffective political strategy. In the PLO's early days, financial leadership was provided by board member 'Abd al-Majid Shuman, a gifted executive who later stepped aside to devote himself to running the Amman-based Arab Bank. The bank is the largest company in Jordan and an ultraconservative institution held by at least 20 percent by the Shuman family. No stranger to adversity, it has lost deposits in the past to Arab government nationalizations and in the takeover of branches on the West Bank and Gaza by Israeli occupiers. Perhaps because of these travails and because it handles much of the PLO's money, the bank is believed to keep substantial sums off the balance sheet, while as much as 70 percent of listed assets are thought to be in quickly available cash and short-term deposits. This level of ready reserves far exceeds levels maintained by most banks in the world. Shuman's successors at the Fund have included Hanna Nasir, former President of Bir Zeit University, and the current Chairman, Jawid al-Ghusain.

Al-Gusain's disenchantment with certain PLO policies is known because he voiced his concerns to the press following a meeting of the Fund's financial directors in Casablanca in June 1986. Without naming names—and loyally disavowing any wish to topple Arafat—al-Ghusain contended that members of the board, including himself, wanted a radical change in PLO policies. "What is the harvest of 20 years of struggle?" he is quoted as saying. "We have managed to create a Palestinian identity and bring our cause to the world's attention. Otherwise it has been total failure."[8] Al-Ghusain also stressed that the board is pressing for budget cuts—especially for the PLO's bureaucracy and military. Savings earned through such cuts, according to al-Ghusain, ought to pay for food and medical care in the Palestinian camps of Lebanon, as well as to fund resistance on the West Bank and Gaza. "We are daily witnessing the blacks of South Africa winning their freedom," the Fund chairman observed. "We must make the occupied territories the center of our activities."[9]

Al-Ghusain's proposals for the reallocation of budget funds, however unlikely their implementation, could bring about profound changes in the PLO. Redirecting PLO or Fatah funds would inevitably reduce the mainstream guerrilla group's strength and importance relative to rivals. More money could be channeled to those in the occupied territories on whose behalf much of the struggle is ostensibly taking place. Reduction of the movement's military budget would liberate funds that could be used to relieve the appalling conditions found in the Palestinian camps of Lebanon. This alone would be a highly significant step. Yet in order for such measures to be implemented, the ethos of revolutionary leadership that suffuses the PLO would have to be fundamentally redefined; a major task to say the least. Thus al-Ghusain's critique should be taken as a barometer of elite opinion, not as a signal of impending change.

As part of its 1984 budgetary review, the board also complains about obstacles to efficient collection of the Palestinian liberation tax. Among these, directors not dryly that, "the amount collected from Libya during the past two years did not reach the Fund. Officials there have been contacted concerning this matter but, until now, without success."[10] It is not clear how much money Libya withheld, but other wealthy Arab states, including the United Arab Emirates, Kuwait, and Qatar, were also blamed in the published report for not meeting publicly made aid commitments, as well as pledges to hand over the liberation tax. Saudi Arabia, on the other hand, is warmly thanked for meeting all pledges.

In a subsequent section of the report, the board discusses accounting procedures and internal audits applied throughout the PLO's "offices, bureaus, departments and organizations." Funding of agricultural projects in Gaza are mentioned, along with the floating of two otherwise unidentified securities offerings valued at $4 million each (no bank is cited, but the Amman-based Arab Bank is believed to handle such transactions). Winding up, directors mention that meager revenues are, for the first time in history, forcing the Fund to cover shortfalls with reserves. Based on this finding, the board issued a plea for spending cuts, consideration of work force reductions and reinvigoration of the tax collection system. More recently, in a July 1985 published interview, al-Ghusain maintained that the Fund deficit has grown to $100 million. He calls for further "austerity programs" and indicates the need to "curb the expenses in all the organizations," citing material losses of "tens of millions of dollars" as a result of fighting in Lebanon.[11]

Although most signs point to the Fund's current account being in serious trouble—albeit with substantial reserves remaining—Arafat's access to other money through Fatah has helped him press ahead with costly military and other activities. Direct and indirect indications are that Fatah accounts, about which the chairman doesn't say much in public, were a principal resource for the PLO's failed 1986–1987 "reconquista" in Lebanon. Looking at the PLO's Lebanese bank assets, it is a peculiar, though well-documented fact that among the many banks plundered in the course of a more than decade-old civil war, the Arab Bank in Beirut has never been touched. As numerous institutions such as the British Bank of the Middle East (BBME) feel prey to militia robberies netting millions, perhaps billions of dollars, Fatah was apparently careful to protect its local strong box.

A 1985 *Financial Times* report cited a large influx of PLO funds as boosting Lebanan's dwindling foreign exchange reserves and bolstering the battered Lebanese pound. Bankers reported that the PLO was bringing in no less than $20 million per month and perhaps more than $50 million per month.[12] Still more recently, the PLO's number two, Abu Iyad, said his organization was sending huge quantities of weapons into Lebanon to back its fighters around the Palestinian camps.[13] Usually reliable reports from the Middle East, as recently as December 1986, indicate payments to Maronite Christians of $3,000 for every PLO fighter allowed to enter the Maronite-controlled port of Junieh for transport to the battle zone around the Palestinian camps.[14] Without such handouts, the war might not have been fought at all.

Despite Arafat's superficial patch-up of PLO unity at the PNC meeting in the spring of 1987, criticism of PLO spending is likely to continue because the chairman's rivals covet his access to large amounts of cash. Among the more prominent Arafat opponents to speak out has been Colonel Sa'id Musa, also known as Abu Musa. A close military adviser to Arafat until 1983, he now controls a breakaway—though little active—guerrilla group based in northern and eastern Lebanon and in Syria. Irritated by reports that the PLO was hovering on the verge of bankruptcy, he charged that Arafat is a "financial emperor," that the chairman has $500 million on deposit in the Arab Bank in Amman and had $1 billion in Lebanese banks when the PLO was evacuated from Beirut in 1982. Other dissidents have charged that, following trips by former Israeli Prime Minister Shimon Peres to black Africa, Arafat distributed millions of dollars in cash payments to African leaders to persuade them not to reestablish relations with Israel. Whatever the truth of such charges, there is no doubt that the attacks struck a sensitive nerve with the mainstream PLO. Writing in a Palestinian publication recently,

Arafat aide Mussalem said the movement had fallen victim to an "international disinformation campaign." He maintained that the PLO has no secret accounts in Western banks and that its budget process is open for all to scrutinize. [15]

CONCLUSIONS

The PLO under Arafat represents a wide and currently unreconciled gamut of Palestinian opinion. The chairman is under pressure from Palestinians in the occupied territories to negotiate with Israel now, but his past failure to resolve internal PLO splits, or to act in spite of them, has often produced political paralysis. Even if Arafat wanted to act decisively, divisions in his organization might prevent it. If anything, the recent reunification of the PLO at the spring 1987 PNC meeting will further limit his ability to take bold actions that might upset the organization's fragile, internal consensus.

PLO finances reflect this state of affairs. And large amounts of money only make matters worse by giving the PLO leadership more latitude and the luxury of postponing difficult political choices and waiting for a better day. If and when that day comes, one hopes Arafat or his successors will respond creatively. But past experience has shown that pressure to respond is, in a sense, inversely proportional to the PLO's financial staying power. It is this staying power which materially guarantees diplomatic and military functions until the next political opening.

As such, PLO financial assets unquestionably represent a potential agent of change, and they are coveted by adversaries and reform-minded sympathizers alike. Although it would be naive to imagine that financial pressure alone could alter fundamental PLO policies, more peripheral PLO actions might be susceptible to such influence. Perhaps the long, bloody, and so far almost fruitless Palestinian struggle in Lebanon would have been less brutal if the PLO had less money and arms with which to fight the battle. Perhaps the PLO would be more eager to control diverse terrorist elements, like Abu al-Abbas and others, if it knew that banks through which it operates might face retaliatory restrictions in the event of continuing terrorist activity. At least such restrictions would have ample legal precedent in the United States, which has already imposed financial limits on Iranian and Libyan activity without unduly alarming other foreign investors. Conversely, on humanitarian grounds alone, consideration ought to be given to doing more to help Palestinian refugees, virtually all of whom are PLO supporters. Finally and perhaps most important of all, attempts should be made to focus greater attention in international fora on

PLO funds and how they are used. This process is now in its early stages, but Palestinians especially should devote greater attention to these increasingly large assets. And because Palestinians are among the most financially sophisticated groups in the Middle East, they are well suited to exercise greater oversight and direct funds to those who need them most.

Even if financial reforms are not implemented, a major weakening of the PLO's diversified asset base is unlikely. Instead, the outlook is for continued growth in line with Western and Western-allied economies where the money is invested. Through painstaking efforts over more than two decades, the PLO has amassed substantial wealth and enough personnel to take advantage of Western financial markets and Third World investments. In this respect, if not in others, the PLO is a status quo power with a vested interest in the prosperity of its US and West European investment havens. PLO wealth also depends in large measure on the continued economic stability of major contributors in the Western-allied Gulf states including Saudi Arabia. Given the organization's secure funding and a lack of alternatives to its leadership, the PLO's long-term survival appears assured.

NOTES

1. *Wall Street Journal,* 22 July 1986, 1; and *The Economist,* 2 Aug. 1986, 33.
2. *New York Times,* 9 June 1988, 14.
3. See *L'Express,* 30 July 1987, and *Wall Street Journal,* 15 Oct. 1987.
4. *The Economist,* 2 Aug. 1986, 33.
5. *Revue d'Etudes Palestiniennes,* no. 21 (Automne 1986).
6. Palestine National Fund financial report, as published in *Falastin al-Thawrah,* 15 Dec. 1984, 28–30.
7. *PNF* report, 28–30.
8. *The Observer,* 22 June 1986, 13.
9. *The Observer,* 13.
10. PNF report, 28–30.
11. *Al-Dustur,* 8 July 1985, 19.
12. Based on the author's private sources and interviews, with the help of an article by Richard Johns of the *Financial Times.*
13. *de Nouvel/Observateur,* 7–13 Nov. 1986, 88–90.
14. Based on the author's private sources and interviews.
15. *Revue d'Etudes Palestiniennes,* no. 21 (Automne 1986).

APPENDIX
SELECT BIBLIOGRAPHY
NOTES ON CONTRIBUTORS
INDEX

APPENDIX:
List of PLO Offices Abroad by the Early 1980s[1]

This list was prepared from information confidentially provided by a British diplomat and from a survey of the *Arab Report and Record*.[2] The list provides information on the status of PLO offices abroad. The information has been subdivided into four classifications: first, those countries that extend the PLO some form of diplomatic status;[3] second, those countries that allow only information offices without formally recognizing the PLO; third, those countries who appear to have consented to an office, but about which there is insufficient information to determine whether or not it is a diplomatic mission. Such occurrences have been labeled as 'unclear'; finally there are those countries for which no information was available.

Country	Status of Office	Country	Status of Office
Africa (N = 41)		*Africa* (N = 41)	
Angola	diplomatic	Gambia	diplomatic
Botswana	—	Ghana	—
Burundi	non-diplomatic	Guinea	diplomatic
Cameroon	unclear	G. Bissau	diplomatic
Cape Verde	—	Ivory Coast	—
CAR	—	Kenya	diplomatic
Chad	non-diplomatic	Lesotho	—
Comoros	—	Liberia	—
Congo	nondiplomatic	Madagascar	non-diplomatic
Dahomey	—	Malawi	—
Eq. Guinea	—	Mali	diplomatic
Ethiopia	diplomatic	Mauritius	diplomatic
Gabon	—	Mozambique	diplomatic

Country	Status of Office	Country	Status of Office
Africa (N = 41)		*Africa* (N = 41)	
Niger	—	Swaziland	—
Nigeria	diplomatic	Tanzania	diplomatic
Rwanda	—	Togo	—
Sao T. & P.	—	Uganda	diplomatic
Senegal	diplomatic	Upper Volta	—
Seychelles	unclear	Zaïre	—
Sierra Leone	—	Zambia	unclear
		Zimbabwe	diplomatic
Asia (N = 28)		*Asia* (N = 28)	
Afganistan	diplomatic	Mongolia	diplomatic
Bangladesh	diplomatic	North Korea	diplomatic
Bhutan	—	Nepal	—
Burma	unclear	Papua New	—
Cambodia	—	Guinea	
China	diplomatic	Pakistan	diplomatic
Cyprus	diplomatic	Philippines	—
Fiji	—	Samoa	—
India	diplomatic	Singapore	—
Indonesia	unclear	Solomons	—
Iran	diplomatic	South Korea	—
Japan	non-diplomatic	Sri Lanka	diplomatic
Laos	diplomatic	Thailand	—
Malaysia	diplomatic	Vietnam	diplomatic
Maldives	diplomatic		
Latin America (N = 29)		*Latin America* (N = 29)	
Argentina	—	El Salvador	—
Bahamas	—	Grenada	—
Barbados	—	Guatemala	—
Bolivia	diplomatic	Guyana	—
Brazil	diplomatic	Haiti	—
Chile	—	Honduras	—
Colombia	—	Jamaica	—
Costa Rica	—	Mexico	diplomatic
Cuba	diplomatic	Nicaragua	diplomatic
Dominica	—	Panama	—
Dominican R.	—	Paraguay	—
Ecuador	non-diplomatic	Peru	diplomatic

Latin America (N = 29)		*Latin America* (N = 29)	
Saint Lucia	—	Uruguay	—
Suriname	—	Venezuela	unclear
Tri. & To.	—		

Western Bloc (N = 24)		*Western Bloc* (N = 24)	
Australia	—	Luxembourg	non-diplomatic
Austria	diplomatic	Malta	diplomatic
Belgium	non-diplomatic	New Zealand	—
Canada	non-diplomatic	Netherlands	non-diplomatic
Denmark	non-diplomatic	Norway	—
Finland	non-diplomatic	Portugal	non-diplomatic
France	non-diplomatic	Spain	diplomatic
Germany (West)	non-diplomatic	Sweden	non-diplomatic
Greece	diplomatic	Switzerland	non-diplomatic
Iceland	—	Turkey	diplomatic
Ireland	—	UK	non-diplomatic
Italy	non-diplomatic	USA	non-diplomatic

Eastern Europe (N = 9)		*Eastern Europe* (N = 9)	
Albania	—	Poland	diplomatic
Bulgaria	diplomatic	Romania	diplomatic
Czechoslovakia	diplomatic	Soviet Union	diplomatic
Germany (East)	diplomatic	Yugoslavia	diplomatic
Hungary	diplomatic		

Table 1: Distribution of PLO Offices by Regions

	East Europe	West Europe	Latin America	Asia	Africa	Total
Diplomatic	8	5	6	14	14	47
Non-Diplomatic	—	14	1	1	4	18
Unclear	—	—	1	2	3	6
Missing data	1	5	21	11	20	60
No. of countries	9	24[a]	29	28[b]	41	131[c]

[a] Includes Switzerland

[b] Includes North and South Korea

[c] Excludes Arab countries. All Arab governments have allowed diplomatic offices for the PLO except Oman.

NOTES

1. On numerous occasions Palestinian and Arab circles were approached to obtain information on the PLO offices abroad. Similarly attempts were made to circulate a questionnaire to the PLO offices. This questionnaire was designed in such a way that it was hoped it would have led to information on not only the location of the PLO offices but also on developments and changes in the diplomatic status of these offices. However, these efforts did not bear any fruit. The list that was finally obtained where possible was crosschecked and expanded.

2. One problem with the information on offices with diplomatic status is that it is often not detailed enough to determine the actual level of the mission. So it becomes rather difficult to tell whether one particular PLO diplomatic mission benefits from a status similar to an embassy or whether it is set at a lower status.

SELECT BIBLIOGRAPHY

BOOKS, MONOGRAPHS, AND PAMPHLETS

Abrahamian, Ervand. *Iran Between Two Revolutions*. Princeton: Princeton University Press, 1982.

Abu Iyad, with Eric Rouleau. *My Home, My Land: A Narrative of Palestinian Struggle*. New York: Times Books, 1981.

Adams, James. *The Financing of Terror: The PLO, IRA, Red Brigades, and M-19, and Their Money Supply*. New York: Simon and Schuster, 1986.

Ajami, Fouad. *The Vanished Imam: Musa al-Sadr and the Shi'a of Lebanon*. Ithaca: Cornell University Press, 1986.

Akhavi, Sharough. *Religion and Politics in Contemporary Iran*. Albany: State University of New York, 1980.

Amos, John, II. *Palestinian Resistance: Organization of a Nationalist Movement*. New York: Pergamon Press, 1980.

Bahbah, Bishara, and Linda Butler. *Israel and Latin America: The Military Connection*. New York: St. Martin's Press, 1986.

Bailey, Clinton. *Jordan's Palestinian Challenge 1948–1983: A Political History*. Bouler, CO: Westview Press, 1984.

Bakhash, Shaul. *The Reign of the Ayatollahs*. New York: Basic Books, 1984.

Batatu, Hanna. *The Old Social Classes and the Revolutionary Movements of Iraq: A Study of Iraq's Old Landed and Commercial Classes and of Its Communists, Ba'thists, and Free Officers*. Princeton: Princeton University Press, 1978.

Becker, Jillian. *The PLO: The Rise and Fall of the Palestine Liberation Organization*. New York: St. Martin's Press, 1984.

Chaliand, Gerard. *La Resistance Palestinienne*. Paris: Seuil, 1970.

Christian, Shirley. *Revolution in the Family*. New York: Vantage Books, 1986.

Cobban, Helena. *The Palestinian Liberation Organization: People, Power and Politics*. Cambridge: Cambridge University Press, 1984.

Cooley, John. *Green March, Black September*. London: Cass, 1973.

Curtis, Michael, et. al., eds. *The Palestinians: People, History, Politics*. New Brunswick, NJ: Transaction Books, 1975.

Dann, Uriel. *Iraq under Qassem: A Political History 1958–1963*. New York: Praeger, 1969.

Dessouki, Ali Hillal, ed. *Islamic Resurgence in the Arab World*. New York: Praeger, 1982.

Dominguez-Dibb, Humberto. *Presencia Y Vigencia Arabes En El Paraguay*. Asuncion, 1977.

Dupuy, Trevor N. *Elusive Victory: The Arab-Israeli Wars 1947–1974*. New York: Harper & Row, 1978.

el-Edroos, S. A. *The Hashemite Arab Army 1908–1979: An Appreciation and Analysis of Military Operations*. Amman: The Publishing Committee, 1980.

Elkin, Judith Lardin. *Jews of the Latin American Republics*. Chapel Hill, NC: University of North Carolina Press, 1980.

Farah, Tawfic E., ed. *Political Behavior in the Arab States*. Boulder, CO: Westview Press, 1983.

Freedman, Robert O. *Soviet Policy toward the Middle East Since 1970*. New York: Praeger, 1975.

———— ed. *The Middle East after the Israeli Invasion of Lebanon*. Syracuse: Syracuse University Press, 1986.

Ghabra, Shafeeq N. *Palestinians in Kuwait: The Family and the Politics of Survival*. Boulder, CO: Westview Press, 1987.

Glick, Edward. *Latin America and the Palestine Problem*. New York: The Theodor Herzl Foundation, 1958.

Golan, Galia. *The Soviet Union and the Palestine Liberation Organization: An Uneasy Alliance*. New York: Praeger, 1980.

Greilsammer, Ilan, and Joseph Weiler. *Europe's Middle East Dilemma: The Quest for a Unified Stance*. Boulder, CO: Westview Press, 1987.

Gresh, Alain. *The PLO: The Struggle Within. Towards an Independent Palestinian State*. London: Zed Books, 1986.

Haddad, Wadi. *Lebanon and the Politics of the Revolving Doors*. "The Washington Papers." New York: Praeger for the Georgetown University Center for Strategic and International Studies, 1985.

Haley, P. Edward, and Lewis W. Snider, eds. *Lebanon in Crisis: Participants and Issues*. Syracuse: Syracuse University Press, 1979.

Harkabi, Yehoshafat. "Fedayeen Action and Arab Strategy." *Adelphi Papers* 53 (1968).

————. *The Palestinian Covenant and Its Meaning*. London: Valentine, Mitchell, 1981.

Hart, Alan. *Arafat: Terrorist or Peacemaker?* London: Sidgwick and Jackson, 1984.

Hirst, David. *The Gun and the Olive Branch: The Roots of Violence in the Middle East*. London: Faber and Faber, 1977, 1984.

Hudson, Michael. *The Precarious Republic: Political Modernization in Lebanon*. New York: Random House, 1968.

Hussain, Mehmood. *The Palestinian Liberation Organization*. Dehli: University Publishers, 1975.

Inter-American Development Bank. *Annual Report: 1985*. Washington DC: IDB, 1986.

Ioannides, Christos P. *America's Iran: Injury and Catharsis*. Lanham, MD: University Press of America, 1984.

Irani, George Emile. *The Papacy and the Middle East*. Notre Dame, IN: University of Notre Dame Press, 1986.

Ismael, Tareq. *International Relations of the Contemporary Middle East: A Study in World Politics*. Syracuse: Syracuse University Press, 1986.

———. *Iraq and Iran: Roots of Conflict*. Syracuse: Syracuse University Press, 1982.

Israeli, Raphael. *PLO in Lebanon: Selected Documents*. New York: St. Martin's Press, 1983.

Jamail, Milton H,. *It's No Secret*. Belmont, MA: Association of Arab-American University Graduates, 1986.

Jansen, G. H. *Militant Islam*. London: Pan Books, 1979.

Johnson, Nels. *Islam and the Politics of Meaning in Palestinian Nationalism*. London: Keagan Paul International, 1982.

Joiner, Charles. *The Fedayeen in Arab World Politics*. Morristown, NJ: General Learning Press, 1974.

Jumblatt, Kamal. *I Speak for Lebanon*. London: Zed Books, 1982.

Jureidini, Paul A. *The Palestinian Revolution: Its Organizations, Ideologies, and Dynamics*. Washington DC: Center for Research in Social Systems, The American University, 1970.

———. *Six Clashes: An Analysis of the Relationship between Palestinian Guerrilla Movement and the Governments of Jordan and Lebanon*. Kensington, MD: American Institutes for Research, 1971.

———, and William E. Hazen. *The Palestinian Movement in Politics*. Lexington: D.C. Heath, 1976.

———. *Revolutionary Perceptions of Harsh Realities: The Democratic Front Takes Stock*. Alexandria, VA: Abbott Associates, 1983.

———, and R. D. McLaurin. *Beyond Camp David: Emerging Alignments and Leaders in the Middle East*. Syracuse: Syracuse University Press, 1979.

——— and James M. Price. *Military Operations in Selected Lebanese Built-Up Areas, 1975–1978*. Aberdeen Proving Ground, MD: U.S. Army Human Engineering Laboratory, 1979.

Kaufman, Edy, Yorman Shapira, and Joll Barromi. *Israel-Latin American Relations*. New Brunswick, NJ: Transaction Books, Inc., 1979.

Kauppi, Mark V., and R. Craig Nation, eds. *The Soviet Union and the Middle East in the 1980s*. Lexington, MA: Lexington Books, 1983.

Kazziha, Walid. *Palestine in the Arab Dilemma*. New York: Barnes & Noble, 1979.

———. *Revolutionary Transformation in the Arab World: Habash and His Comrades from Nationalism to Marxism*. London: Charles Knight, 1975.

Kerr, Malcolm H. *The Arab Cold War: Gamal 'abd al-Nasir and His Rivals, 1958–1970.* New York: Oxford University Press, 1971.

Khadduri, Majid. *Socialist Iraq: A Study in Iraqi Politics Since 1968.* Washington, DC: Middle East Institute, 1978.

Khalidi, Rashid. *Under Siege: PLO Decisionmaking during the 1982 War.* New York: Columbia University Press, 1986.

Khalidi, Walid. *Conflict and Violence in Lebanon: Confrontation in the Middle East.* Cambridge, MA: Center for International Affairs, Harvard University, 1979.

Khomeini, Ruhollah, Ayatollah. *Hukumat-e Islam* (Islamic Government). Translated and annotated by Hamid Algar in *Islam and Revolution.* Berkeley: Mizan Press, 1981.

———. *Selected Messages and Speeches of Iman Khomeini.* Tehran: Ministry of National Guidance, 1980.

Kirisci, Kemal. *The PLO and World Politics: A Study of the Mobilization of Support for the Palestinian Cause.* New York: St. Martin's Press, 1986.

Kopilow, David J. *Castro, Israel, and the PLO.* Washington, DC: The Cuban-American National Foundation, 1984.

Korany, Bahgat, and Ali E. Hillal Dessouki, eds. *The Foreign Policies of Arab States.* Cairo: American University in Cairo Press; and Boulder, CO: Westview Press, 1984.

Kuniholm, Bruce R., and Michael Rubner. *The Palestinian Problem and United States Policy: A Guide to Issues and References.* Claremont, CA: Regina Books, 1986.

Laffin, John. *The PLO Connections.* London: Corgi Books, 1982.

Ledeen, Michael, and William Lewis. *Debacle: The American Failure in Iran.* New York: Vintage Books, 1982.

Lesch, Ann Mosley. *Arab Politics in Palestine 1917–1939: The Frustration of a National Movement.* Ithaca: Cornell University Press, 1979.

Lukacs, Yehuda, ed. *Documents on the Israeli-Palestinian Conflict.* Cambridge: Cambridge University Press, 1984.

Mandel, Neville J. *The Arabs and Zionism before World War I.* Berkeley: University of California Press, 1976.

Ma'oz, Moshe, ed. *Palestinian Arab Politics.* Jerusalem: Jerusalem Academic Press, 1975.

Mehdi, Beverlee Turner. *The Arabs in America, 1492–1977.* Dobbs Ferry, NY: Oceana Publications, 1978.

Melman, Yossi. *The Master Terrorist: The True Story behind Abu Nidal.* New York: Adama Books, 1986.

Miller, David A. *The PLO and the Politics of Survival.* "The Washington Papers" 99. Washington, DC: Praeger Publications with the Center for Strategic and International Studies, Georgetown University, 1983.

Mishal, Shaul. *The PLO under 'Arafat: Between Gun and Olive Branch.* New Haven: Yale University Press, 1986.

Mohajeri, Masih. *Islamic Revolution: Future Path of Nations.* Tehran: Jihad-e Samzadeqi (Reconstruction Jihad) 1982.

Norton, Augustus Richard. *Amal and the Shi'a: Struggle for the Soul of Lebanon.* Austin: University of Texas Press, 1987.

O'Ballance, Edgar. *Arab Guerrilla Power 1967–1972.* Hamden: Archon, 1974.

O'Neill, Bard E. *Armed Struggle in Palestine: A Politico-Military Analysis.* Boulder, CO: Westview Press, 1978.

Owen, Roger, ed. *Essays on the Crisis in Lebanon.* London: Ithaca, 1976.

Pakradouni, Karim. *La Paix manquée: Le mandat d'Elias Sarkis (1976–1982).* Beirut: Editions FMA, 1984.

Palumbo, Michael. *The Palestinians' Catastrophe: The 1948 Expulsion of a People from Their Homeland.* London: Faber and Faber, 1987.

Paolucci, Henry. *Zionism, The Superpowers and the PLO.* Whitestone, NY: Griffon House Publications, 1982.

Peroncel-Hugoz, Jean Pierre. *Une Croix Sur le Liban.* Paris: Lieu Commun, 1984.

Porath, Yehoshua. *The Emergence of the Palestinian-Arab National Movement, 1918– 1929.* London: Frank Cass, 1974.

———. *The Palestinian Arab National Movement, 1929–1939: From Riots to Rebellion.* London: Frank Cass, 1974.

Quandt, William B, Fuad Jabber and Ann Mosely Lesch. *The Politics of Palestinian Nationalism.* Berkeley: University of California Press, 1973.

Rabinovich, Itamar. *The War for Lebanon 1970–1983.* Ithaca: Cornell University Press, 1984.

Rajaee, Farhang. *Islamic Values and World Views: Khomeini on Man, the State and International Politics.* Lanham, NY: University Press of America, 1983.

Randal, Jonathan C. *Going All the Way: Christian Warlords, Israeli Adventures and the War in Lebanon.* New York: Viking, 1983.

Al-Rayyes, Riad, and Dunia Nahas. *Guerrillas for Palestine: A Study of the Palestinian Commando Organizations.* Beirut: An-Nahar, 1974.

Rosenthal, Morton M., and Raquel Schuster-Herr. *PLO Activities in Latin America.* New York: Anti-defamation League, 1982.

Rubenberg, Cheryl. *The Palestine Liberation Organization: Its Institutional Infrastructure.* Belmont, MA: Institute of Arab Studies, 1983.

Rubin, Barry. *The Arab States and the Palestine Conflict.* Syracuse: Syracuse University Press, 1981.

Saddy, Fehmy. *Arab-Latin American Relations: Energy, Trade and Investment.* New Brunswick, NJ: Transaction Books, Inc., 1983.

Safady, Jamil. *Panorama Da Imigracao Arabe.* Sao Paulo: Editora Comercial Safady, c. 1973–1977.

Sahliyeh, Emile. *The PLO after the Lebanon War.* Boulder, CO: Westview Press, 1986.

Said, Edward. *The Question of Palestine.* New York: Times Books, 1979.

Sayigh, Rosemary. *Palestinians: From Peasants to Revolutionaries*. London: Zed Books, 1979.

Sazman-e Cherika-ye Fedayi Khalq-e Iran. *Hast Sal Mobarezeh-e Masalehaneh* (Eight Years of Armed Struggle). Tehran, 1979.

Sazman-e Mujahedin-e Khalq-e Iran. *Tarikhcheh* (Brief History). Tehran, 1979.

Schiff, Zeev, and Raphael Rothstein. *Fedayeen: Guerrillas Against Israel*. New York: McKay, 1972.

———, and Ehud Ya'ari. *Israel's Lebanon War*. New York: Simon & Schuster, 1984.

Sella, Ammon. *Soviet Political and Military Conduct in the Middle East*. New York: St. Martin's Press, 1981.

Shichor, Yitzhak. *The Middle East in China's Foreign Policy, 1949–1977*. Cambridge: Cambridge University Press, 1979.

Sterling, Claire. *The Terror Network*. New York: Berkeley Books, 1982.

Tomah, George, ed. *United Nations Resolutions on Palestine and the Arab-Israeli Conflict, 1943–1974*. Beirut: Institute for Palestine Studies, 1974.

Tsai Chung-lang. *Chinese Communists' Support to Palestinian Guerrilla Organizations*. World Anti-Communist League, Feb. 1973.

Tuéni, Ghassan. *Une Guerre Pour Les Autres*. Paris: J. C. Lattes, 1985.

Vatikiotis, P. J. *Arab Regional Politics in the Middle East*. London: Croom Helm, 1984.

Wilson, Barbara Anne. *Conflict in the Middle East: The Challenge of the Palestinian Movement*. Washington, DC: Center for Research in Social Systems. The American University, 1969.

Yaari, Ehud. *Strike Terror: The Story of Fatah*. New York: Sabra, 1970.

Yodfat, Aryeh. *PLO Strategy and Politics. New York: St. Martin's Press, 1981*.

———, and Yuval Arno. *PLO: Strategy Tactics*. New York: St. Martin's Press, 1981.

ARTICLES

Abugattas, Juan. "The Perception of the Palestinian Question in Latin America." *Journal of Palestine Studies* 11 (Spring 1982): 117–28.

Alpher, Joseph. "The Khomeini International." *Washington Quarterly* 3 (Autumn 1980): 55–74.

Anvari, Mohammed. "Implications of the Iranian Political Change in the Arab World." *Middle East Review* 3 (Spring 1983): 17–19.

"The Arab Contribution to Regional Destablization." *Spotlight on the America*. Washington DC, Center for International Security, April 1984.

"The Arab-Israeli Contest for Influence in Latin America." *Business Week,* 3 May 1982, 52.

"Arafat Says PLO Aids Foreign Guerrilla Units." *Wall Street Journal,* 14 January 1982, 4.

Aronsfeld, C. C. "Jews, Arabs, and Antisemites in Latin America." *Institute of Jewish Affairs Reserach Reports,* September 1983.

Ashraf, Ahmad. "Bazaar and the Mosque in Iran's Revolution." *MERIP Reports* 13 (March–April 1983): 16–18.

Ayoub, Mohammed. "Between Khomeini and Begin: The Arab Dilemma." *The World Today* (July–August 1983); 254–63.

Bahbah, Bishara. "Echeverria on Mexican-Israeli Relations." *Al Fajr,* 22 October 1982, 15.

Batatu, Hanna. "Iraq's Underground Shi'a Movement: Characteristics, Causes and Prospects." *Middle East Journal* 35 (Autumn 1981): 578–94.

Bell, Belden. "The PLO Is at Work Subverting Latin America." *Human Events,* 25 November 1978.

Berger, Joseph. "View of Jews of Nicaragua: Much Debate." *New York Times,* 20 April 1986, 11.

Bill, James. "The Arab World and the Challenge of Iran." *Journal of Arab Affairs* 29 (October 1982): 45.

———. "Resurgent Islam in the Persian Gulf." *Foreign Affairs* 63 (Fall 1984): 108–27.

Bolling, Landrum. "After the Internal PLO Fight in Tripoli: What Hope for Fresh Movements toward Peace in the Middle East?" In Shireen Hunter, ed., "The PLO after Tripoli." CSIS Significant Issues Series, 6(10) (1984): 3–6.

"Brazil and the Middle East." *The Middle East* (June 1986) 31–41.

Bryen, Soshana. "The Sandinistas and the Jews." *Wall Street Journal* 24 August 1983, 24.

Chin, Pao-Chih. "Mao's Plot in the Middle East." *Asian Outlook* (February 1971): 42–46.

Chubin, Sharam. "Leftist Forces in Iran." *Problems of Communism,* (July-August 1980): 10–25.

Cobban, Helena. "PLO Hopes Tie to Nicaragua Will Leave Israel out in Cold." *Christian Science Monitor,* 26 July 1979, 4.

Cooley, John, K. "China and the Palestinians." *Journal of Palestine Studies* 1 (1972): 19–34.

———. "Iran, the Palestinians and the Gulf." *Foreign Affairs* 58 (Summer 1979): 1017–35.

El-Ayouty, Yassin. "Egypt and the Palestinians." *Current History* (January 1973): 5–12, 39.

———"Palestinians and the Fourth Arab-Israeli War." *Current History* (February 1974): 74–78.

Faris, Hani A. "Lebanon and the Palestinians: Brotherhood or Fratricide." *Arab Studies Quarterly* (Fall 1981): 352–70.

Garfinkle, Adam M. "Sources of the Al-Fatah Mutiny." *Orbis* 27 (Fall 1983): 603–41.

Golan, Galia. "The Soviet Union and the PLO since the War in Lebanon." *Middle East Journal* (Spring 1986): 285–307.

Gruen, George E. "Turkey's Relations with Israel and Its Arab Neighbors." *Middle East Review* 17(3) (Spring 1985): 33–43.

Hamid, Rashid. "What Is the PLO?" *Journal of Palestine Studies* 4 (Summer 1975): 90–109.

Harkabi, Y. "Fedayeen Action and Arab Strategy." *Adelphi Papers* 53 (December 1968).

Harris, L. "China's Relations with the PLO." *Journal of Palestine Studies* 7 (Autumn 1977): 123–53.

Heradstveit, Daniel. "A Profile of the Palestine Guerrillas." *Cooperation and Conflict* 7 (1972): 13–36.

Hoffman, David. "Reagan Calls Iran, Libya, and PLO a 'New Danger' in Central America." *Washington Post,* 25 January 1985, 1.

Hudson, Michael. "The Palestinian Factor in the Lebanese Civil War." *The Middle East Journal* 32(3) (Summer 1978): 261–78.

Hunter, Shireen, ed. "The PLO after Tripoli." *CSIS Significant Issues Series* 6(10) (1984).

Ioannides, Christos P. "The Iranian Hostage Takers." *Washington Quarterly* 3 (Summer 1980): 12–35.

"Israel's Arms Sales to Latin America." *Palestine* 7 (1–15 September 1981): 29.

Jabber, Fuad. "The Arab Regimes and the Palestinian Revolution 1967–1971." *Journal of Palestine Studies* 2(2) (Winter 1973): 79–101.

Jackson, Robert L. "Profits from Arms Sales to PLO Put in U.S. Real Estate." *Los Angeles Times,* 13 April 1983, 8.

Janati, Ahmad, Ayatollah. "Defence and Jihad in the Quran." *Tawhid* (April 1984): 39–54.

Joyaux, F. "Le Probleme de la Palestine dans la Presse Chinose." *Orient* 38 (2 Trimestre 1966): 101–10.

Kelidar, Abbas. "The Shi'a Imami Community and Politics in the Arab East." *Middle Eastern Studies* 19 (January 1983): 3–16.

Kilch, Ignacio. "Arabs of Latin America." *The Middle East* (April 1986): 57–59.

———. "Israel and Latin America: Keeping Their Distance." *Middle East International,* 7 January 1983, 9.

———. "The PLO and Latin America: Not Entirely Credible." *Middle East International,* 20 August 1982, 10.

Krauter, U. "Interview with the Mission of the PLO in Peking." *Easter Horizon* 16(12) (December 1977): 20–23.

"Latin America Discovers the PLO." *The Middle East* (December 1981): 31–32.

"Latin America Watch." *National Review,* 24 August 1984, 17.

Lewis, Marlo Jr. "Nicaragua: The Middle East Connection." *Midstream* (January 1986): 3–7.

Macintyre, Ronald R. "The Palestine Liberation Organization: Tactics, Strategies and Options toward the Geneva Peace Conference." *Journal of Palestine Studies* 4 (Summer 1975): 65–89.

Ma'oz, M. "Soviet and Chinese Influence on the Palestinian Guerrilla Movement." In A. Rubinstein, ed., *Soviet and Chinese Influence in the Third World*. New York: Prager, 1975, 109–30.

McLaurin, R. D. "Peace in Lebanon." In W.A. Beling, ed., Middle East Peace Plans (London: Croom Helm, 1986).

Migdail, Carl J. "Radical Arabs Take Aim at Latin America." *U.S. News and World Report* (September 1981): 23–24.

Miller, David A. "The PLO after Tripoli: Prospects for Reorganization." In Shireen Hunter, ed., "The PLO after Tripoli." *CSIS Significant Issues Series,* 6(10) (1984): 7–10.

Muslih, Mohammad Y. "Moderates and Rejectionists within the Palestine Liberation Organization." *Middle East Journal* 30 (Spring 1976): 127–40.

Nahas, Naridi. "State-systems and Revolutionary Challenge: Nasser, Khomeini and the Middle East." *International Journal of Middle Eastern Studies* 17 (November 1985): 507–27.

Norton, Augustus Richard. "Making Enemies in South Lebanon: Harakat Amal, the IDF and South Lebanon." *Middle Insight* 3 (September 1981): 23–24.

Pallis, Elfi. "How Israel Arms the Dictators." *The Middle East* (September 1981): 23–24.

"The PLO in Central America." *The White House Digest,* White House Office of Media Relations and Planning (July 20, 1983).

"The PLO in Latin America." *Swiss Review of World Affairs* (June 1982): 11–12.

"PLO Is Backing Sandinistas." *The Middle East* (August 1983): 11.

"Pro-PLO Paper Indicates Link to Salvadoran Rebels." *New York Times,* 29 January 1981, A2.

"Reagan Calls Iran, Libya, and PLO a 'New Danger' in Central America." *Washington Post,* 25 January 1985, A1.

Rubenberg, Cheryl A. "Israel and Guatemala: Arms, Advice and Counter-insurgency." *Middle East Report* (May-June 1986): 16–47.

Rubin, Barry. "The PLO's Intractable Foreign Policy." *Policy Papers* 3. Washington Institute for Near East Policy, 1985.

————"Yasser Arafat's Tightrope in Arab Politics." In Shireen Hunter, ed., "The PLO after Tripoli." *CSIS Significant Issues Series* 6(10) (1984): 11–17.

"Salvardor Guerrilla Is Reported to Meet Arafat in Lebanon." *New York Times,* 18 March 1982, A16.

Sanction, Thomas A. "Courting the Sandinistas." *Time,* 4 August 1980, 39.

Sayigh, Yezid. "The Roots of Syrian-PLO Differences." *Middle East International,* 29 October 1982, 15–16.

Scully, Eileen. "The PLO's Growing Latin American Bases." Heritage Foundation *Backgrounder,* 2 August 1983.

Sharif, Regina. "Latin America and the Arab-Israeli Conflict." *Journal of Palestine Studies* 3 (Augumn 1977).

Shichor, Yitzhak "The Palestinians and China's Foreign Policy." In Chuin-Tu Hsueh, ed., *Dimensions of China's Foreign Relations.* New York: Praeger, 1977, 156–90.

"Simposio International Sobre La Injerencia Sionists En America Latina." La Havana: Ceamo, 1983.

Stanley, Bruce. "Framentation and National Liberation Movements: The PLO." *Orbis* 22 (Winter 1979): 1033–55.

Stork, Joe. "The War on the Camps, The War of the Hostages." *MERIP Reports* (June 1985): 3–7.

Tamayo, Juan O. "World's Leftists Find a Haven in Nicaragua." *Miami Herald,* 3 March 1985, 1.

Tian, Zhongquin. "China in the Middle East: Principles and Realities." *Middle East Review, 18(2)* (Winter 1986): 7–15.

US Department of State. "The Sandinistas and Middle Eastern Radicals." Washington DC: US Government Printing Office, August 1985.

Wertheim, Peter Howard. "Brazil and the Middle East." *The Middle East* (April 1985): 35–48.

Wolf, John B. "Black September: Militant Palestine." *Current History* (January 1973): 5–8, 37.

Wright, Robin. "Strange Bedfellows: The Pope and the PLO." *Washington Post,* 24 January 1982,1 D1.

Zeitin, Maurice. "Message to Castro: Cuba and the PLO." *The Nation,* 20 March 1976, 338.

NOTES ON CONTRIBUTORS

Robert Thomas Baratta (M.A.L.D. and A.B.D., Fletcher School of Law and Diplomacy) is presently working in the office of the Assistant Secretary of Defense for International Security Affairs, Inter-American Region, in Washington DC. His recent article, "Political Violence in Ecuador," appeared in *Terrorism: An International Journal.* His current research interests include international terrorism in Latin America, the internal politics of Mexico and Panama, and the boundary dispute between Ecuador and Peru in the upper Amazon.

Martin H. Greenberg (Ph.D., University of Connecticut) is Professor of Regional Analysis, Political Science, and Literature and Language at University of Wisconsin—Green Bay. His publications include *Bureaucracy and Development: a Mexican Case Study* and, with A. R. Norton, *Studies in Nuclear Terrorism;* and *International Terrorism: An Annotated Bibliography and Research Guide,* selected as an "Outstanding Academic Book of the Year" by the American Library Association. His *Science Fiction Series and Sequels* was also selected by the American Library Association as an "Outstanding Academic Book of the Year," making him the only scholar to have had books selected in both the social sciences and the humanities. Dr. Greenberg serves as series editor for publishing programs at Southern Illinois University Press, Greenwood Press, and Scarecrow Press.

Chris P. Ioannides (Ph.D., University of Pennsylvania) is Director of the Speros Basil Vryonis Center for the Study of Hellenism, Sacramento, California. He is the author of *America's Iran: Injury and Catharsis* (University Press of America, 1984). His research interests include the politics of Greece and Cyprus, the role of the Greek Orthodox in Middle Eastern societies, and radical movements in the Middle East.

Raphael Israeli (Ph.D., University of California, Berkeley) is Senior Lecturer in Islamic and Chinese History, Hebrew University, Jerusalem, and is the author of *The Public History of President Sadat* (3 vols.), *The PLO in Lebanon: Selected Documents; Man of Defiance: A Political Biography of A. Sadat;* and, *Peace is in the Eye of the Beholder* (Images of Israel in the Arab Media).

Rashid Khalidi (D. Phil., Oxford) is Associate Professor of Modern Middle East History at the University of Chicago. He has taught at the American University of Beirut, Georgetown, and Columbia. He is the author of *Under Siege: P.L.O. Decision-Making during the 1982 War* and *British Policy towards Syria and Palestine 1906–1914,* as well as numerous articles on aspects of Arab nationalism, modern Palestinian and Lebanese history, and great power policies in the Middle East.

R. D. McLaurin is president of Abbott Associates, Inc., a small, private social science research firm. He is the editor of *The Political Role of Minority Groups in the Middle East;* coauthor of *Middle East Foreign Policy,* and *Beyond Camp David;* and, author or coauthor of numerous other studies dealing with Middle East politics.

Augustus Richard Norton (Ph.D., University of Chicago), Permanent Associate Professor of Comparative Politics at the United States Military Academy, West Point, New York, is the author of *Amal and the Shi'a: Struggle for the Soul of Lebanon.* His current research interests include the sociology of religion and politics, US and USSR policies in the Middle East, and the regulation of internal conflict in a number of states, including Lebanon and Cyprus.

John C. Reppert (Ph.D., The George Washington University) has taught Soviet politics for the University of Maryland and the United States Military Academy and has written on Soviet policy for several periodicals. A career army officer, he has served as a Soviet specialist in Germany, the Office of the Joint Chiefs of Staff, and the United States Embassy in Moscow. He is currently on a research fellowship at Harvard University working on arms control issues.

Adam Zagorin (M.A., Columbia University) is the European correspondent of *Time* magazine, based in Paris. A longtime student of Arab affairs, he served in *Time*'s Beirut bureau in 1979 and 1980 and in the Cairo bureau of United Press International in 1977. Zagorin is a graduate of the masters program of the Center for Arabic Study Abroad (CASA) in Cairo. His other publications on economic subjects include articles in *Foreign Policy, The New Leader* and *Manhattan Inc.*

INDEX

with PLO, 110, 132, 133
"Greater Syria," 60
Greece: diplomatic relations with PLO, 5;
  hijacking of TWA Flight 847 from,
  107n. 46
Gromyko, Andrei, 114, 118, 124, 125
Guatemala, 178, 185
Guinea, 88
Gulf Cooperation Council, 90
Gulf states: concern about Islamic revolu-
  tion in Iran, 79–82, 83; financial assis-
  tance to PNF, 197; Palestinian
  population of, 3, 66, 68; role in PLO-
  Syrian negotiations, 22; Shi'i Muslims
  in, 79
Gulf war. *See* Iran-Iraq war
Guyana, 177

Habash, George, 53–54n. 52, 61, 65, 85,
  112, 183
Habash, Yahya, 127
Haddad, Sa'ad, 38, 39, 41
Haddad, 'Uthman, 18
Haddad, Wadi', 58n. 131, 63
Hallum, Rubhi, 191
Handal, Shafik, 183
al-Hassan, Hanni, 74, 80, 81, 82, 84, 149
Havana, Non-aligned conference in (1979),
  83
Hawatmeh, Nayif, 53–54n. 52, 153
Heller, Mark, 4
Helou, Charles, 55n. 76
Hizbollah (Party of God), 86, 93, 94, 98–
  99, 100, 103, 104
Honduras, 169, 184–85
Hua Guofeng, 155, 157
al-Husaini, Haj Amin, 43
Hussein, Ibn Talal (king of Jordan): con-
  cern about Jordanian Palestinians, 23;
  and Jordanian role in Palestinian settle-
  ment, 9, 21, 29, 130, 132; relations with
  Fatah, 25, 27; support for, 28, 65, 90;
  Syrian- and Egyptian-backed attempt to
  depose, 18
Hussein, Saddam, 82–83, 87, 88, 97
Hussein-Arafat Agreement (1985), xi, 9,
  30, 46, 78, 90, 128–29, 133
al-Hut, Shafik, 200
Hu Yaobang, 157

al-Ikhwan al-Muslimun. *See* Muslim
  Brotherhood
Institutional Revolutionary Party (PRI),
  184
Inter-American Development Bank (IDB),
  166, 172
Intifada, 101, 102, 103
Iran, Republic of: American hostages in,
  83–85; Arafat's support of, 74–75; ideological differences with PLO, 75–78;
  leftist guerrillas in, 85–86; pan-Arab
  coalition against, 89; PLO relations
  with, 7–8, 74–75, 83, 86, 89, 91, 96–
  100; relations with Iraq, 83, 87–88;
  relations with Israel under the Shah, 74;
  relations with Lebanon, 91–95; relations
  with Syria, 96–97
Irangate scandal, 100
Iran-Iraq War, 8, 46, 87–88, 89, 90
Iraq: conflict with Egypt over Palestine
  Entity, 23, 42–43; forces in Jordan, 18,
  25, 44; Palestinian population of, 3, 66;
  PLO relations with, 38, 42–46, 82–83,
  87–88, 97–98; relations with China,
  141; relations with Egypt, 88; relations
  with Iran, 83, 87–88; relations with
  Israel, 42; relations with Jordan, 29,
  45–46; relations with Latin America,
  189, 190; relations with Soviets, 116,
  121; relations with Syria, 46; Shi'i Mus-
  lims in, 76, 82
IRM. *See* Islamic Resistance Movement
Islamic Charitable League (*Mujama'a al-
  Islami*), 101
Islamic Conference Organization, 88
Islamic Development Bank, 172
Islamic Jihad, 93, 94
Islamic Jihad Organization, 101, 102
Islamic law: desire for Palestinian state
  under, 65; Khomeini's call for unity
  under, 77–78, 92
Islamic Republican party (IRP), 84, 86
Islamic Resistance Movement (IRM), 95
Islamic Society (*Jama'at Islami*), 101, 102
Israel: arm sales to China by, 10; attacks
  on Lebanon, 34, 35, 36; Communists
  in, 60; as foe of PLO, 1, 12, 60, 62, 80;
  independence of, 22; invasion of
  Lebanon (1982), 9, 29, 39. 40–41, 87,
  91–92, 94–95, 110, 122; Islamic funda-